SWIM

A MEMOIR OF SURVIVAL

This book is partially supported by a grant from the
Illinois Arts Council, a state agency.

ILLINOIS
ARTS
COUNCIL
AGENCY

SWIM

A MEMOIR OF SURVIVAL

CHICAGO, IL

Library of Congress Control Number: 2010911055

ISBN-10: 0-982-90250-6
ISBN-13: 978-0-9829025-0-9

Printed in the United States of America

Bizurich Media books are available for special promotions and rates. For details please go to BizurichMedia.com.

FIRST EDITION

10 9 8 7 6 5 4 3 2 1

This book is dedicated to all of my friends, family, and neighbors who supported me with love and prayers throughout my battle.

I also want to dedicate this book to the entire 8th floor CCU nursing staff.

For it was all of you who gave me hope. You helped me "Swim."

Message From the Author:

To protect the privacy of those mentioned, I changed both the names and descriptions of many individuals within this book. I also changed the names of every hospital to avoid promoting a specific hospital/transplant clinic.

The only names that have remained the same are those of my friends, family members, people within the public domain, and the members of the hospital who I have grown to adore.

"Life is an opportunity—benefit from it.
Life is beauty—admire it.
Life is bliss—taste it.
Life is a dream—realize it.
Life is a challenge—meet it.
Life is a duty—complete it.
Life is a game—play it.
Life is a promise—fulfill it.
Life is sorrow—overcome it.
Life is a song—sing it.
Life is a struggle—accept it.
Life is a tragedy—confront it.
Life is an adventure—dare it.
Life is luck—make it.
Life is too precious—don't destroy it.

Life is life—fight for it." – Mother Teresa

PROLOGUE

As much as I hope the words on these pages find you in good health, in good spirits and without a single burden weighing on your mind, you must be aware that the following pages were not written by someone as carefree. In fact, the sole purpose of this book is to bring comfort to someone who is dealing with my everyday struggles.

This book is not intended to scare you. It is not intended to make you feel pity for me, nor do I mean to make you cry. The following pages are only meant to inspire.

If you are one of the people for whom I intended this book to be read, you are most likely sick. You are not yourself. You are probably receiving negative news about your condition and you are scared and wondering what your life will be like in the coming days, weeks, months or even years. For you, this book was written. I want you to know you are not alone. Though this book may not document your exact condition, I feel you will be able to draw many parallels and find not only similarities, but also hope. Hope that one day you will be yourself again. You will return to the life you remember; the same memory that at this very moment, and with each waking hour, you are desperately trying not to forget.

Right now, you may feel that medication and surgery are the only two things that can help you. I've been there, and at this junction in your journey you are not wrong to feel this way. However, throughout my journey, I have found there is one other weapon you need to have within you to win your battle. That weapon is <u>Will</u>.

But what is <u>Will</u>? <u>Will</u> is the strength to move on. It is the strength to fight and persevere. To put it bluntly, <u>Will</u> is the only thing that you are going to have to get you out of bed someday. You're probably wondering, *What is my <u>Will</u>?* To be honest, I have no idea. It is different for everyone. However, I can tell you how to go about discovering it. You need to think of one short-term goal. I would recommend that you select something to accomplish in the coming three to four months. I want you to then think of one long-term goal that you wish to achieve in the distant future. Finally, think of the one person, group of people, or activity that brings you the greatest amount of happiness and overall sense of joy. Once you do this, you will have discovered your <u>Will</u>.

If you happen to be fortunate enough to be healthy and "fully aware" of the road your journey in life is taking you down, please do not let my words discourage you from reading these pages. I feel that even you will be able to take away something from the lessons I have learned throughout the course of my struggles, or perhaps you may know someone who could use inspiration. Though, much like any battle with any condition, this book will get dark before you begin to see the light.

No matter whom you identify the most with, the healthy or the ill. If you feel compelled to continue at this point, I ask you to proceed.

My name is Bill Coon, and I would like to start by telling you about myself...

MY BEGINNING

Where does one begin when they speak about their life? I can only imagine the average individual would begin their life story with their first recollection. The average person can probably only put into words a minuscule amount of details their underdeveloped brain was able to store at the time. They probably can only speak of colors, maybe shapes. The average person may remember who was with them or they may be able to explain why this memory was their first. Whatever it was, it must have some significance.

I can tell you my first memory. I was on a slide at an unfamiliar park. My dad was pulling me down the slide, he let go, and I fell off. I remember seeing the wood chips as I fell face forward. Why is this my first memory? I couldn't tell you even if I tried. All I gained from this experience was a black eye.

My life is a little different than the average person's. If I told you where my life story began, it would be when my life got very interesting. My life story begins years before my black eye memory, it begins years before I could even speak. My story began at exactly 8:08 AM on April 24, 1989—the exact minute I was born.

I was born at St. Adrian Hospital in Barrington, Illinois to my mother, Ann Coon, and my father, William Coon Jr. My parents, like any other couple, were ecstatic. The story goes that my mom turned to my dad and said, "Honey, it's a boy! You now have someone to play football with in the backyard." Little did my parents know that the son they were referring to was my brother, Gus, who was born years later in 1992. The son my mom was warmly holding onto in 1989, was born with a birth defect. I was born with Hypoplastic Left Ventricle Syndrome. In layman's terms, it meant the left side of my heart was severely underdeveloped. It also meant I would require a heart transplant and my life expectancy clock of twenty-one days had just begun ticking.

I came into this world not breathing. I had a heart attack seconds before I was born. Before I had even seen the light of day, I was in severe pain. I had stabilized, but not for long. The doctors knew I was deathly ill and the next day I was placed a helicopter and flown directly to Lakeside

Hospital in the great city of Chicago. This is where the "King of Hearts" practiced. His name was Dr. Idris. He was a German Pediatric Cardiac Surgeon who had spent the last sixteen years of his life experimenting on puppies and kittens, perfecting his technique at heart transplantation. He had the steadiest of hands and they were going to have to remain steady, for the baby who just arrived on the roof of his hospital was in dire need of his expertise.

Days went by. My parents watched me grow sicker with every passing hour. They witnessed families come and go, many of them with tears running down their faces, as many babies in the NICU nursery did not survive. My parents developed friendships with these couples. Several of them offered their child's heart to me as their parting gift. None of the hearts were ever a match.

My mom could not stay by my hospital bed every night. Instead, she would leave me a wind-up music box that she knew I loved. She had a motherly intuition that told her I enjoyed the music, even though in my first twenty-one days on this Earth I never once opened my eyes, nor did I ever smile. My mom would instruct the nurses to play the music for me as I slept—she wanted to comfort me even when she was not around.

On May 15, 1989, my life expectancy clock had reached its final hours. It had been twenty-one days. The doctors were going to pull the plug because on the twenty-second day my other organs would begin to fail. No one wanted me to experience more pain. I have been told my death appeared imminent that day. I had hit rock bottom, but something was different. The energy of the doctors had changed. They were awkwardly upbeat given the upsetting circumstances. At 4:15 PM, my parents were pulled aside and informed that Canada had just joined The United Network for Organ Sharing (UNOS) and that a matching heart in Ontario, Canada had just been located. "All we can do now is pray for good weather and clear skies," my parents were told. With that, a helicopter and a Learjet embarked on a journey to Canada to save my life.

At midnight, my transplant was performed. I was the eighth infant heart transplant in the nation and the fourth in the Midwest. After the procedure, my entire body was so swollen that I supposedly did not look like myself. I looked like a different baby. My mom watched me in my cradle that night. She wound the music box and it began playing the sounds that I had fallen asleep to the first three weeks of my life. That was when I turned my head toward the music. It was May 16, 1989, the day I opened my eyes for the first time.

IGNORANT BLISS

I must say it feels weird summarizing twenty years of my life in a matter of several pages, but fortunately (or unfortunately, however you choose to view it) I can easily do so. I have led a very lighthearted life. In fact, since the day I returned home from the hospital in 1989, I never once had a single complication. My life was filled with years of easy-going, good-hearted, clean fun.

I lived a pretty sheltered childhood until I was five years old. I was immune compromised and the doctors told my parents when I was an infant that the common cold could kill me. Because of this, my mom made sure I rarely left my house during those first five years. Anyone who came to visit me had to wear face masks. In fact, I have no memories as a kid of ever leaving my house at all. I have plenty of memories, though, of playing with my cousins, Natalie, Peter and Greg. They lived four houses down from me, so up until the age of five, they (along with my younger brother, Gus, and my older sister, Carissa) were my playmates. We had a swing set in our backyard that served as our playpen during those years. I remember using our imaginations a lot, as we created many exciting games using toys for reasons outside their intended purpose. I remember an entire week where Natalie taught us "Safety Town." My mom refused to send any of her children to the "legit," town-funded version of Safety Town, (for fear we would contract diseases from the other children). Natalie would bring home all her papers and art supplies and would teach us how to "look both ways before crossing the street" and all the rules of "stranger danger." Natalie was a very good teacher. At a young age, she was able to make me paranoid of everyone I didn't know. I remember a month of my life going by in which I was petrified of every car that drove past my house because I was convinced the driver was going to abduct me. Of course, it wasn't Natalie's fault. She was only able to teach me what she knew. I guess at her young age she wasn't able to distinguish the difference between somebody you simply don't know and someone who is technically a pedophile rapist. Nonetheless, my childhood was colorful, carefree, and filled with ignorant bliss.

Kindergarten proved to be a smooth transition. I developed many friends on the playground, and after school I was able to branch out and actually visit these friends at their homes for a few hours at a time. I never had sleepovers due to my medication (Cyclosporin), which I needed to ingest twice a day: 7:00 AM and 7:00 PM. It upset me a great deal when I had to decline invitations to sleepover parties, but in retrospect, it was a small price to pay for the normalcy I was living on a day-to-day basis.

The years continued to pass and as I grew older, I broke free of any mandated social limitations. The only limits I had were those I enforced upon myself. For years, I refused to attend any pool parties or take my shirt off in locker rooms because I was embarrassed by my surgical scars. I feared everyone would ask questions and once they received the answers, they would treat me differently. It wasn't until my junior year in high school that I finally overcame my body image issues and told my friends, Jen and Jo, I had a heart transplant. In my mind, junior year is when I finally came into myself. I had matured mentally and I was finally comfortable with "me." It was junior year when I understood that my transplant was a blessing and not something by which to be embarrassed.

The next three years of my life were sensational. I lived my senior year of high school to the fullest. I was chosen by my peers to give the class graduation speech. Months later, I began school at Harper College. Harper is the community college that is only twenty minutes from my house. I spent my freshman year at Harper anxiously waiting for my sophomore year at Columbia College Chicago. Columbia was my dream school, and though I enjoyed my classes at Harper, I couldn't help but fantasize about getting my degree in Radio Broadcasting. I finally transferred to Columbia in the fall of 2008.

My first semester was fantastic. I loved every moment of it. It was during this year that I met a few genuine people who would later play a major role in my life. My life seemed to be on autopilot. Everything was going my way. I learned that if you put forth the effort, you eventually reap the benefits.

It was the beginning of my second semester when my life's autopilot feature shut off.

It was the night of December 31, 2008. I was walking back to my dorm room after a night of festivities when I suddenly experienced a sharp pain in my lower abdomen. I lost my breath and I had to stop walking. I continued to walk, but after about five more blocks the pain re-surged through my stomach. I shrugged off the incident and headed back to my dorm. The pain did not return until March.

I accomplished a great deal before the pain came back. My most note-worthy of achievements was an internship position I obtained in the promotions department of one of the top radio stations in the Chi-cago market. I enjoyed my time interning immensely. The hours were brutal, but the job was always rewarding. The only problem I faced was the pain. The internship began in the middle of March, the very same week the pain returned with a vengeance.

The pain was unique. It was a sensation I had never felt before, and I only experienced it when I would walk. It felt as though a large blade had embedded itself in the lower left region of my stomach. With each step, the blade felt as though it was growing larger. Eventually, it would stretch to an area just below my rib cage, until the blade could no longer expand. It would then erupt, sending needles across my stom-ach. It was when the explosion occurred that I could no longer muster the strength to walk. I would pause, typically for two to three minutes; the needles would slowly disperse and my stomach would begin to pul-sate as though my heart was beating from within my stomach. Warmth would then consume the area and the pain would subside.

When I began my internship, I was able to walk approximately ten blocks until the metaphorical blade exploded. My maximum distance quickly declined. By late May, I could not walk more than twenty steps without needing to stop. I kept the pain to myself, I never expressed my discomfort to anyone. I knew something was wrong with me, but because the pain was in my stomach, I convinced myself it was all stress related and that it would naturally remedy itself at semes-ter's end. I was very naïve. I later learned that each pain was my body having a minor heart attack. When I was an infant the nerves on my transplanted heart were cut, so any pain I should have felt in my chest was being transferred to my stomach. I kept pushing myself, ignor-ing my body's continuous warnings. The pain had gotten to the point where it controlled my life. Opposed to correcting the situation, I stupidly bent my life around the problem, never searching for an answer. It wasn't until June 4, 2009 that I finally gave in to the notion that something was terribly wrong. This was when the pain intensified and I came seconds away from blacking out twice in one day.

The first occurrence that day was at about 1:00 PM. I was walking to the radio station. My job that day was to pack a car and later entertain guests at a sponsored event. I had planned ahead so that I could stop many times along the way and still make it to the station on time. I was taking my first stop to ease the pain when I ran into my co-worker, Mark. We began to walk and talk, meanwhile the pain was growing worse in my abdomen. I couldn't take my breaks and Mark and I seemed to never hit a stoplight. I began struggling to breathe. Mark looked at me with curiosity and asked, "Are you okay?" "Yeah?" I responded, as though I didn't know what he was talking about. We continued our walk. We had made it about eight blocks at this point. This was the longest I had ever walked with the pain. The explosion had already occurred several blocks back and my senses were beginning to shut down. We were at the intersection of Randolph and Wabash. I remember seeing a flock of pigeons tear through the air. I couldn't hear their wings though. The pain was excruciating. I could only hear my heart beating in my head. We eventually arrived at Michigan Avenue when everything went gray. I could only see out of nickel-sized holes. "I'm going to take a break. I'll see you at the station." I said to Mark. I finally gave in. "Are you okay?" Mark asked for the second time. "Yeah! Dude, I'm fine! Just go! I'll catch up with you later!" I snapped back. I waited until he was out of sight before staggering to a nearby ledge. I don't remember what I sat on. I think it may have been a bed of flowers. The heartbeat in my head continued to grow louder. A piercing, high-toned buzz consumed the streets. Pedestrians gave me awkward glares as they passed by during the ten-minute period that it took me to recover and muster enough strength to go the distance to the station. Mark and I eventually drove to the event. I slept in the car each way. The pain had taken so much out of me that I couldn't keep my eyes open.

That evening, the Chicago White Sox played the Oakland Athletics. Actually, the White Sox didn't really play that night. Instead, they were killed 0-7 in their home ballpark, U.S. Cellular Field. I was at this game. However, I only know they lost because I looked it up months later on the Internet. I do not recall a single play from this game. I only remember walking into the ballpark with my cousin, Peter, and my two friends, Doug and Ronnie. Ronnie had won the tickets at his job and was treating us to the game. I should have gone home after my shift, but both Peter and Doug were already on their way to the city and I didn't want to spoil their night.

We entered U.S. Cellular Field. I remember the steps being very large. I had to climb four, but after the first two steps, I was exhausted. We continued our walk, searching for our seats when I was instantly struck with the same ailments that I had faced just hours before at the inter-section of Randolph and Wabash. I paused for a brief second. I looked up and saw Peter sit down in one of the rows. He was relatively close, so I forced myself down the aisles until I finally collapsed in the seat. The next memory I have from this night is of Peter dropping me off on my driveway after the game. I waved good-bye to Peter, before quickly heading to my bed.

Fortunately, I had the next few days free from work. I spent these days lounging around my house, thinking about my prior experience at the station. I was dreading work. I didn't want to be an intern anymore. I wanted to quit and take the summer off from any stress. Little did I know, I would never work another shift again.

It was about 10:00 PM on June 7, 2009. My mom was in the kitchen drinking a large cup of coffee. I was sitting in the adjacent room, watching television, when I felt a tingling sensation in my feet. I looked down and saw that my feet were swollen from my toes to my ankles. I panicked and showed the discovery to my mom. She panicked as well and took me to my bedroom where she stacked multiple pillows on my bed to elevate my feet. She checked on me frequently, but we both noticed the swelling was worsening rather than improving. It was 2:00 AM when the swelling had reached my knees. "Do you think you need to go to the hospital?" my mom questioned. She knew that I was very in-tune with my body and I would be the last person to seek medical help. She knew if I said "yes," it meant that I was scared. I looked her in the eye and gave her the response that she feared. "Yeah, we need to go now," I said. My dad helped me hobble to the car before my parents and I rushed to St. Adrian Hospital.

The doctor evaluated me, took a chest X-ray, and returned to my emergency room with a solemn look on his face. He turned to my parents, and in a sad, but assertive way said, "Your son is in heart failure."
I was given Benadryl to ease the swelling and an ambulance was called to take me to Chicago General, the location of a team of doctors to whom I had just recently transferred my case. I didn't really know them because I never needed to. They were only managing my case because I needed a specialist to review my echocardiogram once every six months and tell me that everything looked fine. This was the first time in my life that a scan did not look fine. A pocket of fluid had enveloped my heart. The water retention had gotten so severe that my heart was no longer strong enough to pump the fluid through my body, thus causing the buildup in my ankles.

My life of good fortune and ignorant bliss had come to an abrupt end. I didn't know it then but my journey had just begun. I was about to enter the darkest period of my life, a period in which I experienced a great deal of pain, heartache, depression, anger and sorrow. I was also entering a new chapter in my life. This chapter introduced me to many incredible people. In this chapter, I learned more about my family, my friends and most importantly, myself. There were moments within this chapter that I wanted to die. I experienced countless moments of fear and frustration. I made enemies with those I love the most, as I struggled to survive each passing day.

Oddly enough, when the chapter ended, I looked back on it all, smiled, and said, "Knowing what I know now... I would do it all over again."

The following is my documentation of that chapter. I hope you're ready to Swim.

Circus de Chicago General

Monday,
June 8, 2009 –
Tuesday,
June 16, 2009

THE PUPPET MASTER

The Puppet Master is a fool. He is a villain. The Puppet Master is a cynical man who sits atop his ivory tower dangling the strings of his puppets. He laughs as he watches them dance. They are pawns in his game. He is a lonely creature, this Puppet Master. He is completely disassociated from the world. He lacks the ability to understand human emotion. He sees no wrong with his greed and tries to make everyone dance to the beat of his twisted drum. Unfortunately for me, the Puppet Master was my doctor. For ten long days I was stuck in his theatre, forced to watch his show.

His puppets are ill-experienced, naive, messengers of his irrationality. I can tell they want so badly to break free. They want to speak their minds and share their thoughts, but they dare not utter a word, for fear of the Puppet Master. They, too, are much like the patients of the Puppet Master, trapped in a world they cannot escape, bound by a reality in which they have no control. Only the Puppet Master holds the key to the theatre, and he chooses who can exit the rows.

Even though his heart is as dark as his theatre, and each one of his props are more eerie than the next, the Puppet Master's greatest flaw is his inability to diverge from the script. Every show is the same. He treats all of his unfortunate viewers with no individuality. He cares not where they come from. He does not mind their differences. He cares only of the price on the ticket and the amount of stubs he has collected at the end of the night. The Puppet Master takes his bow at the end of every show and wonders why nobody applauds.

As much as I want to forget the hospital, my mind won't let me. Instead, I remember every intricate detail. I can picture every face, every sensation, and every needle. I can still recall the poisonous taste of the medications that went through my IV and into my veins. If I try hard enough, I can recollect how many people came to see me, what they were wearing, and the order in which they came to visit. I can tell you how many tattoos each of my hospital transporters had, which ones hated their jobs, and which ones were just happy to still be employed in a hospital that was continuously making budget cuts. I can still hear the sounds of the machines, feel the pulsation of the blood pressure cuff and relive the chill that went down my spine each time the stethoscope touched my bare skin. I can do all this by simply closing my eyes.

During these days, I learned even the purest heart can be filled with hate. I learned that change is inevitable. Whether the change is positive or negative is irrelevant. Change is bound to happen. I learned the harder you fight the negative change, the more devastating its effects become. I also discovered that the faster you embrace the positive change, the more beautiful your life will be.

I learned a lot about myself as I laid helpless in the Puppet Master's theatre. I also learned a great deal about the people I thought I already knew. The Puppet Master didn't teach me a single one of these lessons. He was simply a catalyst who set off a period in my life of personal self-discovery. Ironically, he was my pawn—a miniscule character in a life that is far greater than he will ever be.

AN ANGEL GETS ITS WINGS

I believe everything happens for a reason, that God has a divine purpose for everything He does. It is because of this belief that I am able to find peace with my current condition. I feel I need to have this pain. This belief of mine was only validated days after my admission. I believe I was meant to meet the family of Jennifer.

The day I was admitted was the same day that Jennifer passed. Her battle ended and mine was just beginning. She was a young woman who had gotten into a car accident on the Interstate. Originally, the paramedics took her to a community hospital somewhere on the border of Illinois and Indiana. The doctors began treating her for broken bones. They failed to realize her brain was bleeding. Jennifer was rushed to Chicago General. It would be her second stop and her final place of rest.

Meanwhile, down the hall of the same floor at Chicago General, I was completely incapacitated. I was drugged out of my mind from the Benadryl I had been given during the transport from my community hospital. I recall nodding in-and-out of consciousness. I was fighting to stay awake. I wanted to understand where I was. I desperately tried to study my surroundings.

When I finally regained a grip on reality, I noticed an IV in my left arm and that many hours on the clock had passed. My family members surrounded me. They were all staring at me wide-eyed. They asked the typical questions, "Are you okay?" and "How do you feel?" I told them I felt fine, but really I felt as though I had been crushed by a whale, spun around in a dryer and then injected with cocaine. My nurse entered, she was a blonde woman who had a very bold European name. She was very distraught. Her mind seemed to be in a different world. She looked as though she had been crying. I did not know it then, but she had just witnessed Jennifer pass.

I have come to learn two things about hospitals. The first being that hospitals have power ranks, much like an army. At the bottom of the totem pole are the Residents. They study behind the Fellows, who are trying to work their way up the medical mountain and become Attendings. The ranking system is always enforced. Like a fraternity, the Senior doctors make the Freshman newcomers do all of the dirty work.

I have also learned that when you are admitted into a hospital, not much happens in your first few hours. Once you are stable, it takes a while for your doctors to contact you. This may be due to all the paperwork involved or the doctors are not informed immediately. Whatever the case may be, I recall Dr. Young taking his sweet time to enter my room.

Dr. Young is one of the Puppet Master's pawns. I actually have a bit of history with him. The prior December, I had been hospitalized for forty-eight hours at Chicago General. I was treated for a virus when I began running fevers that surpassed 103 degrees. Much like this second stay, the Puppet Master never once showed his face; he simply sent in his pawn.

Dr. Young is a very fragile looking man. He is very pale, balding, and has a jester-like smirk that never erases from his face. He wears a lab coat and carries an assortment of pens. He never seems to swallow his saliva and does not open his mouth very wide when he speaks. Two Residents accompanied Dr. Young whenever he would enter my room, Dr. Ying and Dr. Yang. They both took orders from Dr. Young. I always thought their jobs must be awful. They had to be the first doctors on the floor every morning and were usually the last to leave. They worked weekends, but worst of all, they were pawns to a pawn. Dr. Young began speaking about how the hospital will immediately treat me for both rejection and Congestive Heart Failure (CHF). He said my heart was failing and I was suffering from Ischemia.

Ischemia is an area of tissue that is not getting enough blood. My Ischemia was causing my heart to ineffectively pump blood to the other organs in my body. I was informed of the procedures that I would have to undergo in the coming days. I was also told that I would need to have a stress test, and pending the results, I may be required to get a stent placed in my arteries.

At this point in my journey, I was afraid. I had lived a life of medical perfection. I was not used to having issues with my heart, and for years, I never had any invasive procedures performed. I was a virgin to any form of surgery. I was inexperienced and had no idea what to expect. Dr. Young and his pawns exited the room and I was left sitting in my bed trying to digest the information, as chemicals poured into my bloodstream through the IV. They were literally destroying my immune system, making me weaker than ever before.

Days passed and I seldom left my bed. Aunts, uncles and cousins poured in and out of my room. They were always around me, consistent in showing their support. Jennifer's family was doing the same, but they were there to support Jennifer's mother. Jennifer's family was grieving, crying over the loss of their beloved angel. The day Jennifer died was the same day as her ten-month wedding anniversary. For some of her distant relatives, memories of Jennifer dancing in her white dress were the last images they were able to cling to. As both our families flowed through our sliding glass doors, the two families met. My family learned of Jennifer's story and offered their condolences. It was during this time that Jennifer's family was deciding if they should donate her organs. My family began to tell my story. They began to share with Jennifer's family about the remarkable life I lived. They began to share stories of my childhood, teen years and of my future aspirations. Jennifer's family listened—they took my life's story to heart.

As all of this was transpiring, I was growing steadily irritable. I hadn't left my room and I was not seeing any progress. I finally stood up, unplugged my IV from the wall and began marching out of my room. It felt good to move around. My legs felt warm. They had been immobile for so long that they may have started losing any form of blood flow. My aunts didn't want me to go anywhere, they were trying to set limitations on how far I could walk. I didn't care though. I tuned them out and continued my march.

There were a lot of corridors. I had many options to choose from. This is where I believe God intervened. I believe He led me to Jennifer's room. There were so many twists and turns that the chance of me accidentally bumping into this family had to be so miniscule that a greater good had to have some force. That was when I bumped into a man. He was Jennifer's uncle. He was dark complected and balding. He carried himself with respect. He had a flashy demeanor as though he came from money. He reached out his hand to me, "Are you Bill?" he asked. I was confused, I thought to myself, *I knew I was a big deal in high school, but I had no idea that my reputation preceded me like this.* Instead, I responded cautiously, "Um, yes?" He looked at me with a smile. "Would you mind talking to my sister? She really wants to meet you."

He slowly guided me down the hall to the room where Jennifer's body laid. Instantly, a large Italian family surrounded me. They resembled mine in a way. They all had bold personalities and similar facial features. The group split and out of the sliding glass door, Jennifer's mother appeared. She walked toward me slowly, trembling, almost crypt like. Tears were pouring down her face. She was a short woman, very thin. The veins in her neck were showing. She reached out to me. She gently grabbed my hand. She held it for a while, examining it. It was as though she didn't believe I existed, like I was a mythological creature who had just risen from the sea. She began telling me how they had just decided to donate Jennifer's organs because of my story. I thanked her and assured them that they had made a great decision. I told them that Jennifer's life would continue through the many individuals she would save. I shared with them how great my life has been and how I am thankful for my donor everyday. The cousins began to usher in pictures of Jennifer. They handed me cameras and shared with me their favorite stories. After awhile, I became light headed. My energy had faded and I knew I had to return to my bed. I said my good-byes and thanked them one last time for making their decision.

The walk back to my hospital room was short, but I remember being amazed. My eyes had been opened. All my life I had only experienced organ donation from the side of the recipient. I never once thought of the emotion involved on the side of the donor, the reassurance a family must need to make that decision.

This day was not a day of medical progression in my journey. This was a day of realization. It was a day I will never forget. I matured as an individual and finally understood the magnitude of the gift I had received as an infant.

WHO'S GOT MY BACK NOW?

Over time, hospitals condition you. Hospitals break you. They give you a new lifestyle, a whole new outlook on life. Hospitals place you in an alternate reality, entrapping not only your body, but also your mind, making you believe there is no other existence beyond the sterile sliding glass door that incarcerates you from the world.

Your room becomes your second home, but it is a broken home. There are no pictures, just hackneyed posters with medical catch phrases, which nauseate you every time you read them. However, for whatever reason, you can't help yourself from staring at them every day. The posters become propaganda, agents of the hospital that only help entrap your mind further into a false sense of reality.

You are given food, but they are meals you do not enjoy. They are tasteless, usually cold, and are served to you on an even colder looking platter. The meals make you not want to eat. They eliminate the body's ability to feel hunger. You starve, but you do not feel the pain. Your body weakens, but you rarely use the muscles to notice.

This broken home is more of a prison, a confinement camp. A world filled with unfamiliar machines. Machines you begin to learn as you spend your days studying them. You watch their technicians operate. They are your torturers, yet your teachers. They unknowingly show you the commands and procedures that must be followed to operate this machinery. Eventually, you don't need them anymore. You become your own torturer, your own administer of depression. Each needle becomes less painful to you and it becomes chillingly easier to fake a smile as the days progress.

You learn who your true friends are when you are locked away in your "home away from home." They are the ones who visit you the most. They are the ones who bend their schedules to see you, even if it is only for a few hours. Your true friends will send you cards, e-mails and gifts. They want only the best for you. They are the ones who cry for you, who share in your pain. Your true friends are the ones who are by your bedside minutes before your surgery and hours afterwards. You discover an undeniable closeness with certain individuals that you would have previously never expected. People come out of the woodwork when you are sick. They are familiar names, but not names that you would consider close friends. Overtime, they evolve into something more. They become people who you want to stay close with, relationships that develop into friendships that can last a lifetime.

You also discover the friends who are fake. The friends who only want to spend time with you when you are on top of your game. They fade into the background. You begin to forget about them, almost as though they do not exist. It is when you escape your prison that you start feeling resentment towards these "friends." They start to reappear. They contact you as though they had been with you through it all. They try to schedule plans with you, but you go out of your way to blow them off, to leave them alone on a Friday night, much like they did to you when you were in your Hell. You begin spending more time with the ones who were there for you. Time spent with them becomes a premium.

You discover the power of silence when you are finding out who your true friends are. True friends do not need to be entertained. True friends can sit by you in total silence when you are sick and feel comfortable throughout the duration of their stay. Silence brings out people's true feelings. Silence proves how committed they are to making you happy.

There are two responses to silence. The first is the response of someone who is uncomfortable—they will begin to squirm. They make a lot of unnecessary sounds as they try to fight against the silence, but the silence always wins. After awhile they can't handle the silence. Fake friends feel awkward. They begin to make up excuses as to why they need to leave in the coming hour. Eventually, they disappear. Typically, they never return. The other response to silence is poise. The ones who truly care about you understand when you are not feeling well enough to speak. They understand that you are fighting to return to your former self and are content with spending hours in silence watching television. These people just want to be near you. They simply want to show their support. These are the people with whom you want to surround yourself. You find that you later need at least one of these people everyday when your health worsens. They are the ones who will give you strength. They give you a purpose and talk you out of slumps on days that you want to give up. These people have your back. They are the ones whom you should call "friend."

IS THERE REALLY A GOD?

On Thursday, June 11, 2009, I underwent a stress test. To this day, I feel that this stress test caused severe damage to my already dying heart. Though I cannot prove it, I firmly believe this test may have shortened my life expectancy by at least two to three weeks. From this day forward, I would lose a step. I seemed to grow sicker much faster; my body seemed to weaken each day.

I don't remember what time the test occurred, but it was in the early afternoon. The transporter came to my door with a wheelchair and I was taken to a lower part of the hospital. I entered the room to find a team of doctors and nurses. A female doctor began to speak with me. Her hair was brown, but it had a streak of grey going through the front near her left bang. She looked aged. She had crow's feet near her eyes and she was beginning to develop frown lines. She showed me three vials and explained that the substances within the vials were going to speed up my heart rate. Meanwhile, I would be placed into a scanner that would quickly take images of my heart. This test was referred to as being "nuclear." I couldn't participate in the standard treadmill test because it hurt too much to walk. I was taken to an adjoining room where two nurses slowly helped me into the scanner. The scanner was like a chamber, barrel-like. My entire body was enclosed with the exception of the sides of my head. Above my field of vision was a calming painting of a tree. Its leaves were purple and it was gently blowing in the wind. The purple leaves were cascading off. They landed in a nearby pond that was surrounded by perfectly nurtured blades of grass. *This is pretty corny,* I thought to myself. Yet, I was unable to look away. The image was the most calming sight I had seen in days. A nurse walked over and injected the three vials into my IV. I braced myself, waiting for my heart to explode with energy. Instead, nothing happened. I just laid there, looking around the room.

The room was tinted yellow. The walls looked aged, much like the doctor. There were two men directly to my right. One was wearing a navy colored polo. *He must be a computer technician,* I thought. The other man was wearing a lab coat. They both sat in chairs, staring at the screen anxiously awaiting data. "Okay, we are going to turn on the machine now," the man with the lab coat said. The chamber was then activated. It didn't move. Instead, it made a loud mechanical noise, an awkward humming sound. That was also when my heart seemed to turn on as well.

At first the test was okay, my heart seemed to be handling the stress well. *This isn't so bad,* I thought. The amount of beats per minute began to steadily climb. Eventually, my heart was pounding harder than I had ever felt before. It was almost like my heart was hitting my rib cage. That's when the pain came back.

I felt like I had been walking for blocks, like I did with Mark. I felt sweat burst from my brow, it trickled down my sideburns. "It hurts!" I screamed at the two men. The man in the lab coat walked over to me, "How bad does it hurt?" he asked. "Really fucking bad!" I yelled back. "Look, we only have a minute and a half left. If you stop now we are going to have to do this all over again tomorrow," he said calmly. "Do you think you can hang on for much longer?" I gave him a dirty glare and began staring at the painting. I took deep breaths in rapid succession. I tried to lose myself in the purple tree. The minute and a half seemed more like a day and a half as I struggled to not black out from the pain. Finally, the humming stopped. My heart continued to race for another five minutes. Thankfully, the pain's intensity slowly weakened.

I returned to my bed exhausted. I took a short nap and was then awakened by Dr. Young, Dr. Ying and Dr. Yang. They used their stethoscopes and asked me how I felt. I explained to them how I felt awful. They of course gave me zero answers as to how I should go about feeling better. All they said was that the results would not be back until later that afternoon, and pending the results, I may require another procedure the following day to place a stent in my arteries. They left, and my mom began to pray.

The room was filled with my aunts, and in harmony, they all said the Lord's Prayer.

"Our Father who art in heaven, hallowed be thy name."

I was shocked. *What, am I dying right now?* I thought. *Has everyone given up on me already?* The room felt like it was in slow motion, I was waiting for the Priest to enter and give me my last rites. *Why are you praying to God?* I thought. *If He even gave a shit, I would be interning right now and walking the streets of Chicago like a twenty year-old should be!*

"Thy kingdom come. Thy will be done on Earth…"

I then exploded, "Shut the fuck up! Are you fucking kidding me?! Get the fuck out of here!" I screamed as I pointed at the door. Everything I said was directed to my mom. The room fell silent. I began to cry. My mom began to cry, too. I looked up and saw the expressions on the faces of my aunts. They all looked scared. Aunt Deme quickly staggered out of the room, Aunt Patti followed after. Within seconds, the room cleared out. My dad was the only one to stay behind. "Do you need anything?" he asked. "No, please, just leave me alone," I responded. My dad began to pick up his computer bag, but just before he left my room, he turned to me and said, "She only did that because she's scared. She doesn't know what to do with herself right now. You're her baby. Her entire life has been spent watching over you and she feels like she has no control. When you were an infant, she would sit by your cradle and say that prayer. She's just confused. She doesn't know what to do, but I understand why you're angry." I couldn't respond because I couldn't stop crying. My dad gave me a saddened look, as though he was holding back his own tears.

My bed was near a window. I looked up at the sky shaking my head in disgust.

THE PAWN ORDERS A PLASTY

When a plane begins a downward spiral, it will typically crash and burn, killing everyone inside. My life had been nothing more than a plane plummeting to its demise for the past three days at this point. My first engine had failed and the second onboard engine was starting to go. That's when Dr. Young entered the room with an awkward grin on his face.

"The results of the stress test came back. Your heart is severely damaged," he said. I heard sputtering and then my second engine shut off. I braced myself for impact. "In fact, one of your arteries is 60 percent blocked, and the other is 90 percent shut." Kaboom! My plane had finished its free fall. Nothing was left but my ashes and a burnt seat from the cockpit.

I glanced over at my mom. She looked stunned, absolutely devastated. My dad shared the same expression. Dr. Young didn't stay in the room for long. Dr. Young answered some questions from my parents, explaining that I had to have a procedure called an angioplasty to place a stent in the 90 percent blocked artery. He also explained that a second stent might be placed in the 60 percent blockage. He left minutes later. The test was scheduled for the following day, so the rest of the evening was spent eating turkey sandwiches and conversing with my aunts. They were choosing their words cautiously as they spoke with me. They seemed to think that I would snap at any second.

My mom didn't leave my hospital bed throughout the entire stay. At night, she slept in a reclining chair, which sat about three feet to the right of my bed. For whatever reason, my mom demanded control over the television. She would awkwardly turn on *Sex And The City* and I would complain throughout the entire program. I don't know if it was because she was overly tired from an emotional day, or if she felt bad for me, but on this night, she let me have the remote.

I turned on the NBA Finals. The Los Angeles Lakers were on the road against the Orlando Magic. My mom had fallen asleep already and I stayed up watching the game. I remember being irrationally angry. I was jealous of Kobe Bryant and Dwight Howard. I hadn't played basketball since I was nine, and when I did play, I sucked. Nonetheless, as I watched the game, I was envious of their ability to run up-and-down the court. I didn't care so much that they could shoot the ball with unbelievable precision, or jump above the rim. I was simply mad that they seemed to have the ability to control every aspect of their bodies.

My nurse entered my room at some point during the game and handed me a sleeping pill. The game ended with an overtime win by Los Angeles. I watched Kobe walk off the court as I felt the pill take hold. I fell asleep.

I awoke the next morning anxiously awaiting the procedure. My dad had arrived early and was pacing the floor. Eventually, all of my aunts returned, seemingly at the same time, almost as though they had carpooled. A few of my cousins came this day as well, along with Carissa and Gus.

In time, two nurses and a transporter whisked me away on a bed. They took me down a hall and into an elevator, which led me to a large area with curtains and a small bank of private rooms. I was placed into one of the private suites, where several individuals slowly filtered in, all explaining to me their purpose.

The first individual was a plump nurse. I wouldn't say that she was fat, but she was certainly "chunky." She had brown hair, brown eyes and rose flushed cheeks. Her job was probably the worst. She was in charge of shaving the incision sight. The incision sight for this procedure happened to be the right side of my groin. She took her time and I feel I must commend her on an excellent shave.

Next, a pair of men wearing blue scrubs entered the room. I learned they were the surgeons performing the procedure. The first man had thick, black, curly hair and was very pale. He had a large nose, and resting above his mammoth bridge was a pair of golden wire glasses. The second man was fat, he wasn't "chunky." He made the nurse look like a spokesperson for Jenny Craig. His skin was red, burnt, as though he had recently returned from a tropical vacation.

They began telling me the steps that would be performed during the surgery. As they were speaking, the final team member entered the room. He was tall and stood like a giant next to the two surgeons. The tanned surgeon began introducing the giant. He explained that he was the Anesthesiologist. Before he finished his introduction, the giant interjected and said, "Hey, I'm Dirk. I'm going to be your bartender today." I smirked.

Now, as I stated previously, I was never myself again after the stress test. I can't explain what happened, but as the surgeons continued their speech, pain unexpectedly consumed my chest. I began scream-ing from the pain. Everyone in the room panicked. I had already been hooked up to a monitor within the room, so the surgeons were able to view my heartbeat. The room became still while they searched for new irregularities in my rhythm. They didn't find anything and the pain subsided.

My mom had been in my private room during the pain. The surgeons pulled her outside and began discussions of possibly canceling the procedure. They later concluded that the surgery should continue as scheduled because they didn't find any irregularities during the pain. The pair of surgeons and my mom returned. They each looked scared. *Great!* I thought to myself. *The two guys who are about to perform an invasive procedure just had their confidence rocked.* I mentally prepared myself for another horrific turn of events, as I was wheeled away into the operating room. My mom kissed me on the forehead before I entered and told me she loved me. I replied with the same sentiment and was then struck with a chill throughout my body.

The room was very cold. It was filled with many people. I would guess there were at least five nurses in the room, along with six others who were dressed in the same scrubs as the two surgeons. I remember feel-ing like I was an experiment. In front of me was a tall wall. Several feet up the wall was a large protruding glass window. There were two men standing in the window. They were both looking down on me. One had a clipboard and he seemed to be writing information about me. The other man was wearing an American flag theme bandana. He was standing with his arms crossed.

Dirk then entered my field of vision and began talking to me about my allergies to medications. I only have one allergy, so it is easy to remember. "I can't take Cephalosporins," I said. Dirk looked at me like I was brilliant, yet like I had wasted his time with my answer. Cephalosporin is a class of antibiotics. Obviously, Dirk only worked with narcotics. I was then startled when I turned my head away from Dirk to find the man with the American flag bandanna directly to my right standing over me. He turned his attention to Dirk, and in a calm voice said, "Alright, let's do this."

I turned my head back toward Dirk and watched him inject a solution into my IV. Dirk smiled as he pushed the drug—Dirk seemed to really enjoy his job. His smile was the last image I remember seeing. The room faded to gray.

I awoke in my private room. It was dark, almost as though they wanted me to stay asleep. A young nurse entered the room and asked how I was feeling. I told her that I was groggy and that I wanted my parents. She then left and my parents appeared. From here on out, my parents, aunts and cousins would take turns walking into the room in pairs. The doctors were strict about how many visitors could come into the private suite. Only two were allowed in at a time. I remember one pair in particular. The pairing was Aunt Deme and my Nouna, (Greek for Godmother). They entered the room and began speaking with me very softly. They told me that the doctors said everything had gone well.

Bear in mind, my heart was not in good shape. Consequently, it was known by all that my heart rhythms were a bit out of the ordinary. I was having PVC's (Premature Ventricular Contractions). On a heart monitor, they appear as giant drops, like out of control nosedives. I found the way the monitor displayed the PVC to be quite symbolic of my own life.

Aunt Deme and Nouna were standing at the foot of my bed when they each looked up at the monitor. Both of their eyes got large as though I was flat lining. I panicked at the sight of their response and I was launched into another painful attack. I bit my lower lip and stared at the ceiling until it passed. My mom had words with Aunt Deme and Nouna. They weren't allowed back into my room.

I instantly grew tired when the attack subsided. I took advantage of my dark surroundings and fell back to sleep. I drifted off assuming I would be sent home the next day. I figured this was the end to all of the surgeries. I thought I would spend the next few weeks at home recovering and my life would go back to normal.

I'm laughing as I write this because I was so naive. I thought my walk through Hell was over.

I hadn't even put on my shoes yet.

ROBOT BOY

It was Saturday when Dr. Kuieffer entered my room. I was on the phone with a friend, staring out my window as we spoke. My view was nothing more than lackluster at best. My window overlooked a rooftop. The particular portion of the roof I could see was the section that housed the hospital's ventilation system. Everything was silver, cold and robotic. I was surrounded by machines; they were both inside and outside of my room. "Is this a bad time?" said the voice from behind me. I turned to find a lanky man wearing a white lab coat. The best way to describe Dr. Kuieffer is to say he closely resembles a turtle. He has an elongated forehead, which is accentuated by his balding scalp that shimmers in the light. He has thin lips, specifically his upper lip. He bites it when he pauses to think. His eyes are small and they appear even smaller under his metallic black framed glasses. His skin is tanned, and when he walks, his poor posture seems to force his neck forward.

"Oh, no, I can talk," I replied as I quickly ended my phone call. Dr. Kuieffer introduced himself and explained he was a surgeon from the Electrophysiology Department. *Okay?* I thought to myself. I hadn't quite picked up on why he was in my room. "After reviewing your angioplasty and stress test, it has come to the attention of the entire staff that you are a candidate for a defibrillator." My mouth dropped open, I was speechless. *Are you shitting me?!* I thought. *Don't sixty-year-olds have those?!* Dr. Kuieffer continued nonchalantly, as though he was not delivering devastating news. "You see… you are a candidate for what is called SCD, or Sudden Cardiac Death. Your heart is throwing irregular rhythms. The rhythms are so severely irregular that any one could potentially kill you." My dad was in the room at this point, he could tell I was stunned, unable to speak. "So what are you saying?" my dad sternly interjected. The turtle got nervous after hearing my dad's tone. He quietly explained that I wouldn't be discharged until I consented to the operation and had the defibrillator inserted into my chest cavity. I finally spoke, "What the fuck is a defibrillator?!" I had a vague idea, but before I got too upset, I needed verification. "Well, it's like a metal box…" he said, "…it's the size of your palm and it has wires called 'leads' attached to it. Those wires will go into your heart and in the event you have an irregular heart beat, the wires will shock your heart and normalize the rhythm." "So its like a fucking pacemaker!" I yelled. A mixture of anger and sorrow was beginning to brew within. "Not exactly, but it's very similar… yes," he replied. I felt the lump in my throat rapidly grow as though my neck was going to rupture from the inside. "Fuck that! I am not doing it!" I exclaimed.

The turtle looked startled by my response. He began to speak but my dad cut him off. My dad escorted the cold-blooded doctor outside of my room. I got up and immediately headed to my bathroom, slamming the door behind me. I stared at myself in the mirror as I felt the lump in my throat release. Tears poured down my face and I lost complete control of my chin as it began to quiver wildly. I turned on the faucet in hopes of washing the tears away with water. Brown, tainted water began to flow into the sink. "Are you fucking kidding me?!" I whispered loudly into the water. "Why me? Why the fuck did this happen to me? What did I do to deserve this?" It was then I had a realization.

Not only was I surrounded by machines, but I was about to become one.

Y/INI

There is a limitation on how much bad news the mind can absorb. After awhile it reaches its breaking point, it snaps. The mind will panic and trigger laughter, its most effective defense mechanism. On June 15, 2009, exactly seven days into my hospitalization, my mind couldn't withstand any more negativity. My mind snapped.

It was the eve of my defibrillator surgery. The room was solemn. Everyone could sense my nerves. The night was filled with small talk about favorite movies, websites, and anything else in the world of pop culture that was shallow enough to keep the conversation light-hearted. This particular night's roster of visitors included my parents, Aunt Lisa, and my cousins Nick and Nicole. My mom had been out of the room for quite some time. She had received word earlier in the evening that Dr. Wiezien wanted to speak with her over the phone. Dr. Wiezien was another one of the Puppet Master's pawns. The day after Dr. Young broke the news of the angioplasty he vanished and Dr. Wiezien then began to follow my case.

I remember glancing up from my computer and seeing my mom and two nurses approaching the glass window. The two escorting nurses looked anxious. One of them kept staring at me, locking eyes, almost as though she was trying to read my thoughts. The other nurse couldn't keep her eyes off the floor as she reached for the handle to slide it open. My mom entered. A sudden chilling silence fell across the room as my mom began to speak, "I just got off the phone with Dr. Wiezien. She has just informed me that six of the Resident doctors that have been in Bill's room have tested positive for H1N1... the 'Swine Flu.'"

The three minutes that followed the moment my mom said those words is a period of time I will never forget. They were the greatest, most entertaining three minutes of my entire hospital stay—it was when my mind snapped.

Immediately after hearing the news, Nicole began to gasp like she was being strangled by shock. She then went into a series of awkward convulsive coughs, followed by a progression of random words and fidgeting. Her awkwardness culminated with her holding her chest like a bad thespian in an overdramatic play.

Aunt Lisa's mouth dropped open. She sat there dumbfounded, her eyes protruding from her head as she continuously muttered, "What the... what the... what the..." she was glaring at the nurses, so taken aback by the complete randomness of the situation.

I looked over and saw my dad. He sat there in his chair, pale, like he had just seen the ghost of Christmas past. He sat there shaking his head, occasionally looking upwards towards the ceiling while rubbing his five o'clock shadow, as if he was looking for an answer from a greater power.

Nick's reaction was the best, though. His face was filled with utter astonishment. I have never seen such a perplexed look on a person's face. It was like someone had unexpectedly taken him from behind. He was looking around the room frantically, as though he was longing for verification that what he had heard was correct. He looked like a mouse who had been baited into its death trap.

That's when I couldn't help myself, I started to laugh. With that every-one paused, turning their heads towards me in unison. I continued to laugh, bent over from pain. They all stared at me as if I were crazy. That's when I mustered enough breath to speak, "What's the next phone call going to be?" I asked, gasping for air, "That Dr. Young has herpes on his stethoscope?" Everyone broke out into laughter, even the timid nurse seemed to perk up. We were laughing because we all felt the same way. We were all stricken by the irony that my doctors, the ones who were supposed to take care of me and bring me back to health, may be the very cause for not only a lengthened period of stay, but they may have crippled me even further with another debilitating disease. The thought of me contracting a disease was not funny to any of us. I think we all just snapped that night. We felt destitute by the unknown. We had to know; how much more could possibly go wrong?

The nurses began to explain how they were going to put me on Tamiflu as a precaution. They also expressed the possibility of my surgery being postponed. They continued to deliver bad news, but I did not care. My mind had already shattered. They could have told me that I was going to grow a vagina on my back or the National Football League was on strike and I would not have cared. I just kept laughing. The remainder of the night was spent calling all of my friends and family who had visited me in the hospital on speakerphone, as we laughed at their reactions when we told them they were inadvertently exposed to one of the deadliest pandemics of the decade. We were riding this high of insanity. We became fiends, chasing our next buzz from the bewilder-ment of others.

As weird as it may sound, I hope your mind snaps. It made for a great night and most certainly, my only good one. It made me feel human, and it was the first time in a week that my tears were not those of sorrow.

THE VISITORS

I was visited one day by a group of strangers. I never got any of their names and I never really got to know any of them. I did talk to all of them though, briefly, and I remember the smallest details of every one of their faces, all seventy-six of them.

As much as I want to believe that everything in this story is my recollection of a dream, I genuinely do not think it was. It may have been a hallucination brought on by the anxiety pill or it may have actually happened. There is a very strong possibility that I may have had an out-of-body experience the morning of my defibrillator surgery.

On this morning, I was awakened at 6:00 AM by my parents and a technician. The technician came in to do a preliminary echocardiogram before my surgery. The process was nothing out of the ordinary. She applied the electrodes to my chest, clipped on the corresponding wires and began to squirt the gel onto her scope. The technician was directly to my left, my mom was in the back left corner of the room, and my dad was standing at the foot of my bed repositioning his laptop bag on his shoulder. I mention this miniscule detail because when the technician placed her scope on my chest, the room faded to white.

The sounds of the hospital were gone. I was alone in a white room, lying in my hospital bed. The IV was gone, as was the television, but then I blinked. Suddenly, the room came back to me. Everything was restored and put back in its place, everything but my parents and the technician. I was not alone though, my visitors had arrived. I looked up and there she was, standing over me on the right side of my bed. Like I said, I never got her name, but she was beautiful. Her skin was smooth, absolutely perfect. She was angelic. She was darker complected, Middle Eastern descent would be my guess. Her hair was pulled back in a ponytail, which was tied together in a large, red bow. The white light above made her hair shimmer. I could see myself in her eyes. They were large, brown and radiant. Her lipstick was also red and it matched her dress perfectly. I can still see the creases on the fabric where the shoulders met the elastic band on her arm. Her dress puffed at the shoulders. It looked old fashion, like something you would see in an old western film. That's when she smiled. Her teeth were neon white, perfectly aligned. Then she spoke, "Hi Bill." Her voice was delicate, very sincere and calming. "Bill, a lot of people come to this hospital and a lot of people have surgeries," her voice remained calm, but her expression changed to sadness, "a lot of us do not make it though." With that, her mood changed. She became very serious but her delicacy did not change. She angled her body and that's when I saw them, all seventy-six. They were standing in a single file line, which flowed out of my room, poured into the ICU, wrapped around the nurses station and ended in the hallway. She turned her body back toward me, "We all came here to see you because we wanted to tell you something." She slowly reached out to me, placing her right hand on my chest, directly over my heart. "You're going to be okay," she said. "You're going to make it." She leaned over, and I felt the moisture of her red lipstick touch my skin as she gently kissed my forehead. She turned and headed straight for the door. She then stopped, looked over her shoulder and smiled at me again with her neon white smile. "Good luck," she mouthed, and then she disappeared.

The rest of the visitors followed, each one from a different walk of life. They were from every culture and every race. There was no limitation to their size or the way they spoke. I was visited by elders, children, and mothers carrying infants. Though they were all unique in their own ways, they all shared with me the same two sentiments. Many of them said, "Good luck." The children would whisper, "You are going to be okay." I just laid in my bed smiling, responding occasionally by simply saying, "Thank you." My last visitors were an older couple. They were wearing matching light blue sweaters with yellow pants. They held hands as they turned and walked out the sliding glass door. That's when the room faded to white again before morphing back into the dark desolate atmosphere I had become accustomed to. "All finished!" the technician said proudly as she began rubbing the gel from my skin. My mom was still standing in the left corner of the room smiling at me. My dad was now seated to my right.

DELIRIUM

Imagine feeling twenty pounds of force holding your left shoulder to a bed. The muscles in your chest have been exhausted. Consequently, you cannot move and it hurts to breathe. You notice you are breathing slowly. Your breath becomes shallow. You begin to struggle for air. You try to breathe faster, but your lungs will not fill, your mind won't allow them to. You are slowly suffocating yourself. You then open your eyes. You can see, but you can only move your pupils. Any movement of your head sends shock waves of pain down your neck, through your left arm, and out your lower back. When you begin to look around with your limited sight, the room is dark. You can see human figures. You can't make out who they are, but the outlines of their bodies look familiar. Two bodies stand at your left foot, another at your right. You can tell they are women accompanied by two men who each sit on opposite sides of your room in chairs. You can feel them staring at you. A female body approaches you from the left. You feel a rough, cool fabric in your mouth and you are told to bite down. The voice is all too familiar, yet you struggle to identify its owner in your mind. You oblige the request. As you bite down onto the fabric, water begins to pour down your throat. The liquid startles you. You begin to choke and your breathing becomes worse. The coughing causes your head to move and you feel the shock wave burst throughout your body. You brace yourself until it is over. When the pain subsides, your vision becomes clearer. It is then you can see to whom the bodies belong.

The water torturer was Nicole. The other body to the left was Carissa. To the right of my bed stood my mom and sitting opposite each other were Gus and my dad. I had just gotten out of my defibrillator surgery and I was experiencing a feeling that I had never felt before, I was delirious. My brain would not work. Though I knew they were my family, for a short while, I was convinced they were trying to harm me.

I had to lay in bed for six hours. During this time period, both Nicole and Carissa would sponge water into my mouth, using a device that looked like a lollipop stick with cheap, green foam attached to it. My mom stared at me with a face that expressed two emotions simultaneously. The first emotion was sorrow. The other was fear. "You need to breathe, Bill!" she would yell at me frequently. I had been given a heavy cocktail of narcotics for the procedure. One of the drugs in particular caused my respirations to slow, dropping my blood oxygenation level far lower than it should ever go. If your blood oxygenation level falls too low for an extended period of time, you run the risk of either going blind, going deaf, or dying.

Carissa walked over and told me to bite down. Both Nicole and Carissa had to give me the same command with each serving because I continuously forgot what I was supposed to do. I bit down again. When I went to swallow the water, I couldn't. The muscles in my throat stopped working. I continued to push until finally the water went down. "I can't swallow!" I whispered to my mom. She panicked and got a doctor. They spoke, but I couldn't understand their conversation. The water feeding continued for many hours until suddenly, as though someone had flipped a switch off on the narcotics, the pain cascaded throughout every limb of my body.

I had never cried over pain in my life, but on this day I instantly broke down into tears. Two nurses ran into my room. I saw one take a syringe to my IV and inject a full dose of a clear substance. It was only moments until the pain dispelled. I felt numb again, but my ability to breath escaped me. I struggled to suck in air. "What did you give him!" my mom scolded the nurse. The nurse looked afraid, as though she had done something wrong. "Dilaudid," she responded sheepishly. My respirations continued to grow shallower; I started forgetting how to breathe. My mom went outside and began speaking with the two nurses. Hours later, I would discover the nurse had "accidentally" administered 2mg of Dilaudid. She was ordered to only administer .5mg. To put into perspective just how drugged I was, 1mg of Dilaudid is equivalent to roughly 6.6mg of Morphine. The sheepish nurse had just re-launched me back into my delirium. Crash carts were pulled into the room and the nursing staff anxiously sweated out the next few hours on the other side of my sliding glass door.

I know now that my family quickly discovered how, when I grew angry, I would subconsciously begin to breathe harder, thus causing my blood oxygenation level to rise. I didn't understand this at the time. Once again, I thought everyone was trying to harm me. My dad took the approach of irritation. He would continuously say, "Hey Bill!" in fast repetition. His voice echoed in the room. To me, he sounded as though he was yelling down an open hallway. I began to yell back at him, finally I screamed, "Would you shut the fuck up!" My heart rate must have begun to rise, along with my blood oxygenation level, because my mom saw fit for my dad to step out of the room.

The hours continued to pass and the Dilaudid began to wear off.

Finally, I was allowed to stand. In pain, I hobbled to the bathroom.
IV pole in hand, I closed the door and stared at myself in the mirror.
Slowly, I removed the green gown from my left shoulder. A large, white
bandage wrapped around my entire chest cavity. Seeping under the
bandage was a bruise that stretched down my torso, past my lower
ribs, and ended just above my hip bone. I didn't cry. I just stared in the
mirror, looking at my angered face. "Your life is over Bill," I said to the
mirror. I stared at myself in silence until my focus was broken by the
sound of my mom's voice. "Are you okay in there?" I didn't respond.
Instead, I punched the mirror with my right arm, opened the door, and
walked back to my bed.

The lights in the room were now on. I sat upright, staring at the wall in
silence. The next day I was discharged.

I was sent home to suffer.

The Lost Days

Wednesday,
June 17, 2009 –
(Approximately)
Saturday,
June 27, 2009

MONSTER

Pain can do a lot to someone. It can tear them down, physically and emotionally. It can make all the beauties in the world seem bleak, distorted. Pain can turn truths into lies, smiles into untrusting smirks. Pain can make the nights last longer than the days. Pain can make you numb.

But pain can also make you stronger. It can test you. As much as pain can tear you down, it can give you second hope, a second life. Pain can revive relationships that once seemed lost.

There is a void in my life, a hole. A period of ten days that no matter how hard I try to piece together, I cannot recall the date, the hours, or the specifics of any conversation I had throughout those days. I do have images, though. Little snippets. Black and white clips of these days that echo in my mind. I don't know what to attribute this lapse in memory to. I question if it is a long-term side effect of the narcotics I was on to ease the pain of the defibrillator, or maybe it was my mind's way of protecting itself from the sadness that captivated my world.

Emotions are what stand out the most in these black and white clips. Not just my emotions, but also the emotions of everyone around me. I noticed a change in people, specifically in my family, mostly in my sister. She seemed humbled by my experience. I used to wonder if her change was in my head, if really she was only being nice temporarily because I was so ill. I had expectations that our relationship would go back to the way it used to be. We were in a constant fight. Every day was a contest to see who had the meanest remark. The comments were meant to break each other down, possibly cause tears. However, as the days have passed and from what I have seen from her since, her change seems to truly be genuine. She has undergone a transformation from one of my biggest enemies to one of my greatest caregivers.

It is because of her transformation that my first memory (though it is far from my darkest) pains me the most. I remember waking up in a horrible mood. I was angry and irritable. What I did next I do not recall, but somehow I found myself sitting at the kitchen table with my mom. She wasn't doing anything wrong, just simply explaining to me my new list of pills that I had to consume daily at both noon and midnight. My shoulder was pulsating. Every miniscule gesture stung and shot waves of pain down my back. I hated it. I hated the way it made me feel. I felt useless, so unnecessary.

Looking back now, I can only assume that ten, maybe twenty minutes lapsed because I remember my mom being angry with me, offended by something I must have said. That's when my sister entered and where my memory comes back to me. Carissa made a comment in regards to our Camry being mostly her car because she had paid my parents a large lump sum the prior summer. For whatever reason, I remember wanting to start a fight. I replied with a comment about her wasting money at The University of Iowa her freshman year of college before transferring to Eastern Illinois University. What that comment had to do with anything still baffles me today, but I do know it received the response I was looking for. My mom exploded, simply lost it. She began screaming at me about how I had to stop treating everyone around me so poorly. I glanced over at my sister and saw such a crushed look on her face. What happened next is another blur in my mind, but I do remember leaving my house. Where I went, I have no idea. How I even got to this unknown destination is lost in the void, but I remember feeling like a monster. I remember hating myself, beating myself up for hours as my mom's words replayed in my head. I felt as though I had to apologize to everyone, but I didn't know where to start. I felt horrible. I couldn't even talk to Carissa. I wrote her a letter instead. I believe I even put it in an envelope, licked it, and slid it under her door. She thanked me for it later and fully accepted my apology. But to this day I still feel horrible about this memory. I am sorry if I hurt anyone else. It was never my intention. I never meant to become a monster.

THE FACE IN THE MIRROR

I remember when I lost the ability to be afraid, the fear had left. Not necessarily the fear of the unknown, but the fear of dying. I believe there is a difference in the two forms of fear. The fear of the unknown still claws at my mind with each second of the day. The unknown is with me when I wake up, when I shower, and when I go to work. The fear is even with me in my dreams. I don't think the fear of the unknown will ever leave me after this experience. I believe the fear has permanently imbedded itself in my mind and will always keep me on my toes, making me search for irregularities, almost paranoid, no matter how healthy I may some day become.

I'm no longer afraid of dying. This I am sure of.

I am not afraid of death anymore because I have realized that death is a certainty. It is a natural stage in life. Though the specific time, or the way you will die isn't given to anyone, I understand that death is going to come. I used to be afraid of death, actually petrified by it. However, I distinctly remember when that fear vanished.

Looking back, I can only assume this black and white memory took place just days after my discharge. I say this because I distinctly remember the pain in my shoulder being worse than it had ever been. I couldn't use the shower throughout the majority of these lost days. I had to settle with sponge-bathing myself in the bathroom. My mom would then later wash my hair in the kitchen sink.

It was during one of my sponge baths when the fear disappeared. I was standing in the bathroom, naked, cold and shivering from the luke-warm beads of water that were rapidly evaporating from my skin. That was when I saw myself for the first time since the hospital. I looked so frail and lifeless. All of the muscle in my body had deteriorated, leaving nothing but the skeleton of the person I used to be. My eyes looked sunken in. Any sign of human emotion was paved away and replaced with a chilling, glazed, disheartening stare.

It was the face of death.

My body looked bruised. Beaten by needles, tubes and leads. Each bruise was perfectly preserved by my blood thinners in the shape of the object that had created them. It was almost like my body wanted to remind me that the Hell I had been through actually happened. That my life had changed, that my devastation was real.

I specifically remember not crying. I held it in. I stood there angry at the world, angry with God, wondering why this had to happen to me. I started thinking about dying and what it would feel like. I don't know if it was because I was in so much pain, but with one look in the mirror I accepted the possibility.

However, let me be clear about one thing. In that moment, I acknowledged the fact that I may die. Not necessarily that day or that week, but I did, for a moment, realize that I may never make it to my twenty-first birthday. I had a choice though, I could give into the notion that death was around the corner, that this disease was going to be my end, or I had the option to keep pushing, to keep struggling and live to see the day when the dark clouds that had been cast over my world opened and the light would shine through. It would be on that day, I would know I had won.

I chose to not give in. I chose at that moment to do whatever it took to keep fighting. I understood that I might encounter some horrible days, that the pain of the defibrillator may become so unbearable I may want to end my life. I knew there were going to be setbacks, but that was when I dug deep down and I summoned the strength. I discovered my <u>Will</u>.

I chose to escape death.

THE HUMMINGBIRD

It's unbelievable how the mind works. It seems the more I write about these snippets of memories, the more the memories come back to me in greater detail than before. There is one memory in particular that I haven't been able to stop reliving. It was the day I was visited by the hummingbird.

I've always believed in a greater being. I believe everyone has a guardian angel. I feel these guardians watch over you and protect you from afar, never revealing themselves until they feel the time is right. They wait until the moments in your life when you are at your lowest. The moments when your mind sinks so low that the ability to pray escapes you. When these angels do reveal themselves, they don't appear as a human apparition. They are much more subtle. They appear in the shape of objects that can go undetected to everyone, but stand out boldly to the ones they protect.

Like all of my memories in this ten-day period, I do not recall my reason for choosing to be where I was or for how long I was there. Though I do know that in this memory I was sitting in my living room, across a large window, which rests above a window seat. I sat there rocking back and forth. I vividly remember the motion. It was very slow, very methodical. It was helping me think.

I was home alone, staring at the pictures on the wall, reliving my life. I was in a trance, as I tried to remember what it felt like to be able to take on the world with gumption. I was thinking about the dreams that I wanted to fulfill, the goals in my life I hadn't yet completed. They were still in sight, but they seemed to be slowly drifting away, further and further from reality as the days on the calendar quickly passed.

That was when I heard the tapping. Immediately, I was ripped from my trance, sucked back into my dark world. I looked around confused, puzzled by the sound. I couldn't find its source. I then heard the sound again, it was even louder than before, "Tap tap!" My attention was quickly turned toward the window. That was when I met the hummingbird.

I remember time freezing. Everything was still, except the wings of the hummingbird. It was beautiful. So blue and so innocent—it was majestic. It floated outside my window in perfect symmetry. I felt a calm come over me. It was a warming sensation I had never felt. All of my concerns and worries began to disperse as though they were melting away. In that moment, everything I had been worried about losing seemed to realign. I experienced total relaxation. Then, as fast as the hummingbird entered my life, it disappeared. I watched it fly away, back into the heavens.

I left the living room and slowly climbed the stairs to the upper portion of the house. I entered my room and sat down on my bed. The lights were off. The blinds were shut. I lay there staring at the ceiling. It was the first time I remember talking to God since the surgery. I thanked him for a second chance. I thanked him for my visitor. Never in my life had I seen a hummingbird.

SYMPTOMS OF A TARNISHED MIND

Every night was a struggle to sleep. I'd lay awake as I listened to the dysfunctional rhythm of my heart—it liked to stop. The beat is all I could hear through my pillow. The room was always quiet, except for the beat. It was a sinister silence.

"Thud... Thud.... Thud.... (Stop!)... Thud... Thud-Thud... Thud... Thud... (Stop!)"

With every pause in rhythm my mind would panic. I would freeze and hold my breath as I'd await the sound of another "Thud." My mind would start to wander and I'd begin to question what would happen if the "Thud" never came. I'd begin to wonder...

Would I simply die? Or would my defibrillator work and I would experience a shock? What would a shock feel like? Would I scream? Could I scream? If I could, would anybody hear me?

These questions were among the many that played through my head every night. They are what I had grown accustomed to while falling asleep.

Nowadays, I only occasionally have nightmares, but during the lost days I feared closing my eyes.

Until you close your eyes, you do not realize how damaged your mind is. You see your heart. You witness your fears. Every scar you try to hide reopens. I discovered in those lost days that my mind was severely scarred. My mind was stained by surgeries and my deepest fears of the unknown.

A damaged mind keeps you up into the wee hours of the morning but won't allow you to sleep past the crack of dawn. There is one dream in particular that has cost me many hours of sleep.

I see the lights overhead shining down on me. The room is hot. I am aware of what is going on but at the same time I am oblivious to reality. I cannot move. I feel as though I am strapped down. I have no control. There's a melodic pulsating chime in the distance. I can hear it, but I cannot see where it is coming from. The hum of the chime begins to fade, as the sound of a cool mist takes over. The mist grows louder until

the chime is nothing more than a faint memory. That's when the faces
appear. They are doctors, but they are doctors I have never seen before.
They all stare at me, but they only communicate to one another. They
don't speak in words but in gestures. Their heads are jittery, like insects,
they rapidly gyrate side-to-side. The doctor on the right reaches for
a scalpel. That's when I spring forward. I scream. Two female physicians rush in. They grab my neck and chest and slam my head into
the pillow. I am then instantaneously transported to my bedroom.
The silent doctors are gone, but I hear crying. I look to my right and
find that everything has been flipped upside down. There are icons of
Saints and the Mother Mary scattered on a table. I slowly start to pick
up the icons. I stare at the faces of the Saints, but they are not the faces
I have grown to know. They are crying; each one of them are in tears.
The paint on the icon begins to run down my finger. I drop the icon. I
watch as it falls to the floor, but I wake up before impact. I'm greeted
every morning by the bright light of the sun, it's always the crack of
dawn.

For ten consecutive days, I had this dream. Each time, the dream
would stick with me throughout the course of the day. It was like a
leech had found its way into my brain and it would begin to suckle
whenever I'd close my eyes. My eyes closed often throughout the lost
days. The exhaustion began to take its toll. I remember dozing off at
inappropriate times. I have memories of finding myself with my head
pressed against my desk in my room or awkwardly positioned on a
chair. I do not know how long these moments of unconsciousness took
place. Time was not a factor in these lost days.

To this day, I still have the same nightmare. The doctors are still
operating on my mind, the paint still drips down my finger, and I still
do not know who is maliciously scrambling my icons. I wonder if the
dream will ever go away. Maybe I need to see the icon hit the floor.
Maybe then my mind will be free and the scars will begin to fade.

THE COTA KID

Not all of my dreams were bad. I had some great ones as well. They
may have been interrupted by the pain, but at least they didn't upset
me. I have one dream I remember even more distinctly than the others.
I was at a podium in front of a large convocation of people who all

seemed distraught. They were staring at me wide-eyed, yet they were confused as to who I was, or why I was speaking. They were talking amongst themselves. I could hear their chatter, judging me, questioning if I could help them.

I wasn't any older in this dream. It was present day, or at the very most, one to two years in the future. I stood there calmly. I was aware that I was a "nobody" and I was going to have to win them over. I shuffled my papers, cleared my throat and began speaking.

The room fell silent as I began to tell them the stories of my childhood, my adolescence, and of my adult years. I preached of miracles and the joys of giving. I acknowledged their sorrow, their losses, and what they had to give to be a part of a tight-knit community. I looked off stage and saw Natalie smiling. The crowd roared with excitement. I walked off the stage where I received praises. I had instantly gone from being an unknown to their leader.

I felt a sting in my shoulder and was instantly awakened, moaning in pain as I glared at the clock. It was six-something, I only remember the "6." But the dream was so distinct that it energized me. My mind was racing and I could not get myself back to bed. I was overcome with this need to make a difference. I felt I had to do something, but what?

I replayed the dream in my mind, searching for symbolism in the most minute of details. I determined that the "loss" the people had undergone was the loss of their loved ones, and that the "tight-knit community" must be the commonality they all share from either receiving or donating organs. What made it all click was my vision of Natalie being at the ceremony. For years, she had spoken at banquets for organ donation, citing my life as her inspiration.

I remember sitting at my computer for hours, researching organ donation and upcoming banquets. I was convinced I had to be part of one. I felt it was my fate. It was like the dream I had was a message from God telling me to give back, but everything I found in my searches didn't make sense. Every banquet and fundraiser had already occurred or was approaching in the coming week. I knew I would be in no condition to speak in a week's time. I couldn't even find events that were to be held in the coming year. That was when I feel fate brought me to a website called "COTA," and the profile of one kid, Jeremiah.

The similarities were eerie. He was an infant, hospitalized for a heart condition at the same place where my journey began, Lakeside Hospital. He had been waiting for an organ donation for months, and on June 16th (the same day that I received my defibrillator), he was discharged. I felt some greater power had brought me to this kid. I felt the need to warn him.

This memory is the only one I have in these lost days that I am able to put an exact date and time on. This is because I am able to see what I wrote to this child on his profile's "Guestbook." I now know this memory took place at exactly 9:45 AM on Thursday, June 18, 2009. At that exact minute of my life, I reached out to a child and I wrote him words that are so true, so gut wrenching to me, that now when I read them, they bring me a sense of pleasure because I tried to help, but also a sense of sadness because I vividly relive the pain that I was in. At 9:45 AM this is what I wrote Jeremiah:

Hey Jeremiah,

I have never met you, nor your family. I too had a heart transplant at Lakeside Hospital. I was 3 weeks old, and it was 20 years ago in 1989.

You may be too young to understand this now, but I just wanted to assure you that you can lead a normal life. You can experience all the beauties in this world and you should NEVER ever be embarrassed of any surgical scars. Though they will fade, they should serve as a reminder to you of how special you are and the miracle that you have been blessed with. This past school year I became lazy with my heart management and medication-taking habits. It led to a recent ten day long battle with rejection at Chicago General (my first rejection episode ever, which could have killed me!) Coincidentally, I was discharged on the same day as you (6-16-09) after receiving a defibrillator.

Learn from my mistakes. Don't ever get lazy (no matter how much fun you will have in college). You were given a miracle because you are meant to create them.

God Bless you and your entire family.

Enjoy it,
Bill

I hardly remember writing any of these words. Though, now when I read them, I can see how my sense of time had already begun to slip away. I told Jeremiah the wrong date of my discharge. Even though I feel that in the scheme of things when he reads it, if he ever reads it, the date will be irrelevant. I only hope that he can live a normal life and that maybe my words will prevent him from ever feeling pain.

I never received a response from his family. From what I can see, they have completely stopped updating their profile page. I'm glad though. I like to think it's because they are too busy living a happy life, enjoying their days with their beautiful son, and looking forward to returning to normalcy. I like to think they have finally found the horizon at the end of their swim.

AMBER

There is a person who thus far has been left out of this book. Her name is Amber and we dated throughout my hospitalization. During these lost days, Amber and I experienced a collapse in our relationship, a collapse brought on by my illness and her need for a boyfriend that I could not be.

Before I continue, I feel I must mention that I was having a hard time dating Amber prior to the hospitalization because each day was a struggle to live. I was very sick, had little energy, and many times struggled to breathe even when I was in a resting position. I was dying, but I was in denial. Amber misinterpreted my change in behavior as an attempt on my part to push her away. This I do understand. I feel the way I was acting merited the response I received. Amber's worry resulted in her questioning me, asking me countless times why I was acting different. She wanted to know why I was changing. I refused to answer the questions and instead would become irritated by her constant demand for answers I refused to supply.

During my hospital stay, Amber was there for me. She was by my bedside almost every day. In my eyes, she was the perfect girlfriend. She came off as being sweet, genuine and sincere. She was what I had always wanted; a cute girl who would love me enough to always be by my side. I became grateful for everything she did.

Amber spent the night with me in the hospital one evening. We were alone in the room. She sat down next to me in the hospital bed as we watched television. I apologized to her. I told her I was sorry for how I had acted in the weeks before my hospitalization. I tried to explain to her how I was not myself, how I was never trying to push her away. I just did not have it in me to admit to her, or myself, that I was deathly ill. She said she understood and I felt our relationship strengthen. I started wanting her near me after the surgeries and in the mornings when I'd wake up. Amber was simply incredible in the hospital. But when I returned home, Amber changed to a completely different person. She was no longer Amber, she was a stranger.

I believe life is full of hurdles. Some hurdles are smaller than others. Nonetheless, every hurdle is placed in front of you to make you stronger. I believe every individual is defined by the way they overcome these hurdles. Do they simply walk around them? Or do they charge full speed, jump and soar above the obstacle? The lost days proved to be an eye opener for me. I learned my illness was too big of a hurdle for Amber. She tried to walk around it.

Amber fought with me constantly during these lost days. I don't remember the details to all of the fights, but unfortunately I have a heavy reel of black and white clips allocated to the memories of Amber. They are not happy memories. The reel is a slideshow of anger, stress and misunderstanding. She would not leave me alone and would become progressively more irritated by the lack of attention that I provided her. I did not intentionally try to avoid her though. She just did not understand.

I have many memories in my mind of wandering around my house as I attempted to avoid people. I didn't want to speak. I was drawn to the quiet. I was in a constant search for solace. It was because of this search that I had many boring days. My life was dull. I had days where I did nothing. I stopped carrying my cell phone on me for hours at a time because I did not want to speak to anyone. Amber did not like this. When Amber would call, she would yell. She would berate me for not calling her and then get angered when I did not have anything to say. I remember her yelling at me because she "always had to be the one leading the conversation!" I would respond by explaining how I simply had nothing to say, how my life was filled with nothing. She still would not understand. She would continue to yell. Eventually, she would realize her insanity.

Amber would apologize, typically the next day, usually through written word in my inbox. I don't recall her apologizing over the phone, but I know she at least tried. The e-mails serve as evidence. I do remember her apologies meaning nothing over time. She fell into this pattern of fighting, apologizing and then fighting with me again over the same subject she had just apologized for.

My most prominent memory packaged into "Amber's Reel" is one in which I was lying in my bedroom with the phone resting near my ear, hearing Amber yell as the fan circulated in the dark over my head. The fan put me in a trance. I was able to tune her out. I suddenly became in-tune with my body and the potentially detrimental effects her negativity was causing. I felt my heart begin to race, my teeth clench, my stomach become nauseous and my blood pressure rise. I was staring at the ceiling fan when I knew I had to cut ties with Amber.

If I remember correctly, we fought for hours on the phone, and it was exhausting. I truly do not remember the details of what was said, but I do recall being very upset. I was finally fighting back. I remember screaming over her, trying to get a word in edgewise. I remember pacing the floors into the wee hours of the night, being so stressed and feeling my heart pound so hard that I had to sit down. I was afraid my defibrillator was going to shock me at any second. I remember feeling beads of sweat go down my face, wanting to stop the fighting, but realizing the end was in sight. Finally, the fighting stopped. There was silence; the quiet that I had grown to love.

We each took turns saying our final words before hanging up. That was the end of Amber.

I chose to include this story not because I am searching for a way to maliciously attack Amber, but because I feel God used this illness as a way of opening my eyes the same way He opened my eyes when I met the family of Jennifer. I am not meant to be with Amber, and He knew that. To this day, I still believe Amber is one of the purest individuals I know. Her mind may be cluttered, but Amber is a good person. Either we simply cannot communicate or she and I have vastly different views on what a successful relationship should be. Regardless of what the case may be, I wish her the best in life. I may never talk to her again, but I hope that God gives her the same clarification that He has given me.

The Journals:

Baby Steps

Sunday,
July 5, 2009 –
Wednesday,
July 29, 2009

Message From the Author:

While compiling my entries into this book, I noticed I never once described six words that are used rather frequently in the following section. For the sake of keeping the entries authentic, I did not want to fill in extra sentences. I chose to leave the pages how they were originally typed. When my mind was filled with sorrow and pain. When I was taking my "Baby Steps."

<u>Vasodilator</u>- A type of drug that dilates the blood vessels, thus helping blood pressure. Though it helps the heart, the same dilation also occurs within the brain causing many side effects, which you will soon read about.

<u>Isosorbide</u>- A name of a drug that falls under the "Vasodilator" group.

<u>Lipitor</u>- A common cholesterol lowering medication.

<u>Lopressor</u>- A medication used in treating high blood pressure.

<u>Norvasc</u>- Another medication used for treating high blood pressure.

<u>Prednisone</u>- The best, but worst drug/steroid ever created. It cures many ailments, but it has potentially some of the worst side effects known to man. This pill will be mentioned a lot, so please know, in my case, it is used for suppressing my immune system.

Sunday, July 5, 2009

Today I thought I was going to die. In fact, I was certain. I awoke feeling so weak and depleted of youth, it took me nearly an hour and a half to muster the strength to put on a shirt.

Everything around me seemed gloomy. I couldn't find the purpose in doing anything. I didn't feel the need to eat, nor did I see the benefits in living. The only task that seemed to make sense was to take my regimen of pills that my mom had laid out so neatly for me on the counter top.

That was when Gus and my dad entered the kitchen. They began to argue over his future in baseball and whether or not he should go to a scouting combine at Ohio State University, or go to an optional high school football camp. Gus, being the stereotypical high school jock with his head up his ass, was debating that scholarship money is not important. For whatever reason, I felt it was my turn to speak. I then went into (what I believe to be) the greatest impromptu speech ever given on the recession, student loan money and how the two combined can equal higher APR rates. Though it sounds like the most random argument, and at the moment I did not understand why I felt the need to share my two-cents about the world of finance, I soon did, when I instantaneously broke down crying.

Everything I had kept locked-up inside spilled out. All of my frustration and anger about my current status gushed out of me. "You have a gift!" I screamed as I pounded my fist on the wall. "You have the God-given ability to play baseball and a chance to earn a scholarship for playing a game and you're throwing it all away!" I had never in my life been this distraught. My voice began to crack as I said my final peace. "Do you know how many people would kill to be able to do what you do?! I wish I could walk down a fucking sidewalk without having to stop and catch my breath, and you're sitting here bitching about playing a sport! You should be ashamed of yourself!" With that, I stormed up to my room, slamming my door. I just sat there shaking, looping Jack's Mannequin's "Swim," searching for strength in the lyrics.

My dad entered and began rubbing my back. He assured me this was not my fault and that I had no control over the circumstances that I was stuck facing. He left, and I found myself in the same position that I was in just hours before. Sitting in my chair, unable to muster the strength to move. That's when I began to do something I never thought I'd be doing, I began to mentally plan my will.

Though it was a twisted thought, it actually proved to be somewhat therapeutic. I began trying to think of all the people in my life who had been by my side or who had offered large amounts of support from a distance throughout my battle. I then realized how blessed I am to have so many amazing people in my life. There are so many people that I began to run out of possessions to will away. I understood at that moment I have so much to live for—I have so many people to fight for. I can't give in to this depression, this Hell, this diagnosis. I need to stay afloat, I need to "Swim."

Monday, July 6, 2009

I just came to a realization this morning; it feels good to cry, to let everything out. It really frees up your thoughts and makes you feel a bit more human. I have been holding back the tears throughout the majority of this ordeal, with the exception of my breakdown yesterday over Gus' baseball camp. That crying episode, however, made me feel really weak. I think there is a difference in the tears you bottle up and those you just let go at their onset.

"Bottled up baseball camp tears," if you will, make your entire body shiver. They put you in this thirty to forty-minute state of paralysis. They make you relive everything. Your mind flashes back to your surgeries, to the nights you spent in the hospital bed. They even make you think about the life you once had, and make you feel that no matter how hard you try you are never going to have the same carefree lifestyle again.

But this morning, I let the tears go. They were triggered by two beautiful e-mails from two beautiful people who have been life-savers for my morale throughout this entire process, Natalie and Aunt Patti. Natalie's e-mail was a very long one. The e-mail was basically just asking me how everything was going. She kept it positive by telling me about all the story plots in her life such as her current boy crush and the people she has been meeting through her job. Aunt Patti's e-mail was a very deep one. It was the second e-mail that I read today, and it was the icing on the cake to make me cry. She went into detail to explain how she feels I have a greater purpose in life, a purpose that I have yet to fulfill.

I love how she ended it, with a Jack's Mannequin line, "Just keep your head above… Swim." Now I know for sure that she is Facebook creeping me.

Today, I have my appointment with a woman named Wendy. She is the manager of the facility that I had leased an apartment in the city from for next school year. My mom and Aunt Patti are taking me down to view the property so that we can make appropriate measurements, and because I would have no idea where to start if I had to select colors off of paint swatches. I think today is going to be a good day, I feel like I'm twenty.

Tuesday, July 7, 2009

Today was by far the biggest roller coaster ride that I have been on since the beginning of this ordeal.

I started out feeling great this morning as I headed into work at Harper College. I have a job this summer as an orientation leader. My job is easy. I simply take terrified youths on a tour of the campus. The day was going smoothly and for the first time I felt like myself again. I felt like I had my old energy level, sense of humor and overall level of happiness back. In a sense, I felt like "I was back." That is until 2:00 PM rolled around and I had one of the most devastating realizations, *I haven't even begun to return.*

I was walking up a flight of stairs towards the main entrance of the building when everything began to spin. I felt my heart beating in my throat and everything around me began to fade to gray, as the ambiance of student chatter became a horrifying buzzing sound. Luckily, I never fell. I was able to grab onto a nearby ledge and regain enough focus to make it to a nearby bench. I didn't hesitate to call my mom for a ride and leave work a couple hours early without telling a single manager. I'm such a good employee…

I later discovered upon returning to my house that my blood pressure was 108/80. Though this may sound fantastic for the average person, but my blood pressure has always been around 130/80 since I was an infant. I believe the drop in blood pressure was a result of my new low-sodium diet, water restriction, and the Lopressor that my physicians have me on.

Once I stabilized my blood pressure, my mom attempted to lift my spirits by taking me shopping for my apartment. She went all out and bought me close to a hundred dollars worth of supplies that I will need for the upcoming school year. It was very generous of her and though I was really happy, I didn't have it in me to show my true appreciation. I found it hard to even fake the usual smile. Even though, deep down, I knew I was happy.

The next few hours were spent asleep on the couch. I was trying to end the day. I just wanted to sleep and hopefully wake up with another chance at feeling normal. Unfortunately, my nap only lasted two hours, and today's roller coaster was just getting ready to make its final free fall.

It was 8:00 PM. Fortunately, my mom was in the room bringing me yet another dose of pills. That's when it happened—the pain. It came on so abruptly. The pain was something I hadn't felt since the stress test at Chicago General. It shot across my chest, piercing the defibrillator. I couldn't breathe. When I tried, the pain seeped deeper into my chest. I kept telling myself, *you're not going back to ICU, you're not going back!* I stood up. I felt a rush of blood consume my body. The room began to spin again, faster than before. I buried my head into my bed so that I wouldn't have to see what was coming next. Then, as if God Himself entered the room, the pain stopped. I was relaxed.

I hope this does not happen again. I pray this is not the calm before the storm.

Wednesday, July 8, 2009

Exactly one month ago today, my new life began. This time one month ago, I was lying in a hospital bed at St. Adrian, naïvely thinking that my swollen feet and "stomach pain" were symptoms of a gastrointestinal problem. Oh, how I wish that were the case.

Today was a great day in terms of energy. I had the same vigor I once remembered tackling life with on a daily basis. I did everything I usually would have done. I was able to go on a three-hour shopping excursion to purchase home theater equipment for my studio, play video games and carry on lengthy conversations with old friends who I bumped into along the way. I believe it was a result of me coming off of the small 12mg dose of Lopressor, which my physicians took me off yesterday.

However, I found the day to be masked by a feeling of uneasiness. I wasn't comfortable feeling good. It was as though the day was dangling a ticking time bomb over my head, a time bomb that was ready to explode at any moment without warning.

I was finishing writing e-mails to a list of family members who had e-mailed me earlier in the day. I planned to close up the laptop and get some rest for another shift at Harper. It was then the time bomb erupted.

Much like the sensation I had experienced the night before, the pain engulfed my chest. My neck began to stiffen but it wasn't as bad as yesterday's attack. I mustered the strength to cross the upstairs hallway into my parent's room. I wanted someone to be near me incase the pain worsened and I fainted.

There I stood, hunched over the foot of my parent's bed gripping my chest. I saw a look of fear in my dad's face and an expression of sadness in the eyes of my mom, as I felt the artery in my neck bulging from my skin. The pain lasted for four minutes. Not as long as yesterday's attack, and not as severe. But the exhaustion afterwards seems to remain constant.

The pain happened at 1:45 AM. Wednesday wasn't a bad day at all, but I have a feeling Thursday is going to be rough.

Thursday, July 9, 2009

I'm starting to wonder if these journal entries are becoming more of a curse than a means of therapy. Yesterday, I wrote that I had a feeling Thursday was going to be rough. "Rough" turned out to be an understatement.

Just after completing my prior entry last night, the plot thickened. My world was shaken with the fear of another unknown ailment. (If these entries are ever published and you are of the type to become squeamish, I suggest you skip to the next paragraph. I actually had to debate with myself if I wanted to include this detail of my day, but I figured that if I was going to do this right, and if my experience was ever going to help anyone get through something like this, I'd have to be willing to share the most embarrassing and private details.)

As I was saying… I continued along with my average nightly routine of brushing my teeth, washing my face, which then culminates with a good night kiss to the toilet… if you know what I mean. Tonight, when I was done "saying good night," I looked down to find blood, just pure blood resting alone atop the water. I stood there in shock, staring at the inside of the bowl. I was so angry, so disheartened that something else could be going wrong with my body. All I could think was:

When is this going to end? Where is this light at the end of the tunnel that I keep hearing about, or this horizon that I need to swim to?

I finally composed my thoughts and marched back into my parent's room for the second time in one night with horrific news.

Because of my late-night chest pains and my unexpected loss of blood, my mom called Chicago General first thing in the morning. My mom woke me up at 11:00 AM. She had gotten my Nouna (who is also a nurse) to come to my house and draw my blood under the request of Chicago General's Nurse Practitioner. Why they needed the blood and what they were possibly trying to rule out is still, at this moment, unclear to me, but I obliged to the request thinking the doctors would take it one step at a time.

That's when I received the news that would devastate the rest of my day. Not only were my physicians demanding I go back on the Lopressor, but they wanted me to go into my primary family doctor to "examine the bleeding situation."

Let me start by saying that from a guy's point of view, the last words that you want to hear when you have blood pouring out of your anus is, "examine the bleeding situation." Because we know the doctors aren't just going to talk to us about it or ask us to describe it. They are going to <u>EXAMINE</u> it.

It's two hours later, and there I am, lying on my side in full glory and feeling every possible side effect from another drug, Isosorbide. I'm dizzy. I can't see straight. I'm starving but at the same time I have an undeniable urge to throw up. I am simply miserable. That's when the doctor began the "examining." I can honestly say the procedure I had to go through was by far one of the most degrading and uncomfortable experiences of my life. I was sitting there thinking, *Wow, I really am like a 62 year old. I have a defibrillator and now this. I might as well have her check my prostate while I'm at it.*

I left the office feeling degraded and drugged out of my mind. When I arrived home I opted for a day of solitary confinement, cut off from the world with the exception of my late night instant messages with my friends, Jo and Marie. Before I knew it, it was 1:00 AM. I began to head off to bed when yet again, another chest pain hit me with full force.

The pain was as severe as the night prior. I was just stunned that it had happened again (considering that I was on Isosorbide, which was to eliminate the pains). I wasn't able to muster the strength to make it to my parent's room this time, so I quickly hit the "video chat" button with Marie and instructed her to call my house if I was to faint. Marie sat there in shock as she witnessed the artery yet again protrude from my neck. Just as the night before, the attack subsided in four minutes. Marie had witnessed it all. She's a good friend. She's one of the many people whom I continue to fight for.

Friday, July 10, 2009

Was today the most eventful day? No. Not by any means. It actually peaked around 2:00 PM. But the morning was a lot of fun. Natalie came home for the weekend from her job in Wisconsin and took me out for coffee. It was really nice seeing her. Since the hospital, I have been getting really excited for her visits. I have been enjoying my talks with her more and more. I think a lot of it is because she understands. She has been dealing with Crohn's Disease for years now, so she understands what it is like to be on medications that tear you apart. She also knows what it's like to have the need to eat everything in sight when you're on Prednisone. As she describes it, "To have a bottomless stomach." Natalie has gone through a lot of the same ups-and-downs that I am experiencing, and I know her battles with her disease have helped shape her into the wonderful person she is today. I also think she is one of the few people who can see me changing, too. I know there are probably a lot of individuals who are sick in this world who are either surrounded by people who don't get it or they are just simply alone. I feel horrible for them. I genuinely think anyone dealing with any disease needs to have a Natalie.

Saturday, July 11, 2009

Today can be summarized with one word - "Change."

"Change" is the perfect word because of the way I feel physically in both a positive and negative sense. Positive, because today was the first day in a long time that I have been able to wake up with energy and maintain that same amount of energy throughout the course of the day. It felt good. I didn't even experience the usual slump that I typically feel around 6:00 PM. It is also my second consecutive day without a chest pain.

The negative side of the word "change" is derived from the difference I feel throughout my body. The swelling has been awful today. My feet are in horrific shape. They are so large that since 4:00 PM they actually hurt to walk on. My stomach is retaining water as well. I feel like I have magically grown love handles, and to make my painful steps worse, I get the privilege of feeling my stomach jiggle with each stride. I basically feel like the one kid at fat camp who is following the diet but not seeing the results.

Ignorant people don't help much either. My suspicions of my changing body were confirmed when a neighbor said to me in passing, "Hey, looks like you're getting yourself a beer belly there. Don't be having too much fun." I did the usual fake smile, but really all I was thinking was, *Wow... go fuck yourself.* I think these kinds of situations are going to happen a lot though. People do not seem to think before they speak.

A couple of girls at Harper have already told me that my arms, "have shrunk," or, "they look like skeletons." I'm learning that I can't dwell on my changing body too much. I can repair it once I am healthy. Someday I will be healthy. When I am, I am NEVER going to make fun of someone's weight or physical deficiencies again.

Monday, July 13, 2009

I did not journal yesterday because for the first time in a long time, I did not feel the need to. I see this as being both a great turning point and a slight problem.

Yesterday was a great turning point in my recovery, because for the first time in over a month I had minimal discomfort from my defibrillator, swollen ankles/feet, medication side effects or overall health. However, I was so bored I played video games for close to eight hours. I can now say that I have the ability to balance a pack of cookies on my stomach, a glass of juice on my ankles, all while I am simultaneously changing the battery pack on a control with one hand and pet my dogs, Max and Joy, with the other (by the way ladies… did I mention I'm single?).

What also made yesterday great was my decision to take myself off of Lipitor, Isosorbide, and I have also officially cut my Lopressor dose in half. Chicago General does not know this yet. That appointment is tomorrow.

Today was a very positive day as well. It started off in a very uplifting manner. I got out of the shower and noticed a deep blue colored residue resting over my defibrillator surgical scar. Part of it was actually dangling from the skin. I gently placed my hand on it and rubbed in a circular motion. That was when I noticed it started to peel off of my body painlessly. There was so much of it, it shed from my body like snakeskin. After a closer examination, I noticed the blue residue was residual bandage that had yet to come off from the adhesive strips. It may sound very unintelligent of me, but prior to today I thought the material was tissue that was going to be a permanent portion of the scar. You could only imagine how ecstatic I was to see such an improvement on just one portion of my body.

I can't help but find symbolism in this morning's event. The shed-

ding of the bandage gave me new light, a new hope. It rejuvenated my
confidence in this recovery process and made me feel like I am going
to overcome this disease. I know in the scheme of things it didn't heal
my heart, but it definitely made it stronger. I'm learning I need to crawl
before I can walk—it's all about baby steps.

Tuesday, July 14, 2009

I had a checkup today at Chicago General with two of my physicians.
First I met with Dr. Nase, my new outpatient doctor who manages my
defibrillator. I like him a lot. Out of my entire team of doctors, he is the
only one who I don't get this "screwing me over" kind of vibe from. He
is always very positive, very one-track thinking process. It's calming.
Dr. Nase liked the progress that my defibrillator scar was making and
went as far as giving me the go-ahead to go in a pool. He also cleared
me to begin working out in two weeks, if I feel ready to.

Shortly after, Dr. Wiezien came in for a full discourse on my medications and overall health. The only positive news from her was that she
firmly believes the swelling in my ankles, feet and torso is due to the
1500mg of Prednisone I was given in my initial three days in ICU.
She also believes the dosage of Prednisone that I have been on since
returning home is having an effect as well. This is good news because I
have been worried the past few weeks that the swelling is a result of my
Congestive Heart Failure worsening. Consequently, she took me down
1mg to 12mg of Prednisone daily.

The rest of the appointment was centered on the fact that I am apparently a horrible and rebellious patient. Dr. Wiezien and her Nurse
Practitioner made it very clear they were upset with me for coming off
of Lipitor, Isosorbide and only taking a night dosage of Lopressor. I
understand why they are upset. I really do. They are trying to prescribe
drugs that will correct my situation, but I struggle to see why anyone
would want to take medication that makes them feel worse than their
actual condition. I have been struggling with this thought for many
days now. I can't help but think to myself, *what's the point in living, if
your quality of life isn't worth living for?* It doesn't make sense to me.
Am I really in the wrong for not wanting to live my days with chronic
muscle aches from Lipitor, impaired vision and asthma from Isosorbide, while having the occasional near-blackout experience and mood

swing from the Lopressor? I am twenty years old, and I'm sorry, but I'd rather have 10 great years of my life with the occasional chest pain instead of 40-60 drugged years of Hell.

Dr. Wiezien apparently "consulted" with the Puppet Master (the same asshole whom I have yet to see). They came up with some new drugs that I will be starting tomorrow night. I'm going to give it a shot, so we shall see what happens…

Wednesday, July 15, 2009

I am starting to lose track of the names of the drugs I am on. With the exception of Cyclosporin and Imuran (the two drugs that I have been on my entire life), I am really only able to name them by their color, shape or most predominant side effect.

About an hour and a half ago, I took one of the newer drugs. I know it starts with a "C" and that it's the replacement for the Isosorbide. So for now I am just going to call it "crap," simply because that is how it makes me feel. It literally drains the life out of me. The worst part about it is that prior to yesterday's appointment, I had a string of about two to three days where I felt pretty good. And today, once last night's "midnight cocktail" of drugs wore off at about noon, I had a lot of energy as well.

As much as my doctors and my mom both claim it will take up to a month for my body to get used to the medications and for the side effects to wear off, I can't help but doubt them and worry. I worry because I don't know how I will be able to function like this at school. This time of night is usually when I do all of my homework. The mere thought of writing a well researched essay right now, or being in a recording studio working on a piece of audio for a radio class is exhausting. Typing this journal entry makes me feel better, but even this feels like a chore.

The unknown is really starting to piss me off. I am tired of not knowing if my feet will ever be normal again or if my heart will correct itself. What's even scarier is that sometimes I wonder if my doctors even know what they're doing.

I know I need to get past these thoughts. As Jack's Mannequin says, "You got to swim, swim in the dark. There's no shame in drifting, feel the tide shifting, and wait for the spark."

Tonight I am definitely drifting, but I just need to believe that my spark will come—hopefully sooner than later.

Thursday, July 16, 2009

I think what bugs me the most about my condition is that I can't do what I want to do. My mind feels so young, but my body feels withered. I want so badly to be able to know that I can make plans two days in advance and not have to break them due to a lack of energy. I want to be able to go to work and then spend the night talking with my friends. Or just simply play video games with someone without being exhausted from the stimulation.

I lash out sometimes in my house by complaining to my mom. I know I come off as completely irrational because she gets irritated by me very quickly—almost upset with me. But it feels good to complain every once in a while. As Natalie said to me once, "Sometimes you need to pity yourself." It sounds lame and immature but it's so true. I think I would do a lot more complaining if it wasn't for these journals; they are kind of a release for me. I am noticing that as the recovery process lengthens, I seem to be writing these entries earlier in the day.

I just received some news; my doctors want me to begin a physical therapy rehabilitation program. They want me to start walking on a treadmill so they can test to see how much my heart can handle. I like the idea because I want to know my limits. One of my fears is that I am going to have to discover my limits on my own when I am away at college in a little over a month. I don't know what is going to happen. In fact, I am even scared to start working out. I don't want to get shocked by my defibrillator, but at the same time I know I need to face my fear because I refuse to live my life restricted by the unknown.

I am not allowed to begin these sessions for two more weeks. I am supposed to be six weeks out of surgery first. Currently, I struggle walking across a parking lot to work. Hopefully in two weeks, I will have enough energy to last fifteen minutes on a treadmill.

Friday, July 17, 2009

"Pain" and "Progress" are the words of the day. I am not certain which drug is causing my pain. It may be the one that starts with a "C" or it could be the little white one that starts with an "N," but since I have been taking the new list of pills, I have been getting "teaser" type chest pains, until today.

I woke up around 10:30 AM still feeling drowsy from my 8:00 PM pill. It wasn't until noon that the drowsiness faded, but was then quickly replaced by another horrific chest pain. I am used to these pains lasting only four minutes, but today they were different mainly because I usually only have one in a given 24 hour period. It is currently 3:49 PM and I have already experienced six. Each pain is progressively more intense, and now the duration of each attack is becoming less predictable. I had one chest pain about an hour ago that lasted close to seven minutes, a new record. However, I have also had two pains that have only stayed with me for a couple of minutes.

Though this pain was awful, it led to a great deal of progress. My mom continued to grow increasingly annoyed by my irritability. She sternly asked me why I was treating her so poorly. With that, I yelled back, "I'm not mad at you, Ann. I'm mad at the whole fucking situation!" She started to cry, asking me to tell her what I was thinking, begging me to let her in my mind. I snapped, "Do you really want to see what I'm thinking?!" She stood there in silence nodding her head. "Well then give me five minutes!" With that, I tore up the stairs and into my room. I began to print everything, all of my journals, all of my thoughts.

I returned to the kitchen where I threw the papers on the table. "This is what I'm thinking, Ann!" She was still crying as she sat in amazement, staring at the stack of papers that lay out on the table in front of her. I paced the house for the next thirty minutes in silence, quietly fighting through the chest pains as she read every thought of mine from the past two weeks.

I didn't want to share any of my journals with anyone until I was done with this battle. I like keeping everyone out of my head, I always have. She finished reading and began to tell me how proud she was of me and that she thinks these journals are healthy. "You really hate Chicago

General?" she asked. "They're a bunch of fucking clowns," I responded angrily.

"Give me two weeks, I'll get you into Mercy Care," she said. "We can leave Chicago General."

There had been nothing I wanted more than to quit Chicago General. Maybe I should start letting more people in my head. Maybe then I'll start seeing a little more progress.

Saturday July 18, 2009

Today was, hands down, the best that I have felt since… well, to be honest probably March, but most certainly since June 8th. I contribute this upswing in both energy and happiness to me voluntarily coming off of yet another vasodilator. Also the reality of quitting Chicago General's "medical practice" is finally sinking in. I am also proud to say I have figured out the name of the drug that has messed me up both mentally and physically for the past three days. It is called Norvasc.

I have decided to come off of Norvasc. This decision has nothing to do with me being the "unruly and rebellious" patient that Dr. Wiezien and her Nurse Practitioner have painted me to be. I have chosen to come off of it for two reasons: life sucks when I am on it. I actually go into a state of depression two to three hours before taking it because I know how bad I am going to feel once I swallow it; and the second reason is because after doing hours of research, I found absolutely zero documentation (not even medical studies) that show any sign that Norvasc is even meant to treat CHF. I did, however, find countless articles on how the drug can cause chest pains. Yesterday, I had six. Today, I had none. Thus once again proving my theory that the Puppet Master is a sham of a doctor. This leads me to my second topic of the day and the second factor that has played a role in making this day a great one.

I can't describe how ecstatic I am now knowing I will have the opportunity to leave Chicago General in the coming two weeks. The mere thought of no longer being the Puppet Master's guinea pig has made me happier than words can describe. It is such a morale boost. The only negative is that I will no longer be able to work with Dr. Nase. I actually do respect that man's opinion, but at the end of the day, the pros greatly outweigh the cons.

Sunday, July 19, 2009

I stumbled upon an old document on my computer today. I thought it was very appropriate given my current situation. It was an extra credit assignment that was due in one of my classes back in high school. The theme of the project was to design a list of the *100 Things That I Want to Accomplish in My Life.* I wasn't really the best student in high school, so it was no surprise the list was unfinished. It stopped at #42. The list was pretty basic. There was nothing too deep; it still had many of my current aspirations listed. The list included goals such as: marry a hot girl; visit Athens, Greece; and purchase Chicago Bears season tickets.

I decided to continue the list and finish what I once had started. I spent thirty minutes in deep thought and made it to #76. I noticed through this assignment that I have really matured since high school. Many of the initial 42 goals are still fun, but they are very superficial. The newest additions seem to be a bit more thought out and much more adventurous. The newest additions include: give something special to a family who has nothing around Christmas; give back to the top 10 most influential people in my life; and go to an airport with spouse, ask for the next departing plane, and make a spontaneous vacation to a random destination. Though I must admit, I stole the last one from the movie <u>Yes Man</u>. Jim Carrey made it look like it would be a lot of fun.

I just realized what I want #77 to be—beat Congestive Heart Failure. Seven has always been my lucky number, so maybe it's an omen. I'm going to keep this list. I'm sure it will be a great source of motivation on the days when I feel down.

Monday, July 20, 2009

It's weird, I am currently stuck in this awkward medium. I am technically a patient of The Puppet Master and his team of pawns at Chicago General, yet I find myself wanting the medical opinion of Mercy Care Hospital more. (Keep in mind, I haven't even met them yet.)

My mom and I were in contact with both teams today. My mom was busy discussing how to go about having my medical records trans-

ferred to Mercy, while I was busy handling business with the Nurse
Practitioner at Chicago General.

My discussion was brief, but I loved every second of it. I left a message
on the Nurse Practitioner's voicemail, "Hi this is Bill Coon calling. I am
just calling to let you know, I took the vasodilator, Norvasc, every night
until Saturday." This was a lie. I stopped taking the medication Friday.
I thought it sounded better. "Well, I am just calling because you and
Dr. Wiezien were not happy the last time I discontinued meds, but the
drug was just as debilitating as Isosorbide, so I stopped taking this one
as well. I had many headaches, I was dizzy, and I was having chronic
chest pains. So I thought I'd call to let you know I stopped taking it and
that vasodilators do not work for me. Please, do not prescribe another
one. If you feel the need to discuss this further, please feel free to call
me." I gave her my number and hung up with a big smile.

Leaving the message felt so good. I felt like I just punched the Puppet
Master in the face. The Nurse Practitioner called me back a few hours
later, I could tell she was nervous. She chose her words very carefully.
"Bill… I spoke with Dr. Wiezien. She wants to make sure you are still
on the other pills that we prescribed you… you're… you are still on
those, right?" I started laughing, "Yeah, I'm still on those." I could hear
her sigh of relief on the other end. "Okay good… well we're not going
to prescribe you anything over the phone, but Dr. Wiezien does want
to talk to you more about this at your next appointment."

I know what that means. Our "talk" will be another lengthy discussion
about how I am not following the doctor's orders, and how I am a very
unruly patient. I am actually looking forward to this talk of ours. I can't
wait to see the look on her face when I come back with some of the
comments I have in store for her. I wonder what her response will be if
I pose to her the question that I had in one of my prior entries. "What's
the point in living if your quality of life isn't worth living for?" Let's see
Dr. Wiezien field that philosophical proposition.

On a brighter note, my mom spoke with Lilly. She is the Nurse Practitioner at Lakeside Hospital. Lilly has known me and my mom for
years, since I was an infant. We only left Lakeside three years ago
because they brought on a doctor who I did not like. He has since been
fired. I like to think I have a gift. I am really good at spotting shitty

doctors. The specialist I am going to see is at Mercy Care. His name is Dr. Krause. Supposedly, he is known for treating patients as individuals, not as test subjects or by a pre-written manuscript. Basically, he is the exact opposite of the Puppet Master.

My mom told Lilly about how I have been beating myself up for my condition. She told her how I fear I may have slightly caused some of this CHF to take effect by missing a dose or two of Imuran while at college. Lilly's reply made my day. She told my mom that there is no way I could have caused all of this in a month's span and knows I have done an excellent job with the cards I have been dealt. She believes my condition was indeed the ticking time bomb that I have been hoping it was.

It's funny, I am not even their patient yet, and already the thought of Mercy Care is making me feel better than the Puppet Master and his pawns ever have.

Tuesday, July 21, 2009

Setbacks are a bitch, especially when you have been on a three-day streak of progress. My life feels like it's on this predictable cycle that I cannot escape. I seem to feel normal from anywhere between forty-eight to seventy-two hours. I do not know if I am just over exerting myself during these "good days" and my body just needs to crash, or if my heart is really so messed up that it just has days where it can't keep me going around the clock. I wish I had a doctor who could give me answers, but honestly, after today's little discovery, I feel there is not a single doctor at Chicago General I can believe in.

I take a very crucial anti-rejection drug (also known as an immuno-suppressant), Cyclosporine. I have been on this drug since I was an infant, and it has been able to sustain my health up until this recent battle with CHF. The drug weakens my immune system so that my body will not recognize my heart as foreign and reject it. Needless to say, the level of this drug in my body has been watched like a hawk and meticulously maintained by my mom and my physicians throughout the course of my life. Last Tuesday, Dr. Wiezien placed me on another blood pressure medication named "Toprol," and told me to take the drug at 8:00 PM along with my Cyclosporine, for fear that if I took it at midnight along with the other "C" drug, my blood pressure would plummet in my sleep. My mom literally asked Dr. Wiezien, "Will this Toprol have any effect on his body's absorption of Cyclosporine if it is taken with it?" Dr. Wiezien replied, "I don't think so."

My mom and I looked at each other with the same look on our faces. It was a dumbfounded face as though to say, "Well, don't you think you should fucking know?" My mom even went as far as saying, "Well, that is not a good enough answer." Dr. Wiezien backpedaled and began to reassure us that it will not affect one of my most crucial medications.

Long story short, I had blood drawn yesterday morning. The results came back today and my Cyclosporine was at the lowest it has ever been in twenty years. I thought of another question for Dr. Wiezien: *How am I supposed to get better when your practice is killing me?*

Wednesday, July 22, 2009

I had a stress test today. Fortunately, it was at St. Adrian Hospital, so I did not have to drive all the way into the city. The point of the stress test was to see how much my heart could handle. They were basically trying to see how far they can initially push me when I begin my cardiac rehabilitation on Monday.

I did not have very high expectations for myself going into the stress test. I know I am in the worst shape of my life, but for some reason my performance made me feel like a failure. The test was supposed to last fifteen minutes. There was a clock to my right measuring how long I could withstand walking on the treadmill. By three minutes I was starting to feel very tired. At the five-minute mark, I was starting to feel dizzy. Once the clock struck seven minutes, I couldn't take it anymore. I told the nurses I had to quit. They stopped the test shortly after.

The test put me in a very bad mood. I was upset and moping around my house for a few hours afterwards. It was another one of those days where I felt I had to pity myself. I know I have been through a lot, and it has only been six weeks since my discharge, but six weeks feels like an eternity when you haven't been able to live your life the way you want to.

Tomorrow is the meeting with Dr. Wiezien. She should apparently have my stress test results for me. According to my mom, this should be the final doctor's appointment with anyone from the Puppet Master's staff. I am very excited about that!

I also found out that I might be able to stick with Dr. Nase, unless Dr. Krause wants me monitored by someone on his own staff. Tomorrow should be interesting.

Friday, July 24, 2009

Thus far, I have received four cards from my Aunt Shea and Uncle Gus. I don't know why this keeps happening, but every time they send me a card, I receive it on a day that I feel like I am hitting rock bottom.

What I did not like about today's step backwards was that I could not explain why I felt the way I did. Typically, I am able to diagnose my own problem. I usually know when it is from the vasodilators or if it is a result of me working too hard at Harper. Neither of those were factors in my day, but still I felt like a train wreck.

I woke up very dizzy and the dizziness stayed with me throughout the course of the day. I was so dizzy I still do not know what the card from Aunt Shea and Uncle Gus says because I couldn't focus long enough to read it. To make matters worse, I had two more chest pains. They are very inexplicable. I truly thought it was the Norvasc causing all of this chest discomfort.

Shortly after the chest pain, I received a phone call from one of the defibrillator clinic doctors asking me for a reading. Dr. Wiezien had mentioned to Dr. Nase that I was experiencing chest pains. I ran a scan for them through a box that connects to my defibrillator with magnets. Shortly after, I was informed they had found a change in the functionality of the defibrillator. Apparently, the output of electricity from the defibrillator has increased slightly since the last check-up. They believe this may be caused by one of the leads in my chest coming loose and dislodging from the heart. I will not find out until Monday when I go in for an emergency defibrillator examination. I really hope they do not find anything. I worry I am going to need surgery, especially after the second chest pain that I experienced tonight. I fear a secondary surgery will set all my progress back and I will lose another ten days of my life from the narcotic pills.

I am so afraid of this happening because of the second pain I experienced around 11:30 PM tonight. This one was different than any I have had. The pain was so severe, that when it finished, I had a feeling deep down in my gut telling me something is terribly wrong. The pain was ruthless. This time it was on both sides of my chest. It shot up both sides of my neck, into my jaw, where it then settled in the temples of my brain for close to five minutes. My neck was stiff. I struggled to breathe. It didn't cloud my thinking though. I fortunately thought to scan my defibrillator results into the clinic from the same box in my room. I sent the scan in during the peak of the pain. I can only hope the information I sent will benefit the hospital and allow them to diagnose me with the correct problem.

It is days like today when I wish I had the ability to see future journal entries. I'm really afraid that if I am going to be hospitalized again, this is going to be the reason why. I know I have enough mental strength, but I don't know if I have enough physical strength in me for round two.

Saturday, July 25, 2009

My family came over to my house today to eat food and drink wine. Since I have been sick, my family has a newfound enjoyment in coming over to my house to spend time with me and socialize. They make for very pleasant days. My only regret of the day is that I did not have the energy I had hoped to. My lack of energy has been mostly due to these mini chest pains I have been experiencing. They are miniature spurts that resemble the typical pains but only last for ten seconds. They are very mild, but three or four of them typically drain my energy much like the standard four-minute episodes.

Earlier in the day, I was speaking with my mom about the pains. I asked her to call the defibrillator clinic at Chicago General to see if they could analyze my transmission from last night's horrific chest pain. The clinic was not open. Apparently, I now have to make sure my defibrillator only has complications Monday through Friday. Thanks, Chicago General, you never cease to impress me!

I told my mom how bad the pain was and how I truly felt something was very wrong with my heart. As the hours went by, and with each chest pain, I began to think the cause for my discomfort was a result of the 60 percent blockage in my other artery, which Chicago General never corrected. I shared this idea with my mom, and she informed me that the only corrective surgery for this problem would be a heart bypass. This was unfortunate because I was convinced this would set me back at least six weeks, cutting my timetable for a September 5th return to school very close. I just wanted to be able to walk through the city without having to stop for breath. It sounds so simple, but that is all I wanted right now.

Later in the night, at the party, I sat at a table with my cousins Peter, Michael and Eleni. They started asking me questions about my recovery. It was nice. With the exception of these journals, I haven't really had an opportunity to open up and speak candidly about what was on my mind. Michael asked me a very intriguing question. He asked, "What do you foresee down the road in your recovery process?" Nobody had ever asked me that. I have thought about it, and I believe in the coming three to four weeks I will have another surgery. It may be a defibrillator correctional procedure or it may be a bypass surgery. Though I hope I am very wrong, I am almost certain this will be the case. Otherwise, barring any additional setbacks, I am hoping to return to half-strength by Christmas. By June 8th, 2010, I am hoping to be able to say that I feel like myself again.

Sunday, July 26, 2009

Today was a day filled with anxiety. I didn't accomplish much, so my boredom allowed my mind to take control. I sat around thinking about tomorrow's appointment at the defibrillator clinic. I started thinking about all of the possible outcomes and I gradually worked myself up to a point where I could not stop envisioning myself having another surgery.

What I do not like is that I have never been this way. For as long as I can remember, I have always felt completely relaxed before a doctor's appointment, regardless of how crucial the results were. It is days like today that I know this disease has changed me.

Today, I am just as battered physically as I am mentally shaken. Today is my third consecutive day with minimal energy. I have started to feel like I did days before my hospitalization. I am very run down and my asthma is starting to come back full force. My swelling is not the greatest either. However, this I am not too concerned about. I realize I could have restricted the amount of fluid intake at the party yesterday a bit more. I am simply paying the price right now. I am a victim of my own stupidity.

I'm having the same miniature chest pains. Not as many as before, but I did have a full-blown episode at 8:20 PM. I am once again exhausted, so I am going to go put my feet up, watch a movie, and hopefully give my mind something else to think about for a couple hours. Tonight, I'm thinking *Ghostbusters 2*.

Monday, July 27, 2009

I had my appointment with the defibrillator clinic today at Chicago General. The technicians wanted to check my defibrillator and verify that the lead in my heart had not moved. The technician analyzed my stats that she uploaded wirelessly from my chest and began manipulating the defibrillator. I hate it when they test the defibrillator, it makes me feel less human. They have the ability to make it vibrate, speed my heart up, and slow my heart down. They can even make alarms and sound effects come out of it. I wouldn't be surprised if they could check their e-mails with it, too.

There was a scary moment when the technician panicked from the results. She was concerned by the large increase in power that the defibrillator began to generate in the past week. She called Dr. Nase into the clinic to analyze the results. He too seemed concerned and ordered a chest X-ray. His major concern was that the lead had moved, and he wanted to compare this X-ray to an X-ray taken the day after the implantation of the device.

Dr. Nase began to choose his words carefully. He explained to me that if the lead had slightly moved, he was going to want me to come in for a procedure in which they shock my heart with the defibrillator after heavily sedating me. The point of the test would be to verify that the defibrillator was still able to sense a cardiac episode and would still serve as a lifesaving device. He also warned me that if the X-ray shows the lead has drastically moved, I was going to need the defibrillator surgery re-done on the same incision spot. This to me, would be the worst-case scenario. Like I have said in prior entries, this is one of my biggest fears. I do not want to relive the pain I felt from the defibrillator surgery, it was too debilitating.

I asked Dr. Nase if he thought the lead could be the cause for the chronic chest pains I had been experiencing. He said it was doubtful, and after I explained to him how the pains felt, he said that they sounded like very bad PVCs. They are the irregular patterns that I hear when I try to sleep at night. They are arrhythmias that cause my heart to stop for a second before it continues to beat. He believes that every once in a while when a PVC occurs, my body's natural response is the pain. What causes the response is unknown. He hinted that I'd either need a correctional procedure (such as a bypass), or overtime, as my heart heals, the PVCs may slowly go away as well. This is a question I will ask Dr. Krause and the team from Mercy Care when I have my meeting with them on Thursday.

Dr. Nase also mentioned he did not want me to do cardiac rehab for another two weeks, just to guarantee the lead has the ability to heal and grow scar tissue to lock it in place. I believe this two-week delay will now cause me to do rehab in the city when I go back to school.

The final portion of the meeting was one I found to be very intriguing and verified all of my thoughts on the Puppet Master. The technician mentioned the Puppet Master's name and saw my negative facial reaction. With that, she immediately went on a rant, candidly disclosing many stories of the Puppet Master ordering tests and procedures on patients and never looking into the results. She literally said, "He just does not care."

If all goes well on Thursday with Mercy Care, I will be making my highly anticipated phone call to the Nurse Practitioner at Chicago General to quit this practice of ignorant clowns.

Tuesday, July 28, 2009

It's one thing for this condition to tear me down emotionally and to give me chronic pain, but when I start to unexpectedly lose hours of my life from exhaustion, that's when I begin to feel defeated and angry.

My day started off bittersweet. I woke up, and as soon as my feet hit the floor, I discovered I did not have the strength needed to go to work today. Luckily, I have Sara for a boss. She has been a Saint throughout this entire struggle. When I was in the hospital, she would write me everyday. She genuinely cares. I text messaged her saying I was not feeling up to working and she immediately responded, "Don't worry about it honey. Feel better. Facebook me later if you want to talk." She is a great boss. I actually have gone into work a few times when I haven't felt up to it just so I wouldn't let her down. I then went back to bed for a few more hours. I was later awakened by my mom with great news. My mom informed me that the X-ray came back negative and the lead had not moved at all! Thankfully, I will not need the defibrillator surgery again.

The rest of the day was pretty lame—mainly because I feel I am getting sicker. Every day since Friday, I feel like I have been taking a major step backwards in my recovery. I feel like I did before I was hospitalized. One of the most devastating symptoms is the asthma, which started today. I am beginning to cough a lot. It is almost as though there is fluid in my throat. Once again, I am attributing this to the other blocked artery. I won't know many more details until Thursday when I meet with Mercy Care. It's kind of sad that I have three doctors on my case already, but I refuse to ask any of them about these symptoms due to their inability to treat me as a human.

The fatigue is starting to hit me full force again. I was writing a passage in the book entitled, "Symptoms of a Tarnished Mind," when I suddenly could no longer formulate sentences. I sat down on the bed to clear my head, and next thing I knew, it was three hours later and I had slept through dinner. My life feels so pathetic lately.

As I was eating the leftovers from dinner, my mom tried to persuade me to lower my fall semester course load from 19 credits to 12. She thinks I can't handle it. She is worried that I may be biting off more than I can chew. I do believe I can handle the actual workload, this I am not afraid of. I only worry that my body will eventually break down after a few weeks of waking up early and commuting twenty minutes from the North side to the South Loop. I have begun to re-evaluate my schedule. I e-mailed my counselor to see if I could take an online course at Harper while also being enrolled at Columbia. My hope is that I can take an entire day off mid-week and use that day to get work done and re-energize myself for the rest of the week.

I hate making plans like this. I can't wait until the day that I return back to normalcy.

Wednesday, July 29, 2009

There isn't much to say about today other than the usual symptoms of CHF and side effects from my medications. My asthma was really bad. I am officially certain that it is getting worse. I am beginning to get light headed whenever I go up or down a flight of stairs. For the last three hours, I have been fighting the exhaustion. I refuse to sleep. It is currently 10:47 PM. I have to wake up at 8:00 AM tomorrow, so I didn't want to take a nap and then end up struggling to fall asleep at night.

Tomorrow is my long awaited appointment with Mercy Care Hospital. Aunt Patti is driving me and my mom into the city because my mom has a fear of expressways and I haven't felt well enough to drive.

My mom questioned me earlier, asking me what I want to speak with Dr. Krause about. I honestly do not know. Obviously, I want to know how he approaches medicine. Is he hands on? How would he plan on treating my case? Does he treat the patient as an individual? Or does he pull a Puppet Master and prescribe the same drugs to everyone?

From what I hear, he seems to be an excellent physician, but only time will tell. I look forward to getting some answers tomorrow. I would also like to know if they think I need another surgery.

Thursday, July 30, 2009

It brings me with great sorrow to say that I am writing this journal entry from my bed at Mercy Care Hospital. I am currently residing in room 1133. It is 1:30 AM and my mom is once again spending another restless night in a hospital room at my bedside.

There is so much to write about today. I think I should begin with the
hope that I find in my new surroundings. These doctors have been
absolutely outstanding thus far. The first doctor I met was named Dr.
Gordon. He is a Fellow that works under Dr. Krause. He really seems
to know his material. Dr. Gordon began the initial meeting by going
through my charts. He asked me about the care I had received at Chicago General and then preceded to go through a very thorough analysis of my history. He was interested in my past, something Chicago
General had never considered since day one. I could tell he was interested in treating me as a unique individual and fully understood when
I told him I could not handle vasodilators. That was when Dr. Gordon
glanced at my ankles. They were bad today, very swollen. He began to
question me about them, asking how long they had been in their poor
state. He seemed appalled by the fact that Dr. Wiezien would even
suggest that Prednisone was causing the swelling. He then began to dig
further into the condition of my breathing. That was when he paused.
He looked up at me and said, "So are you here for just a second opinion?" My mom and I glanced at each other and smiled. "We're here to
actually give you the case," I responded. "I am very displeased with my
treatment at Chicago General." "Well," Dr. Gordon replied, "then I am
going to want to admit you tonight... I suspect an episode of rejection."

I had come prepared for this outcome. My mom told me this morning
before we left that the doctors at this hospital may want to admit me. I
had packed my laptop, some DVDs, and pills—just enough to get me
through the night. It was a sad feeling packing my bags. Even though
it was meant as a precaution, deep down, I knew I was going to be in a
hospital bed writing this entry tonight. I've known since Friday when I
had the horrible chest pain that shot up both sides of my neck. I knew
then that something is horribly wrong with my body.

Dr. Gordon then brought in another specialist, Dr. Janpour. She is
pregnant, very small in stature, but she carried herself brilliantly. She
seemed to radiate intelligence. I instantly trusted her more than any of
my primary physicians at Chicago General. After introducing herself,
she took all my paperwork, the films from my prior X-rays at Chicago
General, and the videos of my echocardiograms. She immediately
went to review them with Dr. Gordon. They returned fifteen minutes
later and began to tell me about the procedures that I may undergo
if I choose to have Mercy Care follow my case. The first would be a

biopsy of my heart, which they would want to perform tomorrow. They believe they could use the biopsy to officially determine what is wrong with me. They can discover how bad my heart is, or they can discover that the situation isn't as bad as everyone, including myself, is anticipating. Dr. Gordon promised to stick with my case the entire stay and to not change doctors on me like they did at Chicago General. I gave them the case. I put my life in their hands, and they put the paperwork through to have me admitted into the hospital. I spent the next ten hours in a secluded emergency room waiting for a private bed to be found on the telemetry floor, "11 West." During my ten hour period in the emergency room, Aunt Patti, along with my sister, came to visit.

I also met another doctor, Dr. Bifnul. He is another cardiologist. He began explaining to me how, if my artery was still only 60 percent blocked, a bypass would not be a method of correction. He simply told me that until the biopsy is performed and the physicians have an opportunity to review all of my material from Chicago General, they will not have a conclusion as to the cause of my exact condition, nor will they know what surgeries I will need to undergo. He did hint at the fact that I should keep an open mind to the possibility of another heart transplant. Oddly enough, I have gotten to the point of no longer being afraid of surgeries. I am awkwardly very open to the possibility.

I have developed a new game plan for this second hospitalization. I am going to keep a clear head. I am going to not only fight my hardest to survive, but I am going to fight my hardest to stay level-headed and positive. I trust these doctors. I have this intuition that is telling me I have found the Promised Land. Whatever life throws at me I am going to try my hardest to take it on with a smile. Nothing is going to bring me down. There is no pill, no surgery, or any news that I will let stand in my way. I'm a fighter, and I am ready for this second fight. Let the games begin.

Sound the bell for round two.

The Journals:

Round 2

Friday,
July 31, 2009 -
Tuesday,
August 4, 2009

Friday, July 31, 2009

I didn't get much sleep last night. Surprisingly, it was not because of the biopsy, but because my bed at Mercy Care has the ability to inflate and deflate on its own. It's designed with the hopes of eliminating unnecessary back pain. It is a great idea, but unfortunately every five minutes it sounded like a plane was taking off from under me.

My day was spent anxiously awaiting my 1:00 PM heart biopsy and visiting with a slew of doctors, including Dr. Krause and Dr. Gordon. The first physician, however, was Dr. Bifnul. He came in briefly to review my vitals and speak with me about my decrease in heart functionality. He then got pretty serious and started to stress the possibility of a heart transplant. He explained that with the progression of my disease, the illness might not be able to be controlled with medication anymore. He then stressed how he was saying this without the biopsy being completed, and that he would not know for sure until he could look at those results along with Dr. Krause and Dr. Gordon.

The next individual who met with me was Dr. Mintle. He is a surgical Fellow to the Attending Dr. Sparih. They are the two doctors who were going to perform my biopsy later in the day. Dr. Mintle brought in the standard release forms for me to sign, relinquishing any liability on the part of the hospital. I find these forms to be interesting. You are basically signing your life away on the dotted line. You give complete strangers the power to do anything they want with your body. You basically state that you are aware you may be the one unlucky bastard out of the ten thousand who receive your surgery yearly, who ends up disabled or killed. To top it off, you are then forced to relinquish your right to sue, and agree to have your unfortunate death studied by students nationwide years later in the chapter entitled, "What Not To Do!"

The biopsy began smoothly, the prep went well and I really liked my nurses. Then the drilling began and I was in utter pain for the next hour. The surgeons drilled a small hole in my neck and sent a catheter down the artery. The catheter went into my heart and snipped out a couple samples of heart tissue. The surgeons successfully completed the surgery. The only problem that occurred was, whatever drug I was supposed to receive to either twilight me, knock me out, or simply numb my skin, failed to work.

I felt this horrible gnawing pain at my neck for an entire hour. It was as though a pack of dogs were chewing on my skin, but I was helpless to do anything about it. I kept swearing throughout the procedure, but Dr. Sparih seemed to be completely against stopping. They kept pushing the same drug, but the drug did nothing to help. Finally, the procedure ended. I was lifted to a secondary bed and wheeled up to my room.

Dr. Krause entered along with Dr. Gordon. Immediately, they began to speak with me about how I am in dire need of a heart transplant. They both feel that I am a perfect candidate for the procedure and that I am also in need of a kidney transplant as well. The news of the kidney transplant was a shock to me. The last procedure I was expecting to need was a double transplant. I am not worried though. Like I said, bad news no longer fazes me. I have been doing my best to keep up the positive attitude and to not stop smiling. So far, I believe it is working. I have been through a Hellish procedure. I have been strapped to a bed by the catheter sticking out of my neck, I found out that I may miss an entire semester of school, and I just had an extremely sharp chest pain. It's hard to keep up my spirits in a time like this, but I truly believe that if I can hang in here and win the mental battle, there is nothing that will stop me from conquering any physical challenges thrown my way. I have been dealt a pretty shitty hand of cards. It's days like today that I need to just hold onto my Will.

Saturday, August 1, 2009

I kicked my dad out of my hospital room tonight around 10:00 PM. He was acting completely irrational, and though I am sure whatever his intentions were, they were only meant to be sincere. I know he meant well. He just picked the wrong way to convey them and he would not shut up. Today was just a bad day and the series of events that took place resulted in an emotional explosion.

My day began much like any day of mine in a hospital, bright and early, with a technician and a nurse waking me up as they demand more blood or urine. I obliged to both requests and continued throughout my morning moaning from the pain of the catheter that is still dangling from my neck as I write.

About an hour later I was struck with a series of five chest pains. Each pain only lasted for about two minutes, but they each severely exhausted me. Unfortunately, I was then forced to start my day feeling very run-down and lethargic. It was a feeling that lasted with me throughout the day and made it difficult to stay awake.

Dr. Gordon later entered the room alongside Dr. Lenair. Dr. Gordon introduced me to Dr. Lenair and explained how he is another member of Dr. Krause's staff. Dr. Lenair took the time to reiterate everything I had been told in regards to my situation, but then the two doctors filled me in on some very interesting details. The first was the result of my biopsy. The tissue samples of the heart came back at a "level zero for heart rejection." What this means, is that the Puppet Master and his pawns had been wasting the last seven weeks of my life treating me for an ailment that I did not have. I was also informed that everything I have been experiencing is a result of Transplant Vasculopathy, a disease in which there is no cure, except for a new heart. Apparently, a small percentage of transplanted organs will begin to fail at random. The failure is a phenomenon and nobody truly understands why it happens. The two doctors then explained to me that all but one of the drugs I am currently taking (Rapamune) has been completely useless in my management, that not a single one would correct Transplant Vasculopathy. This in turn means that every side effect I have been experiencing from the acne, to the blurred vision, has all been in vain. It also means that I have lost seven weeks on the Organ Recipient List.

Words cannot describe the amount of hatred I feel towards the Puppet Master and the entire Chicago General medical staff. They have truly done me an awful injustice and their lack of basic medical knowledge is simply alarming. I am beginning to worry about all of the other individuals who are still under the Puppet Master's "medical guidance."

I had many family members visit me in the hospital today. The list included: my parents, Carissa, Gus, Nicole, Natalie, Peter, Greg, my cousin Anthony, my Uncle George, and finally my Aunt Kathy. It was so nice having such a large support system spend the day with me. However, I couldn't help but feel bad when I struggled to stay awake due to the lethargic feeling that I was experiencing as a result of the morning chest pains. I slept for an hour of their visit. I tried to apologize to them, but they all told me that they did not care and it is not my job to entertain them.

Another issue I faced throughout my day was the consistent bleeding from the incision site. There was apparently a complication in the operation yesterday and the puncture site is slightly larger than the doctors had planned. Blood has been consistently leaking from the wound; I have had the site re-bandaged a total of twelve times since the biopsy. It is becoming very irritating and at times the spot has burned profusely. I have been informed that Dr. Gordon plans on removing the catheter early tomorrow morning for fear of infection.

On top of all this physical anguish, I have been dealing with the mental stress of figuring out my fall semester schedule. Each day, I am faced with the realization that I am going to need to lighten up my original schedule if I am to have any hopes of moving into my studio apartment in September. The truth of the matter is that when I developed my short-term <u>Will</u>, my initial goal was to go back to my internship at the radio station for at least one more shift. This hospitalization crushed my initial plan. I found out that I needed to re-route my thinking. I needed something to keep me afloat mentally. I needed something to hold on to. This is the purpose of the short-term <u>Will</u>. It is days like today, when nothing seems to be going right and you have had a string of events that seem to progressively tear your world into two, that you need something to grasp onto. I decided to make living in my studio apartment and attending Columbia in the fall my new short-term goal. I understand that I may receive the phone call informing me of a matched donor three months into the semester, and I may be forced to finish the fall term courses during the spring. This I am not worried about because in the short-term, I am just looking to prove to myself that this disease cannot control my life. I just want to establish a goal and reach it. I just need a momentum boost. This is what led to my dad being kicked out of my hospital room tonight at 10:00 PM.

I began speaking with my parents about my plan to take two online courses, and three on-campus courses. This is when my dad chose to tell me that he does not think I could handle going to class. From his point of view, I can see him as simply trying to watch out for my well-being. But what he doesn't understand is that I know what I am capable of. I was very insulted, but more so distraught over the fact that he was killing my short-term <u>Will</u>. The only thing I have left to grasp onto at the moment was being ripped away from me so unnecessarily, and simply, he was being an ass about it. With tears pouring down my face I turned to him and said, "Get out!" I honestly did not feel bad about saying it either. He looked at me like I was joking. "Get out!" I repeated. "Take I-90 home. I don't want you here." That was two hours ago and I am still feeling distraught. I'm also pissed because I had been doing so well at keeping the smile, until he decided to fuck it up.

Sunday, August 2, 2009

I slept like a baby last night. The narcotics really got the job done. Shortly after last night's entry, my nurse removed the catheter from my neck. I instantly felt tons of pressure release. It pulsated for a while, but it was a relaxing pulsation. It was a pain that felt so good I didn't want it to stop. It has been a while since I have felt that kind of "good" pain.

The bleeding did not stop though. My nurse re-bandaged the site several more times in a matter of two hours. It was like my neck was having its first period and there wasn't a big enough tampon in the world that could stop the heavy flow. I went to sleep with blood periodically squirting out of my artery.

I awoke this morning to find myself lying in a pool of my own blood. My entire pillow was red, and my chest was stained orange. It looked as though my body was rusting away. I found it to be very symbolic, and eerily true.

Dr. Gordon and Dr. Lenair came into my room shortly after I cleaned off my chest. I like when they are together, they seem to fit together perfectly. They are like a genius duo, almost like Batman and Robin. They were both disgusted in the way my incision was taken care of. They had the Med Students try many techniques. First, they attempted to place an adhesive skin closure bandage over the wound. When that plan failed, they attempted to glue the wound shut. The bleeding proved to be too strong. Dr. Gordon then came back into the room and closed up the hole with two stitches. I was glad he did this. I had been slowly losing a large amount of blood for the past twenty-four hours and I was beginning to feel very faint and weak. I also lost more blood this morning when my nurse had to draw fifteen vials worth of blood for several tests. These tests are all part of the protocol that I need to follow in order for me to get on the Organ Recipient List.

It is my understanding that I must pass the following tests: HIV/AIDS, several blood exams to determine my electrolytes and other elements of my blood, STD tests, a full body CT scan to rule out cancer, two psychology tests, a full dental examination, and finally a colonoscopy. I am really not looking forward to the colonoscopy test. I know from prior experiences during this ordeal that I do not respond well to objects being shoved up my rectum. However, I want to beat this disease so badly that I am willing to do whatever it takes to live.

The rest of my day was filled with guests, nineteen of them to be exact. They were all family members and each one of them made me feel more and more special. I really enjoyed my time with them. The amount of support I have becomes more apparent to me as the days go by, even more so now than my initial hospitalization at Chicago General.

Tomorrow I will undergo a psychology test and the CT scan. I will be injected with dye. Therefore, I will not be able to be discharged until this upcoming Tuesday. The doctors need to monitor my kidneys to make sure they do not go further into kidney failure as a result of the possible detrimental effects the dye possesses. As much as I respect my doctors, I cannot wait to go home. I want to pass these tests and go back to the life I have grown accustomed to. I am filled with this need to live—a feeling that is so refreshing and empowering. However, at the same time, it is a sensation that feels very fragile. I believe that at any second this feeling can be taken away from me. I just need to keep smiling and do whatever I have to do to keep my spirits up. I keep telling myself, *I am going to live, and I am going to be in my studio apartment next month... keep fighting, Bill. Miracles do happen!*

Monday, August 3, 2009

Fuck Golytely! Honestly, it is hands down one of the most twisted forms of liquid ever created. Golytely is a drug that makes you shit profusely. I have consumed a gallon of it in the past three hours for a colonoscopy that has been scheduled for early tomorrow morning. The painful digestion of this drug has topped the list of exhausting procedures I had to undergo today.

My day began at 10:00 AM when I was whisked away for my full body CT scan. The procedure itself only lasted twenty-five minutes, but the entire process took about an hour. I was placed onto a bed. It rotated as a female voice on the intercom gave me commands as to when I should inhale and exhale. The voice then told me I would experience a warming sensation at any moment. Sure enough, I did. Dye was then injected into my veins and I felt a rush of warmth take over. My blood felt like it was boiling. At one point I had to verify I hadn't urinated all over myself. I felt that I had lost total control over my body's functions. After managing to fight the urge, I was wheeled back to my room for ten minutes until my chariot appeared yet again. This time, I was taken to the ultrasound clinic on the lower levels of the hospital.

My body needs to undergo a full inspection from head to toe. The doctors need to be sure I do not have any other ailments before I am given two pristine organs. Consequently, another test is to scan every vein in my body with an ultrasound. I found out that I have so many veins, it takes nearly three hours of cooperation with an ultrasound technician to scan each one of them individually. The technician was really kind. She was spunky though. You could tell she secretly hates her job, but was trying to make the best of it. We did a lot of talking in three hours. She told me a lot about her husband and her career. I fielded many questions regarding my childhood. All my life I have never understood the reason why so many people have been so shocked that I had a heart transplant. I was never able to grasp the magnitude of the situation until this journey of mine began. She seemed mystified by my story and our conversation made the time go by much faster. I was later wheeled back to my bedroom for the final time, but the tests were far from over.

When I arrived at my bedroom, a woman by the name of Carla was waiting for me. She introduced herself as a, "Social Worker for Individuals Who Receive Transplants." Carla then proceeded with a series of questions, which took a total of two hours to answer. The first hour of questioning was simple. It focused on my family life and who I trusted to take care of me if I was ever incapacitated for a given time frame. The questions grew steadily deeper and more intense until she closed with her final inquisition, "Would you still want this surgery, even if I told you that for three months of your life you would be in excruciating pain and possibly suffer from symptoms of depression?" Without hesitation I responded, "I have only felt pain since March. I am ready for whatever is thrown at me. I will do anything to someday live my normal life again." She smiled as though I had answered her question perfectly. She left the room as a fourth-year medical student entered. She was a very attractive girl. "Hi, I was wondering if I could give you a physical?" she asked. "Yeah, if you would like to." I responded. But really I was thinking, *Um, Hell yes! Shawing!* I spent the next forty minutes discussing my entire case with this attractive, young, future doctor of Mercy Care Hospital. I would have attempted to get her number had I not known that I wasn't going to be ill in the coming six months of my life. She thanked me for my help, after a full physical exam of course, and said she would return back with her Attending to go through "tomorrow's procedure." I had no idea what she was refer-ring to, but she was so attractive I really didn't care. As promised, she returned with her Attending, who informed me that tomorrow I would be undergoing a colonoscopy as one of my final exams to make it on the Organ Recipient List. I was given a gallon of Golytely and told to chug it down.

Jen and Jo arrived shortly thereafter. They stayed in the room with me and really lifted my spirits as I tried my hardest to down the horren-dous drink. It tasted like lukewarm saltwater that had already been pissed out by some exotic animal. It was the most sterile drink I have ever tasted. The girls stuck around until about midnight. They are two great friends. It's surprising how much it means to you when people show they truly care. Jen had already done so much research on my condition before arriving, I honestly think she knows more than Chi-cago General does about organ transplantation and management.

This is where I now find myself. I am writing this entry, trying to keep my mind off of the Golytely as I run to the bathroom every three minutes. My ass is officially a wreck. I am experiencing symptoms of dizziness, nausea, and muscle weakness from going to the bathroom so many times. The worst part being that if I cannot consume enough of this stuff before I black out from physical fatigue, the doctors will not be able to operate. I will be forced to spend one more day in the hospital drinking another gallon until the procedure is completed successfully. I have another three or four cups to go. This is one of the worst experiences of my life, but I need to down this. I need to get on that list.

Tuesday, August 4, 2009

Today was one Hell of a day. Ironically, everything came to a head naturally as a result of unnatural force. Since the day I was born, my mom has done an astounding job managing my patient care. She has taken hold of the reins and has monitored every milligram of every drug that has ever gone into my system. I am truly grateful for the way she has taken care of me over the years. I realize that she is one in a million and that she has dedicated her life to making sure I have an outstanding one. She never allowed me to feel different from the other kids growing up. She has simply always been there for me.

A problem that I have been facing with my mom, as I have matured through the years, has been my need to grow and her inability to let go of the reins. This problem has become more apparent to me this summer. I find myself trapped in this horrible circumstance. My body has grown, as well as my mind. I am a man. I am no longer an infant. I know what I want to be done with my body and am able to make my own decisions regarding my care. This is my battle, but my mom sees exactly what I do when I look in the mirror. My body is failing and I am growing weaker. Her grip on the reins of my management have tightened. She is reverting back to the care she provided me as a child. She will not let me speak; at times she answers questions for me in front of the doctors. She has this need to treat me as a child and convinces herself that her wishes are the same as mine. My mom fails to understand that this second time around; she has to sit on the sidelines. I am the one fighting to survive. As much as she wants to believe she is doing the right thing for me, she needs to understand that only I know what it feels like to live in the dark world that has become my life.

There is one doctor whom I have not spoken of in these entries because she isn't the greatest. She is a soft-spoken Asian woman named Dr. Kwan. Though she is soft-spoken, she is one of the biggest alarmists that I have ever met. Since being moved from ICU to the fifteenth floor telemetry wing, I have seen her several times. Dr. Kwan has already told both my mom and me that I may not make it on the transplant list. Today, she told us I may need to undergo a kidney biopsy as well. Dr. Gordon immediately refuted each one of her idiotic comments. He shook his head as though he was astounded by Dr. Kwan's stupidity each time.

Dr. Kwan was the reason for the unnatural force I mentioned earlier. For as long as I have known my mom, she has despised incompetence. Unfortunately for Dr. Kwan, she is extremely incompetent. I would describe my mom as a vulture. For the past few days, Dr. Kwan has been her prey.

My mom has been exhausted over the past few days because she has voluntarily slept in a chair in my hospital room. All my mom has wanted is to go home. She keeps pushing for a discharge but does not listen to me when I passively tell her I am not ready to go home. She took advantage of the incompetent Dr. Kwan today (who I believe has become afraid of my mom) and convinced her to file paperwork for my discharge.

Luckily, I was given so many drugs I have no recollection of today's colonoscopy. I only remember closing my eyes while looking at the blonde nurse. I was severely drugged. On top of the narcotics from the procedure, I was given two immunizations. The first was against Pneumonia and the other was against Hepatitis B. I never received these immunizations before because I had seizures after being given the DTP vaccine when I was an infant. Needless to say, I was unable to move and I slept for seven hours. The time had come for my discharge and my mom shook me from my sleep. Before I knew it, she had packed everything from my room into two little bags and had my nurse ripping the IV from my arm.

I was so disoriented. I couldn't make sense of my surroundings. At one point, I could not determine which side of the room I was on. I just remember my mom's voice echoing, "Go to the bathroom! Lets get going!" I saw my sister. She looked angry and was shooting daggers to my mom behind her back. Carissa understood I was not ready to leave this hospital, but my mom was once again forcing her wishes upon me.

I feel like I am back in the lost days because I only remember staring out my window, looking at the John Hancock building. There was a red construction claw-like object swaying back and forth like a pendulum. It mesmerized me and helped me keep my balance as I listened to my mom's voice echo throughout the room. I have no idea what she was saying, but I deliriously yelled out, "Everybody shut the fuck up! I don't want to hear voices right now!" I believe my sister paged the nurse because she soon came in to speak with me about how I was feeling. I remember the nurse's face. She seemed worried and hesitant to let me go. "Why don't you lie down? You can leave in a few hours if you feel up to it," she said. My mom's phone went off and both Carissa and my mom left the room. My heart began pounding from my chest and I couldn't help but cry. My mom's inability to understand my own individual needs caused my body to hit a point of distress that everything truly erupted. My body became scalding hot, I began to gasp for air. I may have experienced an anxiety attack. Carissa entered the room. She rushed to my bedside and began rubbing my head. "Shh! Calm down. It's okay. It's okay." Carissa looked pissed. "I don't know how you put up with her," she whispered. I was still trembling. My mom entered, she looked hesitant to approach my bed. I then finally told my mom what I have wanted to tell her this entire summer.

"Don't talk!" I said. "Just listen to me! I know you love me and I know you want me to be better, but you have to let go! I am a grown man! I am not a baby anymore! I can make my own decisions and I can speak my own mind! You need to back the fuck down! This is my battle, you need to understand that only I can fix it! You're on the sidelines now! You need to give me my space! There are going to be days that I will be at school, I am going to be so sick that I am not going to be able to go to class or maybe even call you. When this happens you need to leave me alone!"

My mom started to cry. "I never meant to hurt you. I only wanted to help," she said as the tears poured down her face. "I know, but you are only making it worse," I replied. "I love you," she said as she grabbed her bags and left the room. "I love you, too." I uttered after her.

She left my room an hour ago. It is 9:54 PM. I think I have achieved some independence. I feel grown up, even though I am hooked to oxygen and crying like an infant as I write this entry. I hope my mom heard me when I told her I loved her…

The Journals:

Getting On The List

Wednesday, August 5, 2009 - Thursday, August 20, 2009

Wednesday, August 5, 2009

Round two is finally over. I was discharged today around 1:00 PM. I am really glad I stayed the night alone in the hospital yesterday; I desperately needed that time by myself. My family is amazing, but there are just so many of them. They love to support me, but with them always being around and with my mom consistently spending the night, I typically spend an entire hospital stay without a moment of solitude.

I really took advantage of my alone time last night. Even though I felt that I had the flu from the immunizations, I refused to go to sleep. I wanted to savor every second of the silence. I made the room my own domain. First, I opened all the curtains so that I could see the John Hancock building. I love looking at the buildings in Chicago at night. Especially since I have been home sick this summer. The skyline brings me this inner peace and keeps my head focused on the current task at hand. It pushes me to get healthy so that I can return to school in the fall.

I converted my rolling food tray into a desk. I set my laptop up, blared Jack's Mannequin's "Swim," and responded to the large amount of e-mails I received over the course of my hospital stay. I have recently been blessed to be in contact with two fellow organ recipients named Corey and Luke. Luke is the nephew of my Aunt Patti's friend. He received a new heart two years ago and took it upon himself to e-mail me and offer any support I may need. I asked him to describe the process of a heart transplant from the recipient's eyes. I requested that he did not spare me any details. Luke turned out to be a very vivid writer. He shared every miniscule detail he could recall and warned me of which portions of the recovery will hurt the most. It may sound disturbing that I wanted to know such agonizing details, but I needed to know. I have always done the best with situations when I have been able to visualize them beforehand. Luke's e-mail was the perfect medi-cine. It has cured a lot of my anxiety, anxiety that has been brought on from the unknown. I have a feeling I will be reading Luke's response many more times in the months to come.

Corey is another recipient of an organ. However, Corey is the recipient of a kidney, three kidneys to be exact. I met Corey through my cousin,

Natalie. They both graduated from high school together. The poor guy
has had to undergo this process three separate times throughout his
life. I can only imagine how painful and scary that must have been.
I am not ready to speak with Corey though, and I told him just that.
I still have not been able to mentally grasp the fact that I need a new
heart, let alone a new kidney. I am not scared of the surgery by any
means, but I think my mind is still in shock. Corey understood. He
wrote me back saying he is ready to answer questions whenever I am
ready. He is a great guy, much like Luke. I responded to e-mails until
about 2:00 AM before going to bed.

Whenever I come home from the hospital, my life seems to have a bit
of jet lag. I find myself trying to pick up the pieces and get back into a
groove. Today I struggled with staying on my low-sodium diet. I spent
a good half hour trying to re-teach myself what I can and cannot eat. I
think this part of the jet lag is due to all of my meals being ordered for
me while I am on bed rest in the hospital.

The other aspect of jet lag stems from my bedroom. I always forget
how dirty my room is when I return home. I had sticky notes lying all
over my desk reminding me of deadlines that had passed while I was at
Mercy Care. I had to spend over an hour cleaning up and I still feel as
though everything is not in its correct place.

The only other part of my day that sticks out in my mind are people's
Facebook statuses. It seems that three of every five statuses are dedica-
tions to a guy named Brad. Brad is a graduate of my high school. He
was a year younger than I, and today he lost his battle to cancer. As I
read the words of his friends paying homage to his life, I had a chill go
down my spine when I realized that I am unbelievably close to being
the next graduate of Lake Zurich High School who passes away. I had a
vision of my friends posting their favorite memories of me and changing their profile pictures to my image, much like they have done for
Brad. It isn't so much that I am afraid of actually dying. What creeps
me out is the unexpectedness of Brad's death. He had apparently just
been given two weeks to live this past Sunday, he really only got three
days. I just hate how uncertain life can be sometimes. But in a sense,
Brad's passing gave me strength. It helped me realize that my battle is
not a death sentence. My battle is a second chance at a brilliant life.
I view this as a second coming, a rebirth, a chance to accomplish my

previous goals and to raise the bar to a whole new level. Waiting for this phone call is going to be a challenge, but once the phone rings my life will change forever.

Thursday August 6, 2009

My feet are in dire pain. I have water retention from my knees to my toes. My limbs look as though they will split at any second from the pressure of the fluid. I have been out of the hospital for less than twenty-four hours and I already want to go back. Don't get me wrong, I do not enjoy being in a hospital, but at least they can take the pain away. Needless to say, today really was not the best day.

I notice I only have energy for a certain period of time. I can last about four hours until I need to rest for one. If I do not get my hour of rest I rapidly grow very tired. Eventually, I struggle to keep my eyes open.

I spent my four hours of energy with my friend, Caitlin. I have known Caitlin since fifth grade. She recently returned home from vacation and only knew that I was in the hospital. Caitlin was unaware of my new-found need for a heart and kidney transplant. When I broke the news to her, she was shocked. She seemed noticeably upset, I thought for a second that she was going to cry. I tried to stay as upbeat as possible about it because realistically, I am. I am not afraid, so I do not want her to be afraid or upset either. She asked me many questions. Once we were done with our lunch, we parted ways.

I returned home, and that is when I became exhausted. Much like I felt days before this previous hospitalization, I found myself dozing off by my computer. I sat down on my bed, which is when I began to experience the all too familiar chest pains. I hadn't had any chest pain since the night of my biopsy. Dr. Gordon had prescribed a new pill, which had seemed to eliminate them. As I was lying in bed, I realized that I forgot to fill my pill boxes with the added medication. I fell asleep to the pain.

I woke up three hours later and felt re-energized. I was able to do everything I wanted. I spent the rest of the night writing thank you cards. I continued where I left off last night with my mission to restore my room to how I want it. All of the cleaning caused my feet to swell to the massive size they are right now. I am once again exhausted, and I feel like I need to take another nap. I hope I get this transplant soon. I know my energy will only decrease as the weeks go by. This cycle of exhaustion and energy is exhausting on its own… if that makes any sense.

Friday, August 7, 2009

I think the veins in both of my arms have finally collapsed. They have taken so much abuse since June 8th that I believe they have given in. My arms feel heavier, yet weaker at the same time. The vein in my right arm, just above my elbow, has taken the most abuse. It has served as an outlet for six IVs. Now when I touch it, it seems to have a lump in it. It feels so heavy and stiff, I actually had to look down at it a couple of times to verify that the IV was removed. I am assuming I have a lot of scar tissue built up. Hopefully, that will go away with time.

Saturday, August 8, 2009

I am starting to worry. I have noticed a steady decline in my energy level every day since I returned from the hospital. I worry because I am not even on the Organ Recipient List yet. I won't be until this Thursday. I have my final test on Tuesday, which is a meeting with the Nephrology (kidney) team. I honestly do not know what the point of the meeting is. I just know they need to clear some paperwork in order for me to make it on the list.

I think about school, I sometimes doubt myself that I will be able to last a week on my own. But I am going to push myself. I need to go to school. I need to prove to myself that I am stronger than this disease. I feel that even if I only make it two weeks at my apartment before being rehospitalized or needing to live at home, it will be a major accomplishment. I just hate not being myself. And the worst part about it all is that the disease teases me. I woke up today at 8:00 AM. I have since had lunch with Sara and went shopping for my brother's birthday gift. I felt like myself all day. It is currently 2:52 PM and I honestly feel like I can't muster the energy to play video games. This disease will give you a glimpse of the life you used to have, before pulling you into a state of depression hours later. It's almost as though the disease has a sadistic mind of its own. It wants you to think about death.

I discovered the one weapon against this sadistic disease, friends. I just received a text message from Hadi and Maggie, two girls I used to work with last semester at my internship. They simply texted me to say they heard a song that made them think of me. They also wanted to wish me well. It sounds crazy, but little acts of kindness seem to cheer me up. To be honest, I feel slightly revived. It was their text message that gave me the strength to write this journal entry. I hope my friends think of me while I am at school. I am going to need a lot more text messages to get through this.

Sunday, August 9, 2009

I woke up today at 9:00 AM. I have since done nothing with my day. I was just lying in bed a minute ago reading Lucky Man, a book by Michael J. Fox. Peter gave it to me while I was in the hospital a week ago. He said it was inspiring and thought I could use it during my current battle. It wasn't until I finished the second chapter in the book that I realized, *I have not had any human contact today.*

It's 1:24 PM. I have been dizzy all day. My mind seems to be in a funk. I almost feel depressed, but I do not understand why. I feel as though I am subconsciously avoiding the world. I have received a handful of e-mails from friends and family, but I do not have the energy or the drive to respond to a single one.

My stomach has been gurgling for the past two hours, but I haven't cared to silence its moans for food. It sounds sickening, but I think I prefer the hunger pain. It isn't comfortable, but I have allowed it to nest in my stomach because I prefer the feeling over the other pain that I am experiencing. I welcome the hunger. It's different.

Today is my brother's family birthday party. It starts at 3:00 PM. I have become so good at faking the smile that I know I will be able to pretend I am alright. My family always asks how I am feeling. I just make up some bullshit about how I have felt better, but I am feeling fine. That usually appeases them. I have a tendency of pushing people away when they try to get in my head, which is kind of ironic. The mere fact that I am bearing my soul in these journal entries is so out of character for me. I typically like to keep the façade that everything is "A-Okay" and cheerful in the world of Bill. I think a lot of the façade stems from growing up with an emotional shield. All of my insecurities about my scars and my medications built a fortress.

I have just over an hour to mentally pump myself up for this party. I have zero energy right now, so I don't know how I am going to make it through a Greek family party, which typically does not end until 2:00 AM.

On the brighter side, because I have been in bed all day my feet aren't swollen, and I have used 0mg of sodium for the day; I guess there is an upside to depression after all.

Monday, August 10, 2009

I continued my circuit of breaking the news to my friends. Today I met with Sabah and Paul. I have known them since high school. Sabah heard I was sick the day I was admitted to Mercy Care. She has since continuously messaged me to check up on my health. She seems genuinely concerned and had many question as we spoke over lunch. Paul and Sabah were the first friends to really take interest in my feet. It was funny seeing their reaction to my "Shamu" sized ankles. I hadn't laughed about my feet with anyone yet, so it was nice to crack some jokes. I've noticed that you need to be able to keep a light-heart about everything, no matter how hard it gets. Keeping a light-heart not only helps your own personal spirits, but it seems to ease the tension of the people who worry. We also discussed our move-in dates for college. Sabah and Paul are living in an apartment just a few blocks away from my studio next year. We made plans to get together in the coming weeks before we parted ways.

I returned home to learn that tomorrow's Nephrology test isn't much of a test to begin with; it turns out that it is more of a marathon. I will supposedly have to sit through a series of public speakers before I meet with the actual doctors. The speakers will lecture on "how to take care of your body after a transplant" and "how the family aids the patient in their care." The doctors will then draw another fifteen vials of blood, have a mini consultation and answer any questions. I also have a blood draw scheduled tomorrow morning before I go to the appointment for the heart clinic. Something tells me that by the end of the day I will be very lethargic, weak and nearly drained of blood, all after sitting through a program that will take six hours to complete! I also found out that I am technically not guaranteed a kidney. In fact, it is under the sole discretion of the Nephrology team to determine if I'm "a strong enough candidate to receive one." To me, this is kind of ridiculous, but worst-case scenario, I have had several friends and family members offer me one of theirs. However, I do not want to take theirs. I really do not want my disease to cause any other individuals pain, especially my family and friends.

I am sitting at an awkward crossroad in this journey of mine. I am very sick. The only way for me to be healed is by causing others pain. No matter which road my journey takes me down someone has to die. The question now is if I'll be able to take the road that only causes a family of complete strangers emotional pain? Or will this journey place more anguish on my conscience by bringing physical pain upon my family, too?

Right now I just want my life back. I want to be normal again. I just wish nobody else would have to feel this hurt.

Tuesday, August 11, 2009

I feel better today knowing that I have to get my kidney from a donor who has already passed. It's not to say that I feel good at all about the fact that someone needs to die, but I feel better knowing that my friends and family will not experience any pain.

The appointment today was simply a formality. I had to sit through an hour and a half speech about how to take care of a transplanted organ and the medications that are used to preserve such a gift. I believe the presentation itself was very thorough and I'm sure anyone experiencing a transplant for the first time would find it very beneficial. For me, however, I had dealt with everything that they spoke about for twenty years now, so it felt like a giant recap of my life.

I must say, I think the presentation may have done more damage than good for me. It kind of scared me a little and rocked my confidence. I had this image of the procedure going well and my recovery lasting two to three months, which would then be followed by another twenty years of bliss. Then the doctor began speaking about rejection and how the first year you are not out of the "deep end" quite yet. Supposedly, 10 percent of transplanted kidneys need to be retransplanted. The thought of going through this again has now replaced the image of bliss in my mind and has actually terrorized me for the entire day.

I know I need to hold on to the positives and try to think of a better thought whenever I get my confidence rocked like that. There are a lot of scary statistics and I can guarantee I will hear plenty more before this is all said and done. This is when I need to think of my long term Will, grasp onto it and hold it tighter than ever before.

One year from now, this entire chapter in your life will all just be a faint memory... you can't forget that.

Wednesday, August 12, 2009

My life seems so out of check today. Nothing seems clear. My room feels filthy to me, but I lack the energy to clean it. I have a list of things I want to do, such as write thank you cards to my family for the gifts I have received in the past two weeks. I also want to begin writing a paper that is due on August 30th for the internship credit that I took this summer (even though it was short lived). I just can't get myself to do it.

My mom is talking to my sister down the hallway right now. They are not speaking loudly, but I am so irritable, I feel like their voices are echoing and making my head pulsate with each word.

I woke up today to find that my world was in slow motion. With every turn of my head, my body seemed to be moving out of sync. I don't know what caused the feeling. My doctors decreased my dosage of Toprol and Cyclosporin yesterday, but I shudder to think a decrease would have the same effect as an increase! That can't be possible.

I think my slow moving world may be a result of a bad night's sleep. I didn't have the typical nightmares (the ones with the bug-like doctors), but every dream last night was about the day that I get my transplant. I kept waking up in between dreams, and when I'd finally fall back to asleep, the dream would replay. The weirdest part was that each dream's outcome was different from the next.

They all started the same. I would be sitting in my studio in the city. I remember that I would feel okay. I was watching television, but then my cell phone would go off. The phone read, "Mercy Care." For whatever reason I would not answer the call. I knew what it meant, so I would sprint out of my front door. I would feel my heart racing. Then, much like you would see in the movies, I would exit the front entrance of my building to find a taxi conveniently waiting for me outside. "Mercy Care Hospital," I would say to the cab driver. He would then turn and smile at me. He was a pudgy African American man. He wore a sand colored golf hat with an orange-checkered vest. With that, he would abruptly hit the gas and I could hear the tires burning under us. I'd arrive at the hospital, and this is where the dream would begin to change.

In one version of the dream, everything went smoothly. I would hand him the twenty-dollar bill, tell him to keep the change, and I would proceed to meet with Dr. Gordon, Dr. Krause and Dr. Lenair. I'd have the surgery, then I'd awake in a bright room with my family and friends feeling calm.

In another version of the dream, I reached into my pocket to find I forgot my wallet. I would sit in the cab for hours as I debated with the cab driver and tried to connive my way into a free fare. Eventually, I would get another phone call from Mercy Care. This time, they would tell me the clock had expired and that I missed my one chance to live. This particular dream caused me to wake up in a sweat. I was panting, and my heart was beating profusely.

The final version of the dream was one where I had the money. The cab driver and I parted ways on good terms, but the complication in this version was with the surgery. Somehow in this dream, the heart worked, but the doctors found out the kidney wasn't able to arrive in time mid-surgery. I lost a large amount of blood and woke up to a room of my family members crying.

I realize out of all these renditions of the dream, the last one is highly unlikely. The second version is too, but if it did happen, I would probably have him drive me to an ATM instead of stupidly fighting for hours.

The slow motion went away after I took a two-hour nap around 1:00 PM. I am hoping my bad morning was a result of sleep deprivation and not another symptom of this disease.

Thursday, August 13, 2009

I failed again today. I failed to complete my backup short-term <u>Will</u>. After speaking with my mom, I finally came to terms with the fact that I am not physically strong enough to live alone in the city. To be honest, I realized this two weeks ago. I just haven't been truthful with myself. With each passing week, I feel my body deteriorating. It began with my energy level, and now the skin on my feet is beginning to split from the swelling.

I will not give up though. I need to continue to press forward. I will begin speaking with Columbia tomorrow in regards to postponing my enrollment status until the spring semester. Meanwhile, I have signed up for twelve credit hours through Harper College. I will be taking everything online. This way, if the day comes where I can no longer leave my bed, I can still take classes and continue my education.

I am, yet again, faced with developing another short-term <u>Will</u>. Since I have already failed at completing my first two choices, I find it would be a very bad decision to make my next selection, "survive the transplant." I can't help but feel like that choice would be suicide. I am going to go with a safer, less risky bet. I will now say that my new short-term <u>Will</u> is to receive no less than a 3.5 GPA for fall semester. That should be challenging enough.

In other news, I received a phone call today from Dillon. He is the Heart Transplant Coordinator for Mercy Care. Apparently, I still have a few more tests to complete that went under the radar. I have set up appointments with the correct physicians next Thursday. Hopefully, by midnight on the 20th, I will officially be on the Organ Recipient List.

Oh, and I had blood in my ears this morning when I woke up. I have no idea what that means, but unless it happens again, I am going to keep that little fun-fact to myself. I'm not in the mood to be prodded any further.

Friday, August 14, 2009

I am surprised how fast I have been able to come to terms with the fact that I am not healthy enough to return to Columbia. I expected weeks to go by until I was okay with the sudden change in plan. I am no longer angry like I was yesterday. I think what keeps me driven is my cousin Nick's quote, "You just need to cash in your summer." I did cash in my summer. Summer of 2009 will be one that I won't soon forget, even though there were times I wished I could fast-forward through it completely. I am now venturing into fall. I now need to look at it as, "cashing in my fall semester." I am about to lose another three-month interval of my life. However, I have a feeling this next three-month period is going to be far more devastating, both physically and emotionally—mainly due to the fact that all my friends are leaving in the coming week for college. I can only hope this sacrifice of time will result in a lifetime of health and happiness.

Saturday, August 15, 2009

I feel that I should begin this entry by mentioning that I have not experienced anymore bleeding ear problems. I also have not had any more bloody butt issues since my last episode about a month ago. I have done extensive research on all forms of heart failure and Transplant Vasculopathy, "randomly bleeding out of different holes" does not seem to be a symptom of any known condition. Considering this is happening once a month, I am just going to assume that one of my pills is giving me a "Man Period."

Today was an eventful day. I did not leave my house, but it was still very enjoyable. This is due to the fact that Aunt Patti, Nouna and Greg all came over to spend the day with me. They did so because Carissa moved back to Eastern Illinois University today. My parents were gone all day and I was left home alone. Fortunately, I have yet to reach the point in this disease where I need a babysitter, but my family hadn't seen me in a while and they wanted to visit me. I figured that today was the perfect day.

My Nouna and Aunt Patti spent about three hours preparing a low-sodium pork tenderloin meal. Meanwhile, Greg and I watched television. For the most part, I felt really good all day. My energy and spirits were up. Then around 7:00 PM, I felt my body take its typical nosedive. Amongst all the excitement of having everyone over, I found it near impossible to fight the weak feeling. I fell asleep on the couch for close to an hour. I would have slept more, but I had to wake up for my 8:00 PM Cyclosporin.

Everyone was still in my house when I awoke. I took my medications, and then Aunt Patti pulled out the Scrabble board. We played a shockingly low-intelligence rendition of the game. What I mean by "low-intelligence" is that we were able to spell many large words such as "Cat," "Cab," and "Queef." Needless to say, in the end, the scores were not very high.

I had a great day today. I am just really looking forward to the future when I can make it 24 hours without crashing from over stimulation.

Sunday, August 16, 2009

I hate this waiting game, but it feels unfair to say that I am waiting right now considering I am not even on the list yet. Waiting makes your life really dull and out of focus. I can't stop thinking about life after the operation. It is getting to the point where my mind is becoming one-tracked. Waiting makes you not want to do anything.

Monday, August 17, 2009

Keeping up with people my age is exhausting! Seriously, I have never been able to relate to my parents when they would make comments like, "Oh, how it would be nice to be young again," or when they would simply say, "We can't, we're too tired after work." I can really appreciate what they were talking about now. Especially if they were referring to how I feel at the end of the day.

My friends are all leaving for college and I have been doing my best to say good-bye to each of them. I want to spend as much time with them as possible because I will not be seeing anybody until at least Thanksgiving. I can't even visit them at their campuses because I fear that my organs will come on the one weekend I choose to leave the Chicagoland area. I spent today with Jo. We went on a trip to the electronic store. She bought a laptop. It was funny, I have never in my life seen someone so excited to purchase an electronic item before (that says a lot coming from me. I sold computers, MP3 players and video games for three years). We came back to my house and I aided her in the setup process. I taught her everything she needs to know and loaded all of her software before she goes off to college on Wednesday. She left my house around 7:00 PM and I was thoroughly exhausted by the end of it.

Tomorrow I am sure I will spend some time with another friend. Regardless if it's Jen, Jo, Doug, or someone else, I know I will be struggling to keep up. Everyone's gone by this Saturday, so I need to last until then. Honestly, this is getting to be so draining that I have not written a single short story for this book in a week. I'm too mentally tapped-out to put together sentences at this point.

I notice this entry and the prior two entries seem to be slightly less coherent, almost sloppy. Or maybe I am just reading into things too much.

Tuesday, August 18, 2009

I feel incredible right now, almost revived. I want to take time right now to describe in detail how I feel because this is the first day of my life since last February I feel like myself. I forgot how it felt to feel this good! I want to look back on this day in the future when I am recovering so I can remind myself what it is I am fighting for.

Everything is clear. My head feels open. I am relaxed, I am able to be witty without trying. My world is no longer dark. I am able to see the brighter side of everything. I feel as though I can take on any challenge headfirst and accomplish anything I set my mind to.

The muscles in my body feel loose. All my pain has disappeared. I can breathe without effort and I can go up and down flights of stairs without experiencing a spell of dizziness. My voice even feels stronger; I don't hear any sadness in it. Since June, I have noticed that my voice sounds gloomy, less upbeat. I'm sure it is purely psychological and my subconscious has been causing it. Whatever the case may be, the gloominess has left.

Most importantly, my heart feels healthy. I do not feel any irregular beats. Today was the first day that I didn't feel my heart skip beats, nor did it feel as though it was going to pound out of my chest. Typically the rhythms are so strong I notice my body shaking when I am at a resting position. The shaking did not happen once today and I did not feel any pain. I feel as though I can run up-and-down a basketball court without effort. I feel like my heart is healing itself, as though I am experiencing a miracle.

Until today, I forgot what it felt like to be happy. I forgot how it felt to live a normal life. I honestly do not know what to attribute this upswing in health to. My only guess would be the decrease in my recent Prednisone dosage from 5mg to 2mg daily. Or it may be my recent loss of nine pounds in water weight over the past week.

I hope this feeling continues to last and sticks with me until I receive my transplants. Even if I wake up tomorrow feeling the usual ailments of this disease, I feel blessed to be given this day of happiness. I can now cling onto August 18th because now I know how it feels. August is much easier to remember than February.

Wednesday, August 19, 2009

The miraculous energy from yesterday carried into the late hours of today. I continued to feel strong. In fact, today I had to go to Harper to manually register for a course. I had to walk across the same parking lot that I once struggled to cross. Today, I walked the entire distance twice and did not have any difficulty breathing, nor did I have any feelings of weakness. I only felt tired once I got into the building. However, the tiring sensations were not the same as of recent. The sensations were more like I was out of shape as opposed to symptoms of the illness. The fatigue quickly passed and I spent the next two hours visiting with everyone I worked with earlier in the summer.

I left Harper still feeling upbeat and energized. I returned home around 6:00 PM and went about my day feeling strong. It wasn't until about 10:45 PM that my strength left me and I began to feel the illness form of the fatigue. Considering the fact I was able to last almost all day on my high-energy buzz, I am going to chalk today up as a win for The Billness. Bringing the total score to roughly:

The Billness - 2
The Illness - 198

Hey… look at the bright side… I stopped the shutout….

Tomorrow I have (what better be) THE FINAL, AND I MEAN ABSO-
LUTE FINAL DOCTOR'S APPOINTMENT until I make my way onto
the Organ Recipient List. It is my understanding that all I have left to
do is meet a nutritionist, meet the surgeon, meet the transplant coordinator, Dillon and finally read a book about management with the
doctors. Once this is complete, I will be on the list and I will finally be
able to say, "The phone can ring at any second." The appointment is at
11:00 AM. I need to wake up bright and early tomorrow morning so
that my mom and I can meet with Aunt Patti, who is driving us down
to the city again.

I just noticed it's 12:15 AM. I need to be up in seven hours… good
night.

Thursday, August 20, 2009

I learned a great deal today. Actually, I think it's best to say I had a
great deal of information thrown at me. It's just a matter of how much
of it actually stuck.

Let me begin by saying, I AM OFFICIALLY ON THE LIST! The waiting game truly begins now. In order to get on the list, I had to endure
two hours of nonstop discussion about heart transplantation and the
healing process that goes along with it. That was intense, but I must say
Mercy Care does a sensational job "welcoming" you to their program,
or as Dr. Krause phrased it, "their family."

The appointment began with "my family" of doctors entering the
room. I saw some familiar faces such as Dr. Krause and Dr. Gordon.
Many new members of the team were introduced as well. I was able to
finally put a face to the voice that called himself, "Dillon," these past
few weeks. He was a really nice guy, very young. Actually, I know for a
fact he is 35 years old and that he's a Scorpio; Aunt Patti found it necessary to ask him.

Anyway, Dillon is the guy who will be my over-the-phone nurse, and he is the first person I am to contact if I have any problems arise from here on out. If he is ever to deem the situation serious enough, it is my understanding I would have to contact Dr. Gordon or whoever else is on call at the time.

Another member who was introduced, was Tami. She is a Heart Transplant Coordinator who works alongside the head surgeon, Dr. Getty. I met Tami on my last day at Mercy, just before my ride arrived. We spoke very briefly, but I remember her. She is tall, very thin but fit. She has the body of a runner. She has dark blonde hair and fair skin. I really like her and Dillon.

The surgeon, Dr. Getty, entered the room after everyone else. He wanted to meet me and discuss why there is a very high risk of major blood loss throughout the surgery. This is due to my blood thinner, Plavix, which I am on for my defibrillator. He does not want me to come off of the Plavix, but he restated the fact that I am going to need a large amount of blood from the blood bank prepared for me before the surgery.

After finishing their introductions, they all left, except Dillon, who had brought in the nutritionist during Dr. Getty's introduction. She was brief. She basically told me to stick to the diet that I am on for now and, once I am transplanted, I can up my sodium intake safely to 2300mg daily. I am currently ingesting 1200-1500mg daily.

The nutritionist left at exactly 12:30 PM. I was then spoon-fed so much information from Dillon that by the time he was done, my cell phone read, "2:35 PM."

He began by explaining how there are three levels that a recipient can be placed on for the Organ Recipient List:

1A- These are the people who are severely sick. They are on two or more IV medications called Inotropes, which keep their heart beating for them. These people have been admitted into the hospital. They are so ill, that sometimes they have a pump that has been inserted into their chest to pump their heart for them.

I am a bit different though. I can become 1A, but because I do not have my original heart, I am not a candidate for the pump.

1B- Patients listed in this category still live at home, or in a location where other individuals are assisting them on a daily basis. These people either have an IV in their arms at all times and are required to undergo IV medications throughout the day, or they have a pump in their chest as well. It is likely that if I am to wait long enough I will soon get to this level.

2A, 2B- I am a level 2B. At the moment I am sick, but I am not sick enough to need IV medication. These patients are basically much like myself. They have pain, they walk around feeling like Hell, but they are sustained with pills. They are the last group of people to receive organs.

The most interesting part of the day was when Dillon explained the types of organs that I qualify for. The organs are labeled, "High-Risk Organs." They are passed up by all the 1A's and the 1B's. The reason why they are "High-Risk" is due to the lifestyle the donor lived. The donors typically have a history of prostitution, IV drug use, or at one point in their life, they have been incarcerated. This does not necessarily mean they were a mass-murderer. They simply could have had one bad night and were pulled over for a DUI. The catch, however, is that I am not going to be given that information. The reason why these individuals are branded "High-Risk" is because, in theory, they could have had a lifestyle of drug use, which could lead to HIV/AIDS. However, I was assured that the organs go through so much testing, that unless the donor contracted HIV/AIDS hours before their death, the organ would be detected and the donor would be deemed "unsuitable." Dillon explained how the staff would never recommend something they wouldn't give to their own family member, and that if I was to ever turn down an offer, there is a strong chance I will die waiting on the list for a second offer.

Dillon spent a good hour explaining what life will be like after surgery. I already knew a good amount of it. Such as the fact that I will be hospitalized for 7-14 days after surgery, I will need to undergo countless biopsies for the first year of my life, and for a while I will be on several narcotics to ease the pain. Dillon did mention something interesting though. Apparently, research found that older women respond to painkillers the best and are also the most sensitive. Whereas young males have a tendency of needing much higher doses and sometimes will be immune to some drugs. This would explain why I felt my entire procedure during my first biopsy. I must be immune to the drug that they used.

I found the rest of Dillon's information to be a bit dreary. I learned there is a slight chance I will need to have a secondary operation to put the kidney in a day after the heart transplant. The only positive is if this situation occurs, they will keep me fully sedated the entire day, and I will wake up not knowing the difference between four hours and forty-eight hours. The other scenario is I may experience a heavy amount of swelling during the heart transplant and I could be brought back from the operating room with my chest still partially open. In my opinion, this would be the worst-case scenario.

Once I get out of the hospital, I will be back on the Prednisone. Unfortunately, at a higher dose than I have ever been on. The doctors would place me on a dosage that ranges between 20-40mg daily. That was sad news to hear, especially after just learning that I am off of that horrible drug while I wait for a heart and kidney. Once I am placed on the 20-40mg dosage, it will take 12-15 months to come off of it (barring any unforeseen complications). This means, for an entire year, my face will be puffy, I will experience large amounts of acne on my face, neck, shoulders and chest, and I will potentially gain a substantial amount of weight. In addition to the Prednisone, I will be on roughly 19 other medications, which all come with their own side effects. The medications together could mean that at one point I will be on nearly 40 pills a day. I will be slowly weaned off of these medications, eventually leaving three permanent pills, which will hopefully sustain me for another twenty years.

Even through all this gloomy news, I found the one positive. My defibrillator will, without a doubt, be removed! Most likely during the transplant, but worst-case scenario, they will leave the metal box in and a few months after surgery, I would go in for a simple outpatient procedure and they will rip it out of my chest. That will probably be one of the best days of my life.

The Journals:

Trapped

Friday,
August 21, 2009 –
Monday,
August 24, 2009

Friday, August 21, 2009

I was thinking about everything Dillon said yesterday, specifically the portion about how I am going to be knocked out and will have no recollection of the 24-72 hours of my life after surgery. I started thinking about how that could be a problem, considering the fact that I am trying to journal my entire experience each day until I get back to the life that was ripped away from me in early June. I have a feeling that I will experience many flashbacks, that I will be left with snippets of those post-transplant days, much like my experiences with "The Lost Days."

My mind has been interesting today. I couldn't stop thinking about the surgery all day. It's not that I am afraid, it's the anticipation that's killing me. I want to know when. That's it. I do not care about the pain, I do not care about the drugs, bring that shit on. My life has been nothing but pain and drugs for the past three months. Pain and drugs are my life at this point. I just wish I had a date, something I can countdown to.

I mention my mind has been interesting because once 9:00 PM struck, I started thinking about my friends. I forgot about the surgery and I began to get angry that they are all out living normal healthy lives. They are all with their college friends, at their college campuses, surrounded by people our age, enjoying a weekend of partying just before the school year begins. They all have absolutely no stress. Their lives are carefree. They are out enjoying life. Meanwhile, I am trapped in this home, and until I get the phone call I really do not see an end in sight.

Think about it. This is how shitty my luck is. I am one of three children and I am the one child who was born ill. The other two are perfectly healthy and have no idea what it is like to be sick. I recently learned that my parents have known my entire life (but chose to never tell me) that there was a 25% chance that I would experience this disease around this age. I happen to be the one out of four Midwest recipients who ended up getting sick in the end. I am so angry right now that I feel like screaming. But I can't because if I do, I will have to answer forty-some odd questions from my mom as she continues to analyze me like she does on a daily basis. This is why I want to go to my studio so badly. I like solitude, I just want a place to clear my head. But there was a one out of two chance that I was not going to be able to live there at the end of the summer… and we all know how that turned out.

Sunday, August 23, 2009

I made a vow to myself that I would write everyday no matter how sick I got (with the exception of the 24-72 hour coma that I will apparently be in after surgery). Yesterday, I couldn't get myself to journal no matter how hard I tried. I had a really bad day. I did nothing but wallow around the house in my own sorrow. I was very depressed and angry that my life had taken such a sharp nosedive in the past three months. I feel like I was on top of the world for so long, riding such a high, only to be shot down. It's like a bad reality check.

If this disease has done anything positive, it has shown me how fragile both life and health are. I've learned that life could change in an instant; that life is not fair. Bad things don't necessarily happen to bad people, that the good really do die young.

I can't stop taking naps lately. For whatever reason my body seems to be getting on a timed pattern these past few days. At 8:00 PM, I fall asleep. Both days I have awoken at exactly 10:47 PM. It's like my body just randomly decided it needs precisely two hours and forty-seven minutes of rest each day. The phenomenon of my body clock gets even weirder. I have also noticed that for the past four days I have gotten severely nauseous between the hours of 3:00 PM and 5:00 PM. Once the two hours pass I go back to normal. I am able to eat, almost as though nothing had happened to my stomach.

These past two days have been rough. I apologize for not writing yesterday. I just feel really sad.

Monday, August 24, 2009

Typically, I try to write my entries late at night because I want to reflect on the day in its entirety. It is only 6:41 PM right now and I need to write because I don't know if I will be able to in a few hours. Today has been the worst day of my life. I didn't think it could get much worse than July 5th, but today has been awful.

I can't keep my eyes open. When I am awake, I am severely nauseous and the room will not stop spinning. My hearing starts to go. I feel like I am paralyzed for a moment's time. Eventually I get the strength to go downstairs. I seek food for the nausea, but typically it only dulls the sensation. It does not fully kill it. At that point, I cannot move. I feel my body convulsing from within. My mom comments that she sees me occasionally shake. She asks me questions, but my brain does not seem to be moving fast enough to supply answers. I can only make gestures and nod. After I eat, the sensation in my stomach dulls. I become very tired and I fall asleep for two hours. This entire process has happened three times today. I am writing now because this is the only period of time in the day that I have felt strong enough to do so.

In a half-hour I am going to the hospital. We called Mercy, and they advised us that due to rush hour traffic, our best bet is to be evaluated at St. Adrian. If the results do not come back in my favor, I can be transported to Mercy in an ambulance. They do not think today is a result of my heart. All my symptoms are supposedly those of a failing kidney.

Something tells me that for the first time in my life I will be hooked up to a dialysis machine tonight, and if not tonight, then very soon.

The only positive I can find in any of this is that maybe I'll be upgraded to 1B.

The Journals:

Waiting By The Phone

Tuesday,
August 25, 2009-
Tuesday,
October 20, 2009

AN EXERCISE IN SHORT-TERM MEMORY

Shortly after writing the previous entry, I was admitted to Mercy Care Hospital for the second time this summer. The four days that would soon follow were filled with only procedures, embarrassment and incredible amounts of pain. The pain made it nearly impossible to journal my thoughts at the end of each day (Tuesday, August 25, 2009 - Friday, August 28, 2009).

I try to always find the bright side in the bad because when you are ill, you need to be in a constant search for it. Especially if you are hoping to make it through your condition as the same person or a stronger, rebuilt rendition of yourself. The bright side to this four-day period was that I gained experience in memory recall techniques. I now know how to use these techniques once the true test comes and I am transplanted.

My ability to recall is not perfect. My mom has told me that in this period of time, I had twenty different family members and friends visit me in the hospital. Unfortunately, I can only remember five still images of my guests. Each of these images have all been verified to be correct by my mom. The first is of Carissa looking distraught on the chair that rests in the right corner of the room. The second is of Aunt Patti, my mom and Aunt Kathy standing at the foot of my bed. My mom and Aunt Patti were dressed in all black and Aunt Kathy was wearing a glittery yellow jacket. The final two pictures are of my cousin, Rossi, in a white polo standing at the foot of my bed, and one of Greg and his girlfriend standing near my right shoulder. His girlfriend has a flower patterned summer dress on and Greg was wearing a very tight, metrosexual red shirt.

Besides the roster of the visitors, I can honestly say that I recall the most important facts vividly and with extreme detail. Pain helps the mind remember everything. Fortunately, for the sake of this book, to me, pain was my only visitor during this series of four days.

Tuesday, August 25, 2009

I had the honor of having Karrie as my AM nurse for the day. I say "honor" because I met Karrie during my prior stay at Mercy. She admitted me, and was not only by my side, but my family's side; offering her support when I found out I needed to receive a heart and kidney transplant. Throughout this designated time period at Mercy, Karrie was my nurse for a total of sixty hours. It was during this sixty-hour period that I developed a complete trust in Karrie, I grew very close to her. However, on this day, Karrie was distraught to see me.

Karrie is the first thing I remember seeing. I remember being in excruciating pain, sitting on a blue chair near my bed as my lower back felt as though it was burning from within. I can recall feeling a hand on my left shoulder, which prompted me to turn and see Karrie smiling down on me. It wasn't a happy smile, though it was a comforting one. "I was so sad to see your name on the board when I came in this morning. I'm going to go grab something, I will be right back," she said. It was then a doctor entered the room. He was with Cardiology. I do not remember his name, but I remember he was very pale. He began to explain how the results from some blood tests had come back poorly and I would need to have a catheter inserted into the right side of my neck.

A few hours later, I was transported to the operating room. It sounds chilling to say, but I had been in that room so many times up to this point that I was starting to remember the names and faces of the surgeons. What's worse is that they were starting to remember mine. The doctor performing the catheterization came to visit me behind my curtain. It was a woman. A surgical mask concealed her face, and her hair and body were draped in long, sterile attire. She asked me to sign a consent form for the procedure, and began to take note of the drugs I was allergic to. I mentioned how the last time I had this very procedure performed, I felt the entire catheter slide down my neck. I told her how the doctor who performed my colonoscopy did some research at my request, and explained to me that I was given Versed. Supposedly Versed is only effective when mixed with another drug called Fentanyl. The day I had my biopsy, I was only given Versed. I requested that she gave me both drugs. She obliged and wheeled me into the room.

The operating room was cold, ice cold. I must have shown signs of hypothermia because an Italian looking nurse instantly wrapped me in a blanket. "I want to have a lot of drugs!" I yelled to the nurse over the loudspeaker that was blaring acoustic rock. "Don't worry, I'll give you Versed!" The nurse replied. "No! Not alone! That didn't work for me last time! I felt the whole thing! Use Fentanyl with it!" I pleaded. The nurse stared at the doctor, then turned to me, "Okay! We will use Fentanyl!" Moments later I tasted the saline in my mouth. I knew they had just injected me with something. Suddenly, I heard the all too familiar sound of haze. I was drifting into a forced sedation. Everything turned gray around me, until it all eventually faded to black.

I woke up, it was Wednesday.

Wednesday, August 26, 2009

I don't know what can possibly happen to someone to make them fall asleep around 3:00 PM on a Tuesday and not wake up until about 11:00 AM on a Wednesday. Whatever happened to me during this period of time must not have been pleasant. I later learned that Karrie was assigned to strictly be my nurse for the day, so she could offer me complete care. I have asked both my mom and Karrie about Tuesday. Each time, they give me a short, vague answer. Karrie only says, "You were bad that day, really bad."

Regardless of what "bad" means, I know I woke up feeling "okay," or at least better than bad. I was lying in bed when I felt my legs twitch periodically. They would shake without warning. I started to feel a little panicked, but I didn't want to alert the attention of the doctors. I thought it would be a sensation that would just blow over. I convinced myself it was nothing and I began holding my legs in an attempt to wrestle them to the mattress. Little did I know, my parents and the doctors were all aware of these "involuntary movements," so my attempts to be elusive failed from the start. Not to mention that the waves from my legs only transferred through my arms to my shoulders and were making me do a shimmy motion.

My doctors already began taking the appropriate measures. They worried the twitches were a result of a brain defect and sent in two Resident doctors from Neurology. The two asked me to do a series of exercises, which lasted roughly fifteen minutes. I felt like an obedient show dog that was about to take home "First in the Show," as I completed a multitude of remedial tasks. After following both of their fingers left and right, pushing my feet into their hands, and making circles with my legs, they determined that, "Further tests were needed." Twenty minutes later, a technician entered my room to perform an EEG (electroencephalogram). The procedure was just like the familiar echocardiogram, except this time the leads were stuck to my head and my hair smelled like tartar sauce when it was over. The EEG was ruled negative. For the time being, I remained the kid with only two defective organs and not three—lucky me, right?

Based on the EEG results, the doctors were able to determine that due to the skyrocketing amount of toxins in my body, the twitches were a result of my failing kidneys.

Dr. Jampour entered the room. I hadn't seen her since the day I met with Dr. Gordon and looked to transfer my case to Mercy Care. She ordered a catheter to be placed in my groin, and that I begin dialysis as soon as possible.

I remember hearing the word "dialysis." It seemed to come out of her mouth in slow motion, "di-al-y-si-s." My brain flashed back to the prior Monday, an hour before I went to St. Adrian Hospital, when I sat in my office frantically typing my thoughts as I fought the urge to sleep or vomit. I had called it! I felt like a psychic. My gut feeling that I was going to undergo dialysis proved to be true. Unfortunately for my penis, I did not magically foresee her other order, which was to have a Foley catheter placed into my bladder. I heard her say the words, but it was too late for my penis… he was going to have a "bad" day.

The first procedure I had to endure was the second ordered. My nurse for the day, Stacy, had the distinct pleasure of performing the procedure. I have never yelled at a woman before to her face. Amber was really the only woman I had yelled at, and that was when I broke up with her over the phone. Stacy got it bad though. I screamed almost every obscenity at her as she tried to jam something that looked like a rubber stopper up something that should never have to be stopped. The pain was excruciating. It burned and the burn ran up my leg into my lower back. Stacy kept pushing though. Stacy pushed for what felt like an eternity but turned out to only be five minutes, until she determined I was "too squirmy," and that I apparently "clench." Clench or no clench, I felt that I had won the battle, but doctors are resilient. Some doctors don't want battles, they want wars.

My penis and I hung out for a while, reminiscing on the good days. Days where we didn't have to sit in bed, on guard, preparing for an attack. The sliding glass door opened. It was Dr. Blyat. He is a Resident doctor. He admitted me Monday night. Since then I have grown to not like Dr. Blyat. I distrust him. He seems snaky. He's no older than twenty-five, completely bald and has very narrow dark brown eyebrows. His chin is bony. It comes out to a point. He wears workout T-shirts under his white lab coat and has a voice that sounds nasally. He's timid when he speaks, "I need to place this catheter in your groin. It is for your dialysis treatments. I will be joined by Yolanda and Dr. Vividy. It's a small little operation, we're going to do it by your bedside." He stared at me enthusiastically. "Okay, and exactly how many drugs will I be receiving before we do this?" I asked jokingly, but I was actually very serious. "None." he replied. "But we will be giving you a numbing agent on the spot of the incision." I realized I had no choice. There was no way out and after the last ordeal with Stacy, I figured I could take anything at this point. The procedure (which in my opinion should have taken no longer than ten minutes at the very most) lasted close to forty-five minutes as Dr. Blyat, Yolanda, and Dr. Vividy bumbled around with their equipment. I wanted them to stop, but they looked so stupid I felt as though I was watching the Three Stooges. It actually became quite entertaining up until they finally did the procedure right and I felt the catheter slide against the muscle in my thigh. "And we're done!" Dr. Blyat announced as though he had just performed a textbook catheter implantation. "Okay," I replied, but I was really thinking, *Thanks asshole!* The clock read 4:00 PM when the Three Stooges left.

It was about 6:00 PM when my memory of this day comes back to me. My penis was just starting to heal, I could feel the burn subsiding. Dr. Blyat then entered and started to nervously ramble, "Hey, yah know… um… well… we really need to get you peeing, so… I'm going to have to ask you to please urinate in your urinal or unfortunately, I am going to have to insert a Foley into your bladder." "No! I am not getting another Foley catheter!" I rebutted. Dr. Blyat then tried to get all buddy-buddy with me and said, "Yeah… I know… it suuuucks… but you got to start urinating so we can measure your kidney output." At this point I knew he was right. I hadn't pissed since Monday, and the last thing I wanted was to progress further into kidney failure. At this point in the day, or for that matter, this entire summer, I had undergone countless procedures and not complained once. I felt this was the appropriate battle to fight, if not for me, then at least for my penis. "I can't piss right now because my dick still burns from you guys shoving something up it! If I was going to piss, you guys kind of fucked that up, didn't you?!" I snapped back. Dr. Blyat was shocked. He had no idea what to say. "Well umm… yeah… well okay… just, uh, just take your time then… I'll give you an hour or so to pee." He turned and walked out of the room. I reached for the urinal, sat up near my IV and tried as hard as I could to pee. I felt the urge, but no matter how hard I tried nothing came out. "Fuck!" I shouted, and pulled my boxers up.

I tried three more times until Dr. Blyat came back into the room. "Okay, well, I know you didn't go, so we really need to get this Foley catheter in you," he said hesitantly. "Yeah, I know," I said depressed. I was admitting defeat. "If it makes you feel any better, I am going to be helping Stacy with the procedure," he said to me. *Great!* I thought to myself, *He is going to touch my dick, awesome!* Instead, I turned to Dr. Blyat and calmly said, "No, that does not make me feel better." I feel I have to give some credit to Dr. Blyat. He must have spent extensive amounts of time during adolescence, and far into his college years playing with himself because like magic, the catheter went in. It wasn't painless, but it was a much smoother procedure than Stacy's jousting technique.

I can assume that between 6:00 PM and 9:00 PM, the majority of my visitors came. I wasn't on many drugs at the time; I think I was truly so sick throughout this entire ordeal that I was unable to speak with anyone. The more I write I am beginning to wonder if my mind isn't allowing me to remember how sick I was. All I know is that this was the night I had a lot of visitors and this was the night Greg and his girlfriend came to visit. Out of everyone who came this night, I only have the one picture in my memory of the couple by the right side of my bed.

It was then the dialysis machine came rolling into my bedroom. The machine was huge. It was explained to me how the machine was to run a twenty-four hour version of the dialysis treatment. It sounded simple enough, but of course, nothing on this Wednesday could go right. I had an adverse reaction to the treatment.

My body began to quiver. I felt like my blood had been frozen from within. First my teeth started to chatter, then my hands started to rattle. Next to go were my legs, until eventually my entire torso was trembling from the chill. Stacy rushed out and grabbed a thick stack of warmed blankets. She piled the blankets on top of me. They worked momentarily, but the quivers picked up right where they had left off. "I'm st-still cold." I tried to say through my chattering teeth. I was flat on my back and I felt the weight of blankets come down on me. Based on the weight I could tell that Stacy had just covered me in three times the amount of the initial blanket load. I felt warmer, but both Stacy and I realized the blankets would do nothing to stop the shaking. The cold was going to be with me. It was coming from the machine. It had already found its way in.

It was then I lost the ability to breathe. The room went gray for a second. I fought hard through it, and when the gray dispersed I was able to suck in a mouthful of air. Any other breaths from this point on sent a stabbing pain into my back. I grimaced and Stacy asked me what was wrong. "It hurts to breathe," I said. I started to take only short, intermediate breaths but even those scorched my lungs. "He has too much water in his body! We need to angle the bed so that the water flows down!" Stacy exclaimed to the other two nurses who had just rushed into the room.

It was at this moment I thought I was going to die. I had lost total control over any body function, even the act of breathing was becoming tiresome. I felt that I was drowning, that my swim was coming to an end. The bed began to slowly elevate, bringing my head toward the ceiling and my feet closer to the ground. That was when I began to pray.

Please God save me.

The nurses were playing with the dialysis machine, examining it like they needed to repair it.

I feel as though I have led a great life up until now.

My mom was pacing the floor directly to my left.

This cannot be my time to go.

I felt the sheets begin to slide down me, as my body began to angle perpendicular to the floor.

But if it is, please take care of my family.

My head rolled back. I was staring at the ceiling.

Wait... should I try to tell my mom I love her?

With that, the lights in my mind went out. That's all I remember from this brutal Wednesday.

Thursday, August 27, 2009

I have always been a firm believer that certain people enter your life when you need them the most. You and that individual do not know it at the time, but your paths were meant to cross. You both need something from one another at that point in your lives. Your paths may diverge or they may stick together for a lifetime. My path quickly crossed with a pretty girl on this particular day. Her name was Irene, and she was Karrie's student nurse.

Irene is slightly older than me, not by much, literally only a year and few months. She has long blonde hair and a small figure. She is very soft spoken and delicate. She smiles a lot when she talks and carries herself with dignity and respect. I needed Irene on this day. At first I thought she was just going to be fun to look at. She ended up being a great companion for the next twelve hours.

I think I was on some kind of drug this day. I felt extremely lightheaded and the room was always spinning. I should have told Karrie this, but I didn't because I was too busy talking to Irene. She was the perfect antidote. The more she talked to me, the more I was able to focus on her as the center point of gravity and regain my equilibrium.

I had awakened this particular morning not strapped to the twenty-four hour dialysis machine. I remember assuming the dialysis probably continued to go terribly wrong and that they never were able to finish the procedure. As bleak as that sounds, I considered myself lucky to have awoken in one piece as I shrugged off the oddness of the events. Karrie began to explain that I was to have the catheter removed from my leg and have a different type of catheter, a Swan catheter, placed into the left side of my neck (this type of catheter goes directly into your neck artery and is used for very strong IV medications). As added incentive, she mentioned how the catheter that was still sticking out of the right side of my jugular was going to be removed as well. I was relieved to hear this because as she uttered those words I began to feel a pinching sensation near my shoulder.

In my mind, it doesn't make much sense for Karrie to say that and then rip down my pants for a catheter removal, though that is the next memory I have. I will assume it occurred at least a half hour later. The leg catheter removal was relatively painless. It was more embarrassing than anything because I had Karrie (whom at this point, I had already become close with) on one side yanking at my groin, and Irene on the other side staring at the procedure as she did her best to "shadow," even though I could see in her eyes that we were in total agreement of how awkward this moment was. Karrie finished the procedure by applying fifteen minutes worth of pressure to the incision because it was refusing to clot. After a quick breather the same procedure was performed on my neck. The removal was quicker, but another fifteen minutes of pressure was required to aid the clotting process. Irene was great during this portion. She talked to me about school, concerts and movies. She did a wonderful job distracting me from the pain of Karrie's fingers on my neck. Like I said earlier, I needed Irene this day. She was finally someone young and someone I could relate to.

Once again, on this Thursday my ability to recall time escapes me, but my next memory was of the transport to the operating room for the installation of my new neck catheter. I recall coming out of the elevator and entering the ninth floor for the procedure. Karrie leaned over, "Bill, I'm here, and I am _not_ going to leave you." I remember feeling comforted by her words, but confused because I wasn't scared. Yet, with those words I felt the pinching sensation release from my shoulders.

I don't remember this procedure at all. The reason why is a mystery to me because I know for a fact they didn't drug me. I didn't taste the saline—I was waiting for the taste. I only remember the procedure ending and my two lovely nurses standing at the head of my bed. Karrie had kept her promise.

My mind goes black and I am back in my room experiencing the only positive event of this week. Tami is at my bedside. With her light voice, she looks at me and says, "Bill, we have decided to place you on 1B status." I was in shock. I was very light-headed and I couldn't find the right words to say. "Thank you… thank you so much," my voice came out as light as hers. I have a memory of her talking. I can see her lips moving, but there is no sound. I don't know what she said, or if I responded, but I remember I felt like crying. I was so overcome with happiness to be a 1B that I wanted to reach out and hug her. The silent video ends with her walking out of the sliding glass door as my head hit the pillow. The lights go out in my mind.

My memory loses its sense of time again. I flash forward to what I feel must have been a lapse of four to five hours because I find myself staring into the dark sky outside my window. I am alone in the room with Irene. I do not know where my mom is, but I am mid-conversation with my newfound friend. I begin to notice I am struggling to speak, my words are slurring and I lose train of thought mid-sentence. I sit there trying to clear my head, watching Irene stare at me wide eyed, waiting for me to continue my thought. I never finished the thought because that's when Karrie entered. Karrie looked guilty. I could tell she had bad news. "Bill, you-need-to-get-a-picc-line-put-in-your-arm," she said quickly. She didn't breathe between words. Her eyes were squinted, as though she didn't want to see the crushed look on my face. I could tell it pained her to say it because without any response on my part she continued, "I know! I'm sorry, Bill. You have had so much done to you today, but don't worry, I got you the best picc nurse. Her name is Hannah and she will be here soon." Karrie exited the sliding glass door after instructing Irene to stay and watch the procedure. The picc was put into my right bicep. The purpose of the picc was for use if I was ever to be discharged. Supposedly, the picc could stay in my arm without infection for months. I didn't feel much discomfort from this procedure. Once again, I feel Irene got me through it. She talked to me when she knew I was able to focus, and when I couldn't, she watched

Hannah masterfully manipulate the skin on my deteriorated muscle. The procedure ended and my memory jumps ahead to bedtime where my mom was up nursing me into the late hours of the night.

My legs couldn't move, nor could my hands. My hands were bent inward. They looked arthritic. My body was aching from what I thought to be the prior night's trembling. My mom would stretch my legs for me and then feed me a deli sandwich, which she purchased from the cafeteria moments before it closed. This was my first meal all week. I laid in bed, feeling ashamed as I slowly ate it.

There I was, twenty years old. I needed a machine to clean my blood, an IV drug to sustain my heart function, a catheter to urinate for me, and now I needed the assistance of my mom to hold a sandwich to my mouth. I held back the tears, looked my mom in the eye and said, "I've officially lost all independence."

Irene was the perfect girl for this moment in my life. Like I said, I needed somebody young; I was starting to feel old. She gave me the Will power to get through the embarrassment, the pain and the depression that I could only assume would typically overcome someone in my circumstance. I don't know if I did anything for her this fateful Thursday when our paths crossed, but she was my knight in blue-scrubbed armor, and I was one sick patient in distress.

Friday, August 28, 2009

I woke up to discover the pain in my legs and hands from the night before had not left me. It was without a doubt something more severe than aches from the chills. I couldn't move my hands, every incidental bump forced me to scream in pain. I am truly not over exaggerating by any means when I say the slightest touch from a blanket on either my knees or hands induced such a great deal of agony that I almost blacked out twice. These past three months I have prided myself in my ability to describe sensations very accurately. However, this pain was so severe I truly have no words to describe it.

I was forced to lay in bed all day in an awkward fetal-like position. My knees were bent and spread apart as though I was getting ready to deliver a baby. My hands were still stuck in the same arthritic bend:

palms down, thumbs out with my fingers dangling loosely in a con-
torted manner.

"Can I ever get a fucking break!" I shouted into the air hoping someone would hear me. My mom and Dad were both in the room. My dad
was shaking his head in disbelief. "Honestly!" I began to bark orders at
my mom, "Get someone in here so that I can get some fucking drugs!"
I couldn't take the pain. It was torture. My body was officially useless.
The last person I had seen in such a crippled condition was my Papouli
(Greek for Grandfather) weeks before he passed. He was in his eighties.

I awkwardly curled myself in that position for at least two hours until
my dad determined I'd probably be better off sitting in a chair. He
gently grabbed my legs and slid them to the side of the bed for me.
With that, he asked me to stand. I pushed myself to the brink. I fought
my way up. I could feel the tension in my ankles growing. I couldn't
straighten my legs, so naturally my ankles buckled under my own
weight and I collapsed into my dad's arms. My nurse, Leah, grabbed
the Foley catheter and guided me to the chair as though it was my
leash. That's when the doctors my mom paged finally appeared.

Three Residents, one Fellow and one Attending entered. They were
all from Rheumatology. The Attending was a shorter, older looking
woman. She had curly, gray hair, which I could tell was once brown
in her prime. Her mouth was wrinkled and her neck looked slightly
varicose. She began to look at me with intrigue. Her intrigue in my
condition caused me to slightly panic. I remember thinking, *Oh no, in
50 years she has never seen someone look as freakish as I do right now.*
That was when she finally spoke, "I have never seen a case this severe,
but I believe he has Gout." "Gout?" I asked. She began to explain how
in many cases, a dialysis treatment could cause shifting in the body's
Uric Acids. In my case, she believes the Uric Acid in my body was
somehow increased during the process and it found its way to my two
most active joints. She continued to explain how the only way the team
could be certain of this diagnosis was to insert a large needle into my
joint and extract as much Uric Acid as possible. Then, if it were indeed
Gout, they would place me on a large amount of Prednisone until the
pain dispersed. I didn't let the thought of the needle intimidate me.
The pain was too severe to care and it was steadily getting worse. I was
willing to make-out with this old woman for it to go away. I consented

to the procedure and within minutes the Fellow returned with the large needle.

I remember his name was Dr. Noah. I only recall such a miniscule fact because of my recognition with the Chicago Bull's starting forward, Joakim Noah.

Dr. Noah is in his late twenties. He is a well-dressed man. Unlike Dr. Blyat, he wore a suit and tie under his coat. His hair is short. It is styled as though he just returned home from the military. Dr. Noah got down on one knee as though he was about to propose and said, "I'm going to give you a numbing agent so that this won't hurt as bad, okay?" He was speaking to me as though I was a two year-old, but I really didn't mind it. All I could think about was the pain. Dr. Noah injected the numbing agent. I recognized the feeling. It was the same numbing agent used on me by Dr. Blyat during his leg catheter implantation. Dr. Noah was much more efficient though. Moments later, the needle went in. Much to my surprise, I didn't feel a thing. "All good?" Dr. Noah asked. "Yeah, that wasn't bad at all," I said in pure disbelief. The Attending chimed in. "We're going to go run this under a microscope. If we see sharp, crystal-like objects, then we know for certain you have Gout."

I don't think much time passed before the entire team came back into the room. Dr. Noah was smiling ear-to-ear like he had just struck gold. "He has Gout!" he exclaimed with utter exuberance. The Attending began to detail her exact Prednisone prescription and forewarned it could be a while until her prescription was approved. Dr. Krause and his staff had the final say on all prescriptions. The fact that Prednisone was going to compromise my immune system, meant it could take hours of deliberation on their part. Unfortunately, she was right.

I returned to my bed and this is where the rest of the day completely escapes me. I do know why I can't remember roughly seventeen hours of this day. Leah was able to convince a Resident to give me constant amounts of Morphine throughout the day. Morphine makes me sleep, so for hours I drifted in-and-out of drug-induced sedation.

I ended this week the same way I started it—drugged out of my mind, still waiting for a second chance at life.

Saturday, August 29, 2009

Today was a pretty mellow day, but it was a day of vast improvement. The Gout pain in both my knees and hands dramatically decreased. The pain is not fully gone. However, I was able to not only wash myself, but I was able to walk around the ICU with minimal pain.

I continued my dialysis treatment. Luckily, it was not the typical twenty-four hour treatment. Today I only did the four hour version. The two treatments are the same. The only difference is the four hour dialysis treatment is much more intense in terms of how fast the blood filters through the machinery. In both versions of the treatment, I was able to get two liters of blood cleaned. I think my body is becoming used to the dialysis because I only get cold throughout the procedure. I no longer experience shortness of breath or chest pains.

The other major highlight of my day was my ability to return not only to my cell phone but also to my computer. I deeply missed journaling on these days. Especially when I was mentally aware that the only thing stopping me was the crippling pain from the Gout.

Meanwhile, I sat up in bed and entertained my large amount of guests. Today was the first day in a while that I had the energy to speak with them.

Sunday, August 30, 2009

My day started a bit late because I did not get to bed until 4:00 AM. I ended up staying awake into the wee hours of the morning with my mom as we talked about an assortment of topics.

I have been itching a lot lately. The doctors believe the itching is a sign of severe kidney failure, so they gave me a pill to stop the itching. They were afraid I would itch myself into a condition of Cellulitis. Unfortunately, I later discovered this pill is in the same family as Benadryl, the same pill that destroyed me during my transfer to Chicago General back in June.

I was delirious. I was supposedly talking in my sleep to two nurses and the Resident doctor who was on-call. I apparently said something to the effect of, "No, I don't want an echo! I cannot navigate an echo right now!" Who knows what the Hell that means?

I spent the rest of my day in La-La drug land. My aunts and uncles came to visit, but I struggled to carry conversations with them. I had a difficult time responding to their questions and processing any answers they provided. The medication wore off about two hours ago.

It is 12:55 AM and I am lying in bed awaiting the sleeping pill that I sweet-talked my way into this morning. I am also doing my typical nighttime routine, which I have been doing since the day I made my way onto the Organ Recipient List. I go to bed praying to God. I promise Him that I will do great things with the organs if He is to bless me with them. I promise to take my medication and to continue the perfect medical habits that I exhibited up until spring semester of college last year. I pray for the surgery and then I do my cross. In a little bit I will finish the rest of my tradition. I will lay in bed feeling horrible that I technically just prayed for someone to die.

Monday, August 31, 2009

The sound of the phone ringing has stopped my heart three times already. Tami told my family when I was moved up to 1B, that the first number they would call if a donor was located would be the room phone number. The past two calls have been from distant relatives who do not have my parent's cell phone numbers. Today's call was for Garth, the nurse who was in charge of running my three-hour dialysis treatment.

The ring is very boisterous. It pierces the room with every chime. The ring is digital, high pitched and makes my stomach drop as remorse instantly consumes me. I always think the same thing, *Shit… someone died.*

It's weird knowing someone's life clock is ticking down with every waking hour. For all I know, this is someone's last Monday on Earth. God bless the family who loses their loved one. I promise I will honor their loved one's life and continue to honor the life of my infant donor as well. I have two shoulders, and I know I have enough strength in me to bear the burden of two coffins. It's all about strength and sheer resiliency.

Tuesday, September 1, 2009

Kidney dialysis really takes a toll on the body. When you think about it, how could it not? For anywhere between two to four hours, two liters of your blood are being run through a machine that looks like it is from the set of a bad 80's action film.

My body aches from my neck to my ankles. I know the expression is, "From my head to my toes," but my head is fine and so are my toes, so it would be a lie for me to say that.

I can't see very well. My vision has been almost perfect this entire stay, but today I can only view my surroundings through blurry eyes.

I had an interesting occurrence happen a few hours ago. I took a narcotic pill, Norco. The pill was taken with the hopes of eliminating some of my muscular pain. When I took it, I started hearing music. I swear, I started hearing 90's rock music coming from the corner of the room. It sounded distorted though, like there was a pillow over the speaker. I asked my mom and Aunt Kathy if they could hear it, too. They both stared at me like I was crazy and then desperately began searching for a sound—a sound they would never hear.

I could distinctly hear parts of the lyrics though. The chorus went, *The leaves on the rose are shaking...* The vocalist was high pitched, sounded a little like Motley Crüe. The best part was when the original pill wore off and I popped a second one, the genre of the music changed. I started to hear jazz music—a good fifteen minutes of jazz music. I sat in my bed and watched my mom interact with Aunt Kathy as an upbeat quartet provided the soundtrack for their actions.

I am now hooked up to another dialysis treatment. I am forced to recline. Refusal is not an option.

Wednesday, September 2, 2009

You do a lot of praying when you're sick, especially when you are given an opportunity to experience solitude. I prayed tonight as I walked the quiet halls of the CCU (Cardiac Care Unit). I reached out to God and told him my plan.

I have this vision that when I am done healing and the day comes when I know I am strong enough, I want to return back to this very CCU and walk the same halls I did tonight as a better man. "Better" not only in the physical sense, but better because I want to help the people who need comfort behind these glass doors. I want to speak with Dr. Krause and Dr. Gordon about developing a lasting relation-ship with the people this hospital treats. I know there will be many others like me. Some may be my age, some may be more sick. I just want these people to know there is a light. Sometimes you just need to see a survivor.

Thursday, September 3, 2009

Not much to write about today except for the fact that I am anxiously awaiting the phone call and that I was moved to 11 West again. It's lower intensity. Dr. Krause believes I am stable enough to drop down a bit. It sucks because I was enjoying the company of Karrie and Irene. However, I must admit, I am not enjoying the company of my mom.

The silence and tension is starting to build. The anxiety is getting to me, and I think it is having an affect on my mom, too. We are starting to bicker a lot, like an old couple. Everything I do seems to irritate her, while everything she does annoys the Hell out of me. I love my mom to death, but I am quickly learning she is one of the <u>WORST</u> roommates.

Friday, September 4, 2009

I understand why people need support when they are ill more than ever tonight.

I needed a night off from my family. Actually, I needed a night off from the world. That is, I thought I did. Since I checked into this place, roughly twelve days ago, I haven't had a moment of silence. The only break I received from human interaction was when I went to fill up my plastic urinal in front of the toilet as IV wires and heart rate monitors dangled from my skin. Even then a nurse or two would accidentally walk in on me.

I've always realized how lucky I am to have as much support as I do. I have an extended network of family members and friends who would put themselves on the line to visit me for a couple of hours at a time. Because of this, I never get to be alone, until tonight.

You start thinking about death when you are ill and alone. Not so much your own personal death, just "death" in its most general sense.

You start thinking, *Why do things die?*

A simple question, which should merit a simple answer, right?

But really, why do things die? Is there really a divine purpose? Does God really have a flow chart that has everyone's expiration timed down to the perfect second? If I was to kill a fly, did God plan for that fly to die by my hand? If so, was it both the fly's and my own destiny to meet at that moment?

Do accidents happen? Are there occurrences that upset the balance? Then, do more things die or live as a result of that upset?

You also start thinking about life. Once again, not your own life or your own mortality. You start searching for a definition and a grand meaning behind the term "life."

What determines life? I know the whole debate that exists between the concept of life beginning at the time of conception and those who say life begins when the heart starts to beat. I'm not interested in that debate. I just can't help but wonder:

What keeps a life going? Is there something deeper? Does human interaction truly play a role in sustaining life? Can words keep someone fighting, pushing to survive to maintain that very life?

I like to think they can. I just received a message from Irene on Facebook. She wrote to say that I am an inspiration to her, that she has not met many people my age who see life the way I do.

I already had plenty of motivation, but today I will admit I felt myself slipping. I started losing sight of the light. My family calls me an inspiration, but they know me. The fact that a girl who I have only met three times would say such kind words to me really keeps me afloat. I wasn't anywhere near drowning. I felt myself sinking, but Irene just held my head out of the water. She just gave me the much-needed boost to keep me swimming.

Saturday, September 5, 2009

I want to give back to organ donation. I have mentioned this desire before in previous entries. Over the past week I have made small steps towards sharing my story with as many media outlets as possible. Last week my cousin, Natalie, (who is a morning anchor in Wausau, Wisconsin) put together a two-part series dedicated to my life story and the education of organ donation. Natalie interviewed both Dr. Krause and my mom for both of these segments.

My friend, Jen, has even gotten involved. She contacted a large newspaper in my hometown. This morning, I awoke to a story about my struggles and how organ donation can help save families from the distress that my family is currently undergoing.

Today's newspaper triggered many people from my past to come out of the woodwork. I received an onslaught of e-mails and phone calls from people who I haven't spoken to since high school. I haven't responded to many of the messages thus far, only a select few. I am still deciding if I will respond to the rest. Honestly, I don't know if I have enough energy to do so.

I can feel myself bottoming-out again. Yesterday, I was very dizzy. Today, I am very weak. If the cycle continues like it has the past two times, tomorrow or Monday will be a very bad day. Eventually, I am going to become extremely nauseous for a few days. Inevitably, I will end up downstairs with Karrie and Irene in the CCU again, most likely with another catheter in my neck. That's when I'll be moved to 1A. This is my prediction. I hope I am wrong about the nausea, but sadly I can't help but feel certain that I am right.

Sunday, September 6, 2009

I notice my nurses and doctors have been asking me stranger questions lately such as, "Do you feel stable?" I feel like Hell, so I must look like it, too.

I feel like I am living in a very blurred world. I can't see straight. In fact, I am having a difficult time seeing what I am typing right now. I have been suffering from nausea all day and I'm beginning to wheeze when I breathe in. The room is silent right now, so all I can hear is the clatter of the keys and the whistle of my lungs as they slowly drown in water from my decreased heart and kidney function.

I think my prediction is going to come true.

I had a large assortment of visitors today. Many of whom were the usual guests (Greg, Aunt Patti, Nouna, etc.) But I did have one group of visitors that I enjoyed immensely. It was my dad's best friend, Mitch, and his family. They drove in from Wisconsin to see me, nearly two hours. Mitch has three children, two of them came. One is a girl named Lori. She is my age and I have known her since I was a kid. It was really nice seeing them, especially because they were new. I love my visitors, but when you are in the hospital, new faces seem to spice up the atmosphere a bit more. Mitch's family came at the perfect time. I had just awakened from a two-hour nap and I felt refreshed. However, I spent all my energy fighting through the nausea and weak spells as I reminisced with them. They left and I was preparing to nap once more, until an unexpected family of visitors came.

By this point, my energy level was at a bare minimum. I felt appreciative that this second family came to visit me, but I truly did not have the strength to converse. They were not here for long, but it seemed like an extended stay because I was progressively drifting deeper into my blurred world. The room was spinning and I must not have looked good because both my Aunt Patti and Nouna asked me if I'd like everyone to leave. I faked a smile and said I was enjoying their company for the sake of being polite. Finally, they left and my parents followed shortly after.

I waited until my parents were far enough on the road until I called them and requested that they did not come tomorrow. I need a day off from guests. I need a day of solitude so I can clear my head. I love my parents, but all they talk about is my illness. I need to take control and break free for a day. I need twenty-four hours where I do not hear the words "heart" or "kidney."

Monday, September 7, 2009

It's interesting how you lose your sense of time when you are in the hospital. I have missed a lot while I've been hooked up to this IV.

I have a program on my computer that is a virtual calendar. Before this entire fiasco happened, the program ran my life. I had every summer plan written on this calendar. Everything was color coordinated to differentiate concerts from traveling plans and schoolwork from parties. I stopped looking at this calendar two weeks ago when I was admitted for the third time this summer. I just glanced at the calendar for the first time today.

It's funny, just a month ago I was bent out of shape about not moving into my apartment. My move-in day was this past Friday. The day came and went like all the others.

The 30th of August was the date of a Creed concert that I was highly anticipating. Instead, I spent that Sunday very drugged in the CCU, watching the Chicago Bears Preseason game from my hospital bed, listening to the sounds of the crushing tackles faintly echo out of the bed remote's tiny speaker.

Tomorrow I was to begin my first class of the fall semester at Columbia. That means today was the day I was to make my rounds through the city, stopping at the apartments of my friends where we would share stories of our incredible summers of interning, working and entertainment.

I am currently lying in my hospital bed. I have two drugs going into my body via IV. One drug is to eliminate the Urinary Tract Infection I was diagnosed with this morning. The other is a drug that keeps my heart beating. I am dressed in an outfit that does not match, wearing socks that have grips on the soles. Meanwhile, I'm trying as hard as I can to muster the endurance to complete homework for my online classes.

It's interesting how life can send you for a loop. This time last year I was enjoying my new apartment and meeting people who I thought were like me. I realize today that I am a bit different than everyone else. I can never relax in life. I can never take my health for granted.

Tuesday, September 8, 2009

And so the poking and prodding continues…

I am temporarily off the list. My white blood cell count is too high, so my doctors feel that a transplant would not be in my best interest until my white blood cell count lowers. My count is currently 25. My doctors will not transplant until it declines to the 12-13 range.

I am back in the CCU because Dr. Gordon elected to have both my picc line and my dialysis catheter removed. He fears the bacteria that is causing the rise in my white blood cells may be resting on the catheters themselves. I had two IV's inserted into my arms. The one on the left is for my continuous stream of Dopamine (the drug that makes my heart beat) and the picc line on my right will serve as the outlet for all my blood draws and IV antibiotics. I can stand the IVs, those I have gotten used to. I can also handle the blood draws that are straight from my veins (I had an additional stick today for 60cc of blood cultures). The pain that I cannot get used to is the pain from a blood gas removal.

Since being re-admitted to the CCU, I have begun to develop dull chest pains whenever I breathe. The pain is not severe by any means. It is just deep and uncomfortable. The Residents on staff are concerned I may be developing a blood clot in my lungs from my continuous bed-ridden inactivity. Apparently, the only way to determine if there is a blood clot is to stick a very large needle deep into your forearm, past several layers of tissues, until they finally hit the artery, which then releases some form of amazing rich blood. The pain was excruciating. I forewarned the nurses that I may scream. It was a good thing I did because for about three minutes, all I could think to scream was, "Fuck, fuck, fuck, fuck, fuck, moooooother fucker, fuck, fuck, fuck!" Well, you get the gist... I said, "Fuck!" a lot.

I don't know why humans swear when they are in pain, it just comes out so naturally. Why don't we scream nice things like, "Pony, pony,

pony, rainbows, gumdrops, fruit roll-ups, apple juice!"

I hope I do not have to experience any more pain. Now that I am down in the CCU, I have confidence in my team of doctors that they will not let me bottom-out. I think they will catch me before I fall. Hopefully, when I start to slip they will put me on another Inotrope and move me up to 1A status.

I could potentially have two good days coming up. Tomorrow, Natalie, Aunt Patti, Greg, Nouna and my Yia Yia (Greek for Grandmother) are all coming to visit. Then on the following day, now that I am back in the CCU, I should have Karrie and Irene again as my nurses. They make the days very enjoyable.

Wednesday, September 9, 2009

Today was a test. Not a medical test, but a test on my <u>Will</u>. I almost feel as though God was making sure I was willing to fight for my life. My morning began with the chills. I got up to bathe myself much like I do every morning. Today, I suddenly became flushed. My body became very warm, then instantly began to quiver. I felt the sensation of a quality throw-up coming to a boiling point. I rushed to the trash can where I dry heaved for close to five minutes. My body began to ache and my temperature started to spike around 100 degrees Fahrenheit. The room was spinning and I was forced to return to my bed with heated blankets where I slept for the next two hours.

It was when I awoke that I noticed my heart was beating extremely hard, almost as though it was struggling to hang on. My body was shaking from the intense rhythm. This was the first time in a while that I acknowledged how precious time is for me. At that moment, I realized I might be just weeks away from dying.

I requested Dr. Gordon's presence at my bedside. He arrived very quickly and I expressed my feelings to him. I had planned out what I was going to say to him, so I can remember verbatim what I said:

"I have been through a lot of shit these past three months and I have only spoken my mind once. It was when I demanded I leave Chicago General and transfer my care here. Thus far, that has been my best decision this summer."

Dr. Gordon smiled, he seemed flattered.
"Now, I am not trying to push myself to 1A, even though that would
be a dream come true right now, but I just want to feel better. My heart
is getting so much worse; I can feel my body shake. I need a second
Inotrope in me now. I know I have an infection so that's 20 percent of
the problem. The other 80 percent is my heart crashing. When you put
a Swan in me I know you will see my pressures have worsened and that
can validate the Inotrope. But in the meantime, I need you to just put
another one in me so I can feel better."

Dr. Gordon smirked. He said he agreed and would speak with the rest
of the Cardiology team. He left and my nurse entered.

Thus far at Mercy, I have had close to twenty nurses. Each one of these
nurses has been spectacular. I can truly say that they have all treated
me with dignity and have always been able to aid me with any situation. Today, however, I found the black sheep of Mercy Care nursing.
Her name is Maud.

Maud is an old, haggard woman. She looks and sounds as though
she has been a chain smoker for decades—long before cigarettes had
filters. Maud does not like me, nor is she fond of my mom. Throughout the day she has treated me poorly. Maud has rolled her eyes at me,
acted unbelievably unprofessional, and even left two vials of blood in
my bed as I slept. I had an IV in my right arm, which was very sensitive. Regardless of my request for her to gently use the site, she would
continue to roll her eyes and carry on her business in the same routine,
rough manner. Shortly after Maud left, my IV blew. Blood began to
drip from my arm. My night nurse was left cleaning up the mess and
re-inserting another IV into my arm.

Throughout all this commotion, I had to undergo a Nuclear Medicine
procedure, so my doctors could rule out a blood clot in my lungs. Due
to the recent development of chest pain when I breathe, my increased
temperature and my abnormally high white blood cell count, my doctors are looking at all possible scenarios.

The Nuclear Medicine procedure was painless, very simple. I'd say my biggest complaint was that it was time consuming and very boring. I had to breathe in a tasteless mist for five minutes and then lay in a bed for close to an hour, as a large machine that resembled a CT scanner circled my body in a jerky, robotic motion.

As I was bored out my mind in Nuclear Medicine, Dr. Gordon returned with Dr. Shao (the newest Attending doctor) and explained to my mom that they will be looking to place a picc line back into my arm sometime tomorrow.

I returned from the procedure to hear the sound of alarms. The woman in Room 806 was very ill and a "Code Blue" was called. Doctors rushed in-and-out of the room until I heard the family cry. Priests flooded the halls of the CCU shortly after. They were there to give the woman in Room 806 her last rite. I was reminded of how my clock is quickly ticking down as well. I need to get this transplant soon. I'll be damned if I'm going to be the next Code Blue.

Thursday, September 10, 2009

My morning was, yet again, a bad part of the day. I began to experience a sensation I never felt before. My heart felt as though it was speeding up rapidly. The room would begin to spin and I could do nothing but lay down and press my head against my pillow. These sensations lasted ten seconds each time, but happened at a rate of once every three minutes. This cycle repeated for an entire hour, until finally, the sensations ended as quickly as they began.

I was a little down. Whenever I begin my day with a medical problem, such as today's sensations, my day is usually ruined. I become angry and depressed that I am not normal anymore. Today I was lucky. Irene saved me from my depression.

She entered my room, smiling with her wide eyes. "I was upset to hear you're not on the 11th floor anymore, but I bought you these," she said as she handed me a box of cookies. Irene had decorated them. She made them look girly by embellishing the box with smiley-faced stickers. I was very touched by her kindness. We talked for a while until she had to return to work. Sadly, Karrie was sick. Consequently, Irene had to shadow a different nurse. The day wasn't as entertaining as usual.

Karrie needs to get healthy A.S.A.P.

Friday, September 11, 2009

It has been eighteen days since I have felt the warm touch of the sun on my skin, went to the bathroom without collecting my urine in a plastic container or simply used a shower.

I experienced a great deal of pain today. Every inch of my body aches, and to make matters worse, the pain is being caused by four ailments, two of which can be rectified.

The Gout is steadily coming back. My Uric Acid levels increased again. As a result, my knees, hands and jaw began to feel tight and arthritic. Fortunately, I caught the pain before it worsened. The Rheumatology doctors were called in. They increased my Prednisone dosage. It's now 11:18 PM. The pain has finally begun to subside.

Every muscle in my body feels not only weak, but also sore. The sensation is comparable to the pain you feel the day after a high-intensity workout. It is a struggle to get in-and-out of bed. Everyday activities, such as going to the bathroom, are becoming a battle in-and-of themselves. My doctors informed me that the pain I am experiencing is a result of the toxins in my body rising from my inability to receive dialysis. In addition, the fact that I have had so much water pulled off of me from the use of diuretics has caused my body to be "too dry."

On top of all these problems, my potassium levels are at an all-time low. I was given IV potassium and warned that it can be uncomfortable. My warning proved to be right as my entire vein burned up through my bicep and into my shoulder. I finally couldn't handle the pain, especially because I knew it was not a mandatory drug. My nurse removed the IV and placed an ice pack on my bicep. It helped to subdue the pain.

Though today was filled with discomfort, I have a strong gut feeling that tells me the surgery is around the corner.

Sunday, September 13, 2009

I finally see the light at the end of the tunnel. Today I was upgraded to 1A status. This means that at any moment, from here on out, the phone can ring. What I enjoyed most about being upgraded to 1A was the manner in which I was moved up. I feel the increase in status is a major milestone in this battle of mine. I had the privilege of sharing the milestone with the people I have grown to trust with my life over the course of the past three months.

In order for the status change to occur, I needed to have another Swan placed into the right side of my neck and have an additional Inotrope drug pumped into my system through the Swan. This procedure is usually performed in the operating room and I am typically sedated for the entire day. However, this time around, Dr. Gordon wanted to operate bedside, and he wanted to make sure his hand did the procedure correctly.

The prior two Swan procedures did not go smoothly. The first attempt was a large failure and caused me to bleed out of my neck profusely for days afterwards. The second attempt was successful, but the physicians gave me too many drugs and caused me to be a physical wreck for twenty-four hours. Because of these bad prior experiences, I was a bit scared to undergo this procedure for the third time. I began to suffer anxiety attacks beforehand. I had to continuously tell myself, *This is a means to an end. You're so close. You can't quit now!*

Knowing both Karrie and Dr. Gordon were performing the procedure helped ease a great deal of tension. Since the moment I met Dr. Gordon, I liked him a lot. I understood him and I think he completely understood me. I felt comforted by his demeanor. I respected the way he treated me like an adult and did not ignore my individuality. As time passed and I quickly grew sicker, Dr. Gordon never let me down. He was always there for me when I needed him, and he would take his time to answer my questions. I will honestly say that if someone asked me right now to put my life in the hands of one human being, I would choose Dr. Gordon without hesitation. I struggle to describe just how much admiration and trust I have for that man.

Karrie has been a driving force behind my recovery, as well. The way she cares for me is almost motherly—it feels weird to say that because my mom has been with me each step of the way.

Karrie and Dr. Gordon made sure the procedure was painless. You could tell they had my best interest in mind. Dr. Gordon went out of his way to create a Bicarb/Lidocaine mixture, which made the procedure nearly painless. My face was covered throughout the procedure by a sterile cloth, but I could hear both of their voices. The few times that the procedure got rough and I started to squirm from the pain, the sound of Karrie's voice calmed me down.

After the procedure ended, Dr. Gordon immediately left to report the findings to the transplant team coordinators, Tami and Chloe. I later received a phone call from Chloe. The phone went off when both Karrie and Irene were in the room.

My two lovely nurses were smiling as I picked up the phone and listened to Chloe's sweet voice explain to me that I was 1A. She also told me to make sure I prepare myself for an operation because it is going to come very soon. I felt my face beam with happiness. I couldn't stop smiling, and all I could think to say once again was, "Thank you." "You don't have to thank me," Chloe would reply. But I still couldn't stop uttering those two words. I hung up the phone and immediately began to celebrate with Irene and Karrie.

Dr. Gordon re-entered and began to explain how if the operation happened tonight, he would be at the surgery. If the operation happened on Monday or Tuesday, he would not be able to take part in the transplant because he needed to take his Board exams.

This fantasy of transplant is becoming a reality. I'm so close to returning to life. I'm so close to being happy again and I'm so close to beginning my newfound dream of helping other people.

Monday, September 14, 2009

When you feel semi-decent and you are not undergoing any procedures, you have a lot of free time to think. Today I could not stop thinking about how weird it is that Dr. Getty will be cracking open my chest.

The chest cracking is the only aspect of the surgery that blows my mind. For whatever reason, I have no preconceived notions in regards to the actual kidney or heart transplant. The thought of my heart being cut out and another individual's heart being sewn in seems very standard and eerily normal to me. It's the sound of the **crunch** that keeps playing in my head.

I know I will be knocked out before Dr. Getty even puts a finger on the saw; Dr. Gordon assured me the other day that I will be obliterated with drugs almost instantaneously when I enter the operating room. But I just can't begin to fathom the fact that this rock-solid bone that I can physically touch will be split into two pieces. What amazes me more is how the human body heals so rapidly. Before I even leave the hospital the bone should already have fused itself back into one piece.

It is currently 2:25 AM. The waiting is a horrendous part of the illness. I am currently sitting next to the phone in my room. I placed it on my food tray just in case. I can't stop thinking of the crunch and my breathing feels like it's worsening. I am going to hit the sheets now. I hope the next sound I hear is the sound of my room telephone going off.

Tuesday, September 15, 2009

My life has become this miserable existence. Don't get me wrong, I feel blessed to be sitting at 1A, but the little amount of independence I had in this hospital has been stripped away with the implantation of this Swan catheter. It is a very debilitating device. I am strapped to numerous wires, which are all dangling from my neck. Those wires are then plugged into a giant gray machine, which resembles an old fashioned cable box. The system of wiring is so intricate that I need to get permission from my nurse each time I have the need to get out of my bed so that she can release me from the cable box. Basically, whenever I have to go to the bathroom, I need to inform an adult as though I am a toddler.

Another issue, which is pissing me off, is the mere fact that my life is completely on hold. I cannot move forward with my life and pursue any of my dreams or aspirations until a phone rings. I think what is really getting me down is the fact that I truly do not believe I ever deserved this. I have mentioned this before, and I do believe that everything happens for a reason, but whenever I get down I start to wonder why I was born with the defective heart as an infant. What made God choose me?

I really am not bitter for my current circumstance, I'm just frustrated by the unknown. I shudder when I realize this could all happen again when I am 40 years old, then again at 60. At what point am I not going to be saved? Is there a limit on how many times the human body can be sliced open and transplanted? I wonder about my future relationships. I technically can never look the woman who I am going to marry in the eye and guarantee her that I am going to live a long life.

Really though, it just makes life that much more intriguing. When I get out of this hospital, I am going to live life like each day is my last. I feel this aspect is a blessing. Very few people can say they live life in such a vigorous manner. I have a feeling I am going to see the world in a whole new light. I am going to be more adventurous. I am going to try new things, I am going to go for what I want and I will not let anything ever get in my way.

Wednesday, September 16, 2009

Waiting for the phone call that will save your life is far worse than knowing you are slowly dying an emotional death.

Anxiety builds as you wait for a phone call. Your mind begins to play tricks with you. You begin to think everyone is keeping secrets. You become convinced that everyone around you, including your nurse, knows something. The gestures and actions of the Residents begin to seem awkward. You wonder why they are talking to you as you convince yourself that they are a part of a secret society—a group of individuals who know your fate, but are sworn to hide the facts.

I'm getting tired of everyone texting me, asking if I have heard anything yet. It seems as though whenever I am able to get my mind off of the phone, no sooner does someone contact me begging for an update. I think I need to send out a broad message to all my friends and thank them for their support, but at the same time ask them to stop questioning me about my phone call status.

Today was not an enjoyable day. I can't stop thinking about life after transplant. It's so close, but it seems so far away. I just want to spend a night alone in my studio apartment and have a day go by where I do not hear the words "kidney" or "heart." I want to be normal again. I hate being the center of attention. I just want all eyes to be on someone else for one day. I want to be Bill again. I'm tired of being the brave one.

Friday, September 18, 2009

I had another Swan put in today. Dr. Gordon agreed to do the procedure and he met me in the operating room around 1:45 PM. Much like the last Swan that Dr. Gordon "installed" in my neck, the procedure was, for the most part, painless. I was then forced to spend the rest of the day much like the last Swan installation, high as a kite on Morphine. Then much like the last procedure, I spent a good portion of the day coming down off the Morphine. I become very nauseous and tired when I withdraw from Morphine. I ended up falling asleep to the silence of my bedroom.

I awoke from the Morphine crash at 6:30 PM in considerable pain. Fortunately the nausea was gone and because I was no longer sick to my stomach I refused to take any more narcotics for the pain. I fought through it even though it felt unbearable at times.

Irene saved me again, she took away the pain. Irene escorted me through the halls of the CCU. We had a long discussion. I learned a little bit more about her life. In turn, she learned a little bit more about me. It seems the more I speak with Irene the more genuine and dignified she becomes. Irene continues to be medicinal. I know for sure I was destined to meet her.

Saturday September 19, 2009

The wait for a double transplant is much longer than I anticipated. I thought for sure I would have been transplanted by today. For the sake of not getting another infection, I have not accepted any visitors since I was moved up in status. Due to the unanticipated length of my wait at 1A status, I needed visitors again. Mentally, I needed to see someone besides my mom and dad.

Natalie came into town today, so I couldn't help but feel that today was the perfect day to have visitors. I kept the group small by only allowing Natalie and Aunt Patti access to my "mini-suite" in the CCU ward. Both Natalie and Aunt Patti were fantastic visitors. They kept my mind off the phone and aided me in passing the time quickly.

Dr. Gordon is off all weekend and I slept through Dr. Lenair and the Cardiology team's visit this morning. Therefore, I unfortunately do not have any updates on anything medical or news on my transplant status. I can only provide an update on my mental status.

I am still staying strong, optimistic and looking forward to getting on with my life. I still believe that miracles happen, that everything happens for a reason and that someday I will understand why I was chosen to work with this crappy hand of cards I was dealt.

I have a few guesses that I am currently clinging onto. I believe that this is all happening to me, if not for both of these reasons, than at least one of them:

1. **SWIM**: I believe this book will help many deal with challenges in life. I hope this book spreads hope, joy, and confidence to many. If my struggle or my words help at least one person swim and find something to live for, then all of the pain I am feeling is well worth it.

2. **To Relax Me**: Before I was diagnosed I was very high strung. I spent countless hours every day worried about my finances, scholarships and student loans. I used to go as far as having panic attacks when I would think about my future. I was only a sophomore, but I was already worried about my career. I pushed myself to the brink almost every day. This disease has opened up my eyes. I realize now that life is too short. If you spend too much time worried about the stresses of tomorrow, you will miss out on the beauties of today. I know I have a lot on my plate right now, so it would make sense that I am currently not stressing out over my career. Yet realistically, I have changed so much that I can give a rat's ass about my future employer. Work in general seems so mundane and meaningless.

Someday I will enjoy life again. Out of the darkness there will be light.

Sunday, September 20, 2009

My doctors have decided to administer my Plavix and Aspirin every other day in hopes of a transplant coming very soon. They are tapering the drugs because my doctors fear I will bleed too much during the operations. I have been thinking a lot lately about what could go wrong during the procedure, however, it wasn't until tonight that I realized I could potentially die on the table. It is my understanding that Dr. Getty has a sensational track record. I believe he has not only encountered a similar situation before, but he has never had a patient die on his table.

I started thinking about things in my life that are incomplete, projects that I want finished. This book is my main goal at the moment. I want this book to get into the hands of people in my situation so badly that I decided to develop a back-up plan in case I do not make it out of surgery alive. I chose to write Peter. I want him to finish the book, but I don't want to worry him or the family too soon. I wrote the e-mail, but I do not plan on sending it until I receive the phone call. This is what I wrote:

Hey Peter,

This is going to sound very morbid and I don't need you to (nor do I expect you to), respond to this letter.

It is currently 12:07 AM on 9-20-09. I obviously have not received the phone call yet for surgery and I don't think I will for many days.

I am pre-writing this letter because I plan on sending you this in an e-mail moments before I go into surgery.

When I first began writing this book on July 5th, I never imagined that it would become one of my driving forces throughout my battle with my condition. In fact, if it were not for my dedication to completing this book, I do not think that I would have been able to stay as positive as I have been throughout these past three months.

There was a time in the infancy stages of my journaling that I almost stopped. I almost gave up because I doubted this book could help anyone. It was your complete understanding of my vision and your words that kept me going. In a way, you inadvertently gave me some of my initial strength.

I am on Plavix right now, so it is known by my team of doctors that I will potentially have a slight complication from the bleeding. A double transplant is a major operation, and with every major operation there is, of course, a slight risk of death.

Like I said, this is going to sound morbid, but I know you understand my vision for the book. If, God-forbid, something is to go wrong during the surgery, I want you to complete the book. I have written enough thus far where I feel I have expressed everything that I have learned thoroughly through my journal entries.

Everything that you need is located on my computer, on the desktop, in a folder entitled, "SWIM." The files are clearly labeled, dated, and separated into sections. All I ask is that if something were to go wrong during surgery, you finish my "memoir section" by collaborating with the family to share stories of my life leading up to the hospitalization on June 8th. Then possibly write something for the end of the book to explain the final outcome.

I have full confidence in my entire team of doctors, and though it may not seem like it based off of this letter, I know that I will be fine. I simply have too much time on my hands and I have always spent my free time planning for the future.

Thank you once again for the early motivation. I hope I do not creep you out with this letter. I just wanted to make sure this book is complete and I trust your artistic vision more than anyone in the family.

Love yah man,
Bill

I don't know if I will send Peter this e-mail when the phone call comes. I just want to be ready. I don't know what emotions will run through me, but at least I know I am ready if I get a negative feeling.

Monday, September 21, 2009

I realized yet again today that I am not myself, no matter how hard

I try to believe I am. I have energy, but it only comes in spurts. The energy I feel is a fake high, induced by the two Inotropes; Dobutamine and Dopamine, which run through the Swan in my neck. At times, I feel like I am a dog being walked around the CCU by my IV pole. The Swan is my painful leash—a choke chain.

I had this realization when I was talking to my three lovely nurses for the day, Ashley, Karrie and Irene. I was having a great time joking around by the nursing booth. We were laughing and sharing stories. They were helping me forget about my current predicament. Sadly, reality always seems to hit me the hardest whenever I begin to escape it. I began feeling heart failure weakness and I was forced back to my bed where I found myself needing to take short ten-minute naps or just rest in silence for twenty minutes. The downward spiral has begun yet again. I know my body and I know I am going to bottom-out soon. I have called it the past two times, but I am hoping that because I am on these two drugs the cycle will take longer to complete. I don't know what the next step will be. I am already in the CCU and I am already 1A status, so do they just put me on another IV Inotrope? More importantly, when is this heart going to finally crap out?

Tuesday, September 22, 2009

"Do you believe everything happens in threes?" were Dr. Gordon's first words to me this morning. I stared at him baffled. "What?" I replied. There was a group of Residents sitting next to him, staring at me as though I was crazy for not understanding what he had said. I replied with either yes or no, but really I don't remember what my response was. I was legitimately dumbfounded by the oddness of his question. Dr. Gordon continued, "There is a transplant going on right now. Whenever there is one transplant, the next two happen very quickly." I was shocked. Honestly, I was still rocked from his original statement. "That's great, so I'm no longer number ninety-six, I'm going to be number ninety-seven." I said with confidence. (Mercy Care Hospital is anxiously awaiting their milestone one-hundredth transplantation. I think it would be cool to be the one-hundredth, but at this rate I will settle for ninety-seven. It's a boring number, but I really do not care.) Dr. Gordon responded by telling me that I could be ninety-eight as well, but he seemed strangely certain that this theory of three was going to pan out.

The conversation somehow switched to football and fantasy sports as I compared my online roster with the Residents. I eventually went back into my room where Karrie later came in and started telling me about this theory of three. She seems to be a believer in it, too. Karrie explained that whenever a nurse gets pregnant, two more get pregnant shortly after. Supposedly, if someone dies on the CCU ward, two unlucky patients die weeks later. Finally, when one person gets a transplant, two more patients will soon be transplanted, as well (though this rule only applies to hearts).

To answer Dr. Gordon's question, I really do not believe in this theory. I believe everything happens for a reason, but I do not think his particular superstition is true. I used to enjoy these forms of superstition. Sometimes I would buy into them. However, since being in this hospital and hearing my family try to rationalize reasons as to why I'm going to get a transplant on a specific day, I am losing my belief in superstitions. My family has been making such comments as, "It's going to happen on September 21st because you were transplanted on your twenty-first day of life. This is your fourth week of being in the hospital and you were the fourth baby transplanted in the Midwest. Not to mention you're going to turn twenty-one soon!" Obviously that superstition did not come true. As much as I respect what Dr. Gordon says, I am going to have to disagree with him on this one.

I hope to God I am wrong. I want Dr. Gordon and Karrie to be eerily right. However, I just realized something. Two weeks ago a man who owned a designer clothing store on Michigan Avenue passed away in Room 808. A week later a woman in Room 806 passed. If someone else dies and another heart is transplanted soon, then maybe I will buy in.

Thursday, September 24, 2009

I didn't see the point in journaling yesterday. The day as a whole was very monotonous. My only visitor was my mom. She just sat in my room all day as I walked the halls of the CCU and worked on my homework.

It seems the longer I wait for my transplants, the more I begin to think about the life of my donor.

What are they doing right now? What will cause them to die? If they are driving in car when they are killed, where were they going? Were they happy when they died? Did they find inner peace before they passed? Or did they just finish fighting with a loved one and will never get a chance to say they were sorry? Is my donor a good person? Do they have many regrets from their past? What are their future aspirations that they want to accomplish but will never get a chance to complete? Do they have a family? Are they alone? Were they scared when they passed?

My mind races with these questions on monotonous days. I find it shocking to believe that my donor's life is so rich at the moment, so normal. They have no idea what is to come in the near future, nor do they have any idea as to who I am and how horrendously awful my life has become in a matter of three and a half months.

Like always, I am trying my hardest to push those thoughts aside, look for the bright spots in my life, but I still can't shake the thoughts.

I hate monotonous days.

Friday, September 25, 2009

My mom noticed something today. She noticed that this room is bright. You feel as though there is life in this CCU room. She and I started to reminisce and compare this room to the room at Chicago General.

You felt as though there was no end in sight at Chicago General. The room was dark and it pulled your mind into its darkness. The nights were long and sometimes scary. Everything and everyone felt cold.

Here at Mercy, I feel alive. Everyone is so warm and the nights are short. I feel like as soon as my head hits the pillow, the loving face of one of my nurses awakens me with breakfast in hand.

Looking back on it all, the transition from Chicago General to Mercy Care was like stepping out of the infernos of Hell and into the Pearly Gates of Heaven.

Saturday, September 26, 2009

I want to go home. This is the first day that I have felt this way. I have had many days where I missed normalcy or have been anxious to continue my life, but never have I truly missed home. I want to lie down in my own bed, play with my dogs and just relax in the kitchen as I tap my fingers against the black granite counter top.

I wish I could watch football on my flat screen television or simply put my feet up on the ottoman while I indulge on a plate of home made nachos. I even miss the very small things about my home that I never appreciated, but now wish I could simply touch.

There is a room in my house that connects to the kitchen. My mom has meticulously designed this room to have grape décor. Everything from the place settings to the wallpaper has purple grapes woven into its pattern. I used to think these grapes were meaningless, almost obnoxious. Now, after over a month of staring at the same hospital walls, I see the grapes in another light. The grapes now symbolize home, a place filled with warmth, love and comforting nourishment.

I am beginning to wonder if I am ever going to get out of this hospital. Will I be eating a hospital-style, low-sodium Thanksgiving dinner with the nursing staff? Will I be decking the halls of the CCU with boughs of holly? I honestly can't see the light today. It seems the light is fading in-and-out as the days progress.

My nurse just said, "It only takes one phone call." She's right, but I don't think the phone will be ringing today.

Sunday, September 27, 2009

There are a few topics on my mind to discuss today in this journal entry. The first being my fear of getting cancer from all of the X-rays I have undergone in the past five months. Lately, I have been receiving a chest X-Ray in the middle of the night so that my doctors can verify that my Swan has not shifted in my heart. Every time the X-ray camera is pointed at my chest and the light from the machine shines on my torso, I get this vision of me going through chemotherapy sometime in the coming years. On the weekends, Dr. Gordon and all of my regular physicians are usually not working. The floor is run by a group of Resident doctors whose opinions I typically do not trust. When I see Dr. Gordon tomorrow, the first thing I will speak with him about is the possibility of discontinuing these X-rays, or if at the bare minimum, making them a little less frequent.

As I stated, Residents run the floor on the weekends. Last night, I was able to sweet-talk my way into getting the nursing staff to eliminate my dietary restrictions for one meal. I ordered a ham and cheese sandwich, cheese pizza and a hotdog. I have not had any of those meals in the past four months. All I have eaten has been this God-awful, low-sodium diet. Everything is tasteless. I have lost thirty-five pounds in the past four months. Most of it has been muscle, but I believe a portion of the weight loss has been due to my lack of desire to eat. Needless to say, I enjoyed my meal immensely. I hadn't been that happy eating in what feels like ages. Unfortunately, there is a reason I am not supposed to eat the food I like. The sodium makes me retain water. Both my heart and kidneys are too weak to push the water out of my body, so I retain it.

Tonight, I began to wheeze hours after feasting and I started to feel short of breath. I haven't felt short of breath since my first admission here at Mercy. I told my nurse about my breathing problem before I went to bed. Overnight, the Residents overreacted and shot me up with large amounts of IV diuretics in my sleep. Consequently, I awoke this morning feeling extremely parched and drained of life. I walked six steps to the toilet first thing in the morning. When I was finished, I lacked the strength to walk the same six steps to my bed. Instead, I walked three steps to a chair, where I sat in my boxers awaiting my nurse, Melissa, so that I could complain about how I felt. I knew at that moment the Residents had gone overboard. I was just waiting for Melissa's verification. Sure enough, I was correct and my fluid restriction for the day was lifted so that I could rehydrate. I drank everything that was handed to me. It is 9:26 PM and just now I am no longer craving water.

The final topic of the day is how depressing it is that I got a new bed. I know this sounds weird. The average person is usually extremely excited to get a new bed, but in hospitals you apparently "qualify" for a bed upgrade after being in the CCU for over a month. I must admit, the bed is very nice. It is extremely high-tech and much quieter than the standard model. The saddest part about the whole experience is how excited I was to be upgraded. Typically, twenty year-olds do not get excited about such events. This excitement is usually something you experience when you are forty and have been married for seventeen years. I don't know why hospitals have an ability to make you feel so old.

I need to get out of this place; I need to feel young again. Irene is here tomorrow. She always cheers me up. She is quickly becoming a very close friend of mine.

Monday, September 28, 2009

I'm really going to miss Irene when she is gone. This upcoming Thursday is her last shift at Mercy Care. We were talking today and we both agreed that it feels like we've known each other for months. She has become such a close ally to me throughout this battle. I would go as far to say that she ranks as high as my mom, Aunt Patti and Natalie in terms of people who have helped keep my spirits up the most. I know I will see her when I am out of here though, that's a given. I think our friendship grew too strong in the past month for it to break. I know only time will tell, but like I have stated already, I know I was destined to meet her. She has already helped me greatly. I'm looking forward to seeing how I can someday help her.

Tuesday, September 29, 2009

The only way I can describe today is with two wretched words, "HEART FAILURE." The cycle toward my eventual bottom-out is at full force. I think I will need my Inotrope dosage upped this Thursday or Friday in order to sustain my typical energy level. I really hope they find a donor soon. The wait is devastating. My doctors and nurses will slip me the occasional story of how close my team of doctors have gotten to pulling the trigger and transplanting me. In the past two weeks, I have heard eight different stories.

The first few stories I heard were from Dr. Gordon. I apparently received a series of donor offers from individuals with "histories of heart attacks." Why someone would want to replace their damaged heart with one that seems slightly dysfunctional is beyond me, but those were the original offers I was receiving.

I then heard another story about a male who was 5'11" with my blood type, who crashed his motorcycle somewhere in the city of Chicago. The kidneys were pristine, but the heart was bruised, making the donor no longer a match.

A donor who enjoyed cocaine passed away from... yeah, you guessed it, a stroke caused by a cocaine overdose. My doctors received word before the blood results came back, and sure enough, the man's body was so overloaded with drugs, Dr. Getty didn't want to even touch the body. This, of course, was another let down.

Yesterday, one of the newer Fellows to join the team, Dr. Derma, informed me that this past Sunday night the transplant team was buzzing over an absolute perfect match for me. It was a female, but she died while she was sick. She apparently had contracted an infection and the team determined that the risk of infection after transplanting me with her heart and kidney was too high.

Finally, I just found out tonight (from my nurse) that a man came into Mercy yesterday. It was apparent that he was going to die. The team ordered a stat echocardiogram. Not only was his heart too big, but he was also currently battling multi-organ failure, much like myself.

I mention all of these tales not to be crude. I simply find comfort in the fact that the strangeness of these individuals' deaths are becoming slightly less reckless. I am receiving the best possible offers. I think with the rule of odds, something has to click eventually.

Thursday, October 1, 2009

I've stated in prior entries that I wait until the very end of my day to journal, so I can reflect on all the events that transpired as a whole. Last night, I was unable to do so. Due to faulty equipment and a glitch in the hospitals heart monitoring system, my night nurse, Lauren, requested I stay in bed. The monitoring system was reading that I was dropping 95 PVC's a minute. I knew this was not true because whenever I have 30 PVC's in a minute, I experienced crushing chest pains. Last night I was fine, but for the sake of appeasing Lauren I chose to stay in bed and not journal.

Yesterday was not very eventful anyway. I had my sixth Swan inserted into the left side of the neck. Dr. Gordon was not available at the time, so I opted to take Fentanyl and sleep through the procedure. Miraculously, I awoke when the surgery was complete and did not lose the rest of my day to the drugs. I did, however, receive consistent Morphine for the pain—a pain that would carry into today.

I woke up this morning automatically upset. I knew today was Irene's last day. The thought of her not being around truly depresses me. She has been my rock through so many episodes of pain. On days where I would have been depressed, she cheered me up. I wanted to spend time with her all day, but due to a mishap in the scheduling, she was paired with a different nurse. My nurse for the day, Melissa, somehow ended up teaching a male nurse. I awoke to Melissa's face this morning saying, "Hey Bill, I'm going to be your nurse for the day. This is my student nurse, Abdul." I responded by saying, "Oh, sweet," but in my mind I was furious to not see Irene in her dark blue scrubs.

The rest of my day was rather meaningless until 7:30 PM. Irene entered my room and we began to talk. For the most part we were saying our good-byes. I thanked her for everything she did for me. I tried my hardest to explain to her how grateful I was to have met her. I still am not sure if she fully understands just how much she helped me, but she smiled and told me how inspirational my optimism and resilience was to her. We shared a big hug and I honestly had to fight back tears. I concealed them beautifully, but it was hard. I never once was that emotional over seeing somebody leave my side.

Dr. Gordon is not going to be around all weekend. He leaves tomorrow for a banquet in Texas. His departing words to me were that if I get the surgery this weekend, he would make a special trip into the hospital to see me late Sunday night. Otherwise he would see me Monday morning and he would be participating in the surgery alongside Dr. Getty.

I would love for Dr. Gordon to be a part of the procedure, but at the same time my desire to go home outweighs my comfort with Dr.

Gordon.

Friday, October 2, 2009

It's amazing how history repeats itself, how the generosity of the people who I never met in one story can be duplicated in front of my eyes.

I met a woman last night. I'd say she was in her late fifties or early sixties. Her husband was admitted because his defibrillator had shocked his heart 27 times and he was left unconscious from the pain. He was experiencing strange arrhythmias and he had to undergo multiple procedures.

I do not know the details of these procedures. I only know that during his first trip to the operating room the procedure did not go smoothly. There apparently were some complications with his heart, and before his second procedure, his wife and kids were warned that he might not make it through the operation.

Let me backtrack by saying that last night his wife and I bonded for a short period of time. I wished her the best of luck, told her to stay positive, and mentioned that I'd keep her in my prayers. She, in turn, offered the same support and then we parted ways.

This woman was so touched by my story, and enjoyed her time with me so much, that during her time of stress she approached Melissa while I was asleep. She offered her husband's heart and kidney to me if he did not make it.

I am amazed not only by this woman's pure generosity, but by the fact that today's events mirrored my parents' experiences when I was an infant. This woman was much like the grieving parents in the NICU nursery twenty years ago at Lakeside, who offered the hearts of their deceased newborns to me. Much like those infants, the heart of this man was not going to be a match due to his obvious history of heart problems. Nonetheless, I am stricken by the eerie similarities.

Right now the man is no longer on the CCU floor. He has been moved to the seventh floor, the same place I will go after my transplant. I can only assume the procedure went successfully and he is on the road to recovery—anxiously waiting to go home.

The generosity of strangers amazes me.

Saturday, October 3, 2009

I sat down to journal tonight with the intention of writing an entry that summarized my week. I planned on writing a piece that would bring all of the smaller stresses of my life to light, such as my battle to find the energy to keep up with school work. I wanted to mention that today is my fortieth day in the hospital. Forty days is equivalent to one Lent. I intentionally sat down in front of my computer an hour before I planned to go to bed, for I expected this entry to be a larger one. That's when the alarm went off. The man in Room 803 began to crash. A Code Blue was called.

I have heard this alarm many times throughout my stay. Typically, it's a false alarm or the code only lasts moments. The man in Room 803 wasn't so lucky. He crashed for a good twenty minutes. I know this because I witnessed the code from a distance.

I do not know the man in Room 803, nor have I ever heard him speak. I have seen him on my walks though. He is never in his bed. The nurses have told me that he prefers his wheelchair and becomes angry when anyone tries to move him. He is African American, bald and very thin. I do not know what his face looks like because he always has his back toward the door. He stares out the window, but at times I wonder if he can see. His head is always drooped to the left. It dangles as though he has no strength in his neck, almost as though he has Cerebral Palsy. Typically, there is a woman sitting at his bedside in a green chair toward the window. She looks to be in her late thirties, old enough to be his daughter. Each time I see her she is wearing the same sorrowful look. I recognize the look. It's the same look my sister wore when I was admitted. Carissa's face, along with the others from that week, are still burned in my memory. I did not see the man tonight. I only saw the medical staff rush in-and-out of his sliding glass door.

Doctors from all departments consistently poured into the CCU. It was almost as though I was witnessing a reunion, as familiar faces from my two stays showed up at the man's bedside. Equipment I have never seen before was wheeled in-and-out. Olivia (one of the nurses on the floor) ran through the halls frantically grabbing equipment from each room. That was when I heard another nurse scream from within Room 803. "Charge to 300!" I had seen too many hospital television shows and movies to not know what was coming next. "Charge is at 300... Clear!" With that, I heard the man's body hit the mattress as his bed rocked. It sounded as though thunder had just touched down in the CCU.

Time continued to pass, I progressively felt less wanted roaming the halls. With IV pole in hand, I turned around and headed back to my room as I listened to the harmonic sound of the alarm continuously loop overhead.

The man in Room 803 reminded me of something tonight, he kept me level headed. He was living proof that at any second everything can change. I can be in surgery in the blink of an eye, or things can change for the bad and I could end up like him, convulsing on the floor.

I just asked one of the nurses if the man in Room 803 survived. She turned to me, paused, and with a stone face said, "For now, he is still with us."

Sunday, October 4, 2009

I fell asleep today for close to three hours. My parents came to visit, but unfortunately today was a heart failure day. I struggled to find the energy to stay awake.

Consequently, I am still up at 1:22 AM and I do not foresee myself falling asleep for another two hours or so. I feel as though almost every girl I knew from high school was up late tonight, as well. I had many conversations on my web cam, many of which lasted twenty to thirty minutes a piece. The last video chat was with a friend of mine named Kylie. I hadn't talked to Kylie in quite sometime. The last time I saw her was when Chicago General was still following my case. I was out shopping for furniture to decorate my studio. Little did I know then my studio would be a small room in the CCU of Mercy Care Hospital. Kylie and I talked for about ten minutes. She was shocked to find out about my current situation. Kylie had no idea I was even sick when I saw her earlier in the summer. I was still keeping my illness very quiet from all of my friends. Kylie said she was going to come see me this upcoming Friday. One of her last questions to me was, "So wait, how long do you have… like, how serious is this?" I told her I was in good shape and not to worry. I explained how I am currently on two medications that are keeping me alive and well and that if the situation got really bad, I think my doctors would be able to sustain my life long enough. Soon after, our chat session ended, but Kylie's question left me pondering.

Like I have said, when you are stuck in isolation, you lose total sense of time. You almost forget that it exists. You remember the times of your medications, but the times are just numbers, they begin to lose significance. It dawned on me when Kylie posed her question that I had forgotten the simple truth that I may be running out of time. I may go to bed in a couple of hours and never wake up in the morning. It is a grizzly thought, but it is a thought I have not considered for many weeks. The Inotropes almost make you cocky. They make you feel somewhat invincible. Inotropes are only temporary. Kylie reminded me of that. She sobered my perception of everything with one intuitive question.

I began to think about my past. I worry that I may die with regrets. I started thinking of my life very thoroughly. I flashed back and tried to think of every person who I may have wronged in the past—people whom I have upset, or at the least, left on bad terms. It was then that I realized that something beautiful had come from this dark disease. There were three individuals who I parted with on bad terms. Each one has contacted me in some form to send their well wishes. Each time I have been able to re-establish a friendly connection.

The initial two relationships of regret are with two friends from high school, Ben and Kurt. These awkward relationships were completely my fault, simply because I spent all of senior year tearing them apart and making fun of their girlfriends. I really never had anything against their girlfriends. I just got a sick enjoyment from watching them get embarrassed when I'd talk about them. The jokes were never too crude. Ben and Kurt were just two very introverted guys, and what made the jokes even better, was that I happened to be friends with their girlfriends. Most of the time the girlfriends would chime in with my insults and feed me personal information about their boyfriends in an attempt to heighten the humor. The end result to a year's worth of insults was a strained relationship with both Ben and Kurt. The two have contacted me wishing me the best. We are now on much better speaking terms. They both actually mentioned that they have forgiven me for my sense of humor.

The other individual was named Maureen. She lived across the hall from me last year at Columbia. I was good friends with her the entire first semester. I was single then, Amber and I were on a break. Amber and I got back together over winter break. When I returned for the second semester, I lost touch with Maureen. I did so intentionally. Amber did not like Maureen and instead of hearing Amber complain, I opted to keep my distance from Maureen. I feel I wronged her and since last semester I have felt horrible about losing touch with her. A few weeks back I received a message from Maureen. She heard about my illness through the grapevine and wanted to send her best. To make a long story short, she and I are now on good terms. We are planning on getting lunch sometime next semester.

It feels good having no regrets. I find it astonishing that I was able to go through twenty years of life with such minimal mental anguish. Hopefully, this next heart lasts me twenty years and I am able to have the same success.

Monday, October 5, 2009

I am struggling to keep up with school. There are days where I need to muster every ounce of energy in order to simply write my teacher an e-mail asking for an extension.

For the most part, my teachers have been phenomenal. However, there is one teacher, who after hearing about my condition, simply wrote back saying that she doesn't care and she will not give me any different treatment than other students. She said, "I don't make exceptions for any students." Needless to say, I refer to her as, "Professor Bitch."

The other three teachers have been unbelievably compassionate. Each of them have made exceptions and have allowed me to turn in my assignments weeks late.

A lesson I have learned from this illness is that there are many compassionate and good-hearted individuals in this world. However, for every three decent people, there is one cold-hearted cunt.

Tuesday, October 6, 2009

I had yet another Swan put in today. Like usual, I took Morphine to ease the pain. Today, I needed a little extra narcotic boost. Dr. Gordon allowed a Resident doctor to place the Swan in my neck. This is the one thing I hate about Mercy Care. It is a teaching hospital and unfortunately there are many Residents who need to learn.

The Resident began the incision by screwing up dramatically. The pain was severe. I screamed very loudly. Dr. Gordon then took the reins and did not let the Resident continue until the very end of the procedure. Though the Resident was only allowed to work on the Swan for a total of ten minutes, enough damage was done that I later needed both Morphine and Fentanyl to ease the pain. Consequently, I fell asleep for close to four hours. I awoke with the chills and have not felt very well since. It is currently 7:00 PM and I am eating dinner as I type this. I plan on getting to bed within the next hour.

I am really beginning to question if I have any more space on my neck to put another Swan in five to seven days from now. My neck is currently covered in scabbed over incisions.

Wednesday, October 7, 2009

I went to bed last night around 8:00 PM after learning that I was running a low-grade fever. I spent the entire night very uncomfortable. Around 2:00 AM I awoke covered in my own sweat. I paged my nurse and she changed my bed sheets as I put on a new outfit. I went back to bed slightly more comfortable until I awoke this morning to Karrie's face and the same low-grade temperatures.

Dr. Lenair and Dr. Gordon entered this morning and began to bounce ideas back-and-forth as to what illness I could have possibly contracted this time. I tried to pay attention to all of their suggestions, but I found it difficult as I began to worry that their next words were going to be, "We're taking you off the list."

Fortunately, they informed me that they were not going to take me off the list. In fact, if an offer was presented to them in the next hour they would not hesitate to operate on me. I was feeling relieved, achy, irritable and overall "shitty" at the same time. That was when my mom entered.

She was in a good mood. She began to show me different foods she purchased and the clothing she had brought me from home. She sat down on my bed and showed me an e-mail that a woman by the name Casandra Ropers wrote. Casandra began to tell me I was a major inspiration to her. She said that I am having an impact on so many people and changing lives. I thought it was a pretty deep message from someone whom I had never met, but nonetheless I was flattered.

My mom spent the day in my room knitting, talking to the nurses as they passed and doing what we have both been doing for too long now, waiting. I haven't felt well all day. I feel like I have the flu.

Thursday, October 8, 2009

I have a tendency of ignoring symptoms. I first did this when I ignored the "stomach pains" for three months. I obviously didn't learn my lesson then because today when my back began itching profusely, I waited three hours to tell Karrie. Karrie rubbed some anti-itching agent on my back. It was very cool and sticky. I felt a sensation that I can only describe as my muscles relaxing. Finally, the itching stopped, it was like the calm before the storm.

Two hours later, I began to scratch my scalp, forearms, and eyes excessively. The itching sensation had returned full force. Like an idiot, I again ignored the obvious symptom for nearly three hours until I finally told Karrie toward the end of her shift. Karrie and Dr. Derma discovered that the antibiotic I had recently been placed on to clear up my newly discovered Urinary Tract Infection was causing my body to breakout in a splotchy rash. The rash then led to my throat closing. I began to have difficulty breathing. I wasn't suffocating, but my inhalations were significantly restrained.

The patient in Room 812 is not doing very well at the moment. Unfortunately for Dr. Lenair, but fortunately for me, Dr. Lenair has chosen to stick around much later than he typically would. I was able to show him my current condition and he prescribed a Hydrocortisone shot, coupled with 25mg of Benadryl. I just received the shot. In a few minutes I will swallow the Benadryl. I have chosen to write this entry as I continue to ignore the symptoms because I know what Benadryl does to me. Within an hour's time, I will be in a medicinal coma.

October 8th was an interesting day. The above description of my day was one that occurred externally. I also had quite an eye-opener today. Internally, I found slight peace with a current situation of mine.

Exactly one year ago, there was a man on this ward who waited, much like I am, for a new heart. Many months prior to receiving his heart, he had received a kidney from his brother. Chloe, from the transplant team, thought he would be a perfect person for me to meet. His name is Tim. For three hours, Tim sat with me in my room and not only discussed life after transplant, but we also compared stories of our stays inside these hospital walls. I enjoyed my time with Tim. He alleviated a great deal of mental anguish.

Friday, October 9, 2009

Another day has passed without a new heart and kidney. It's a weird feeling when you truly trust your doctors, yet you fail to see any light in sight. I can't sleep tonight. Lauren is my night nurse. She is one of the younger nurses on the ward. She is twenty-three to be exact. It is kind of funny. It's currently 3:34 AM, Lauren is struggling to stay awake, whereas I am struggling to merely yawn. I have been talking to Lauren almost all night. I can't tell if I am annoying her or if she is actually enjoying my company. I do know that she is helping me pass the time as I try to end this boring day.

It seems as though the duller my days are, the harder it is to sleep at night. It is almost as though the lack of mental stimulation throughout the day finally catches up to me when the nurses switch their shifts. My mind begins to race and I cannot help but lay awake wondering about my future. I question if I am ever getting out of this hospital or if I am going to feel guilty while I am walking around with another person's organs inside me. Most of all, I question why I feel like someone else's heart is going to be so different. I think I never truly came to terms with the fact that I had a donor before any of this happened. I always considered this current heart to be mine. I guess because I grew up with it, I never fully appreciated it for its full value. I have always tried to live life to its fullest for both myself and my donor, but I don't think I ever truly took the time to appreciate the sacrifice that was made twenty years ago by an anonymous man.

I hate boring days in the CCU... they really fuck with your head.

A ROUND TRIP TICKET TO HELL AND BACK

I can tell you what Hell looks like. I've been there. I took an eleven-day trip through the fiery gates. I stared the Grim Reaper in the eye, laughed at his scythe, turned my back on him and kept pressing on until I found the hidden exit that was concealed by the flames.

Everything disappears when you're in Hell. Your family, your friends, anybody who supported you is gone. In reality they may be there. They may be crying at your bedside, but mentally, you are alone. It is you versus the devil, a one-on-one battle to prove that you want to live. You need to fight to survive and show that demonic son of a bitch that you still have a full life ahead of you.

You live your entire life as you search for this hidden exit. Your eyes are opened to the many mistakes you have made. You relive your regrets, you relive the happy moments, but mostly you see your future. You see everything your life has in store, everything that is going to be taken away from you, as your body continues to deteriorate and the horizon at the end of your swim is pushed further away by the changing tides.

It is at this point when you find the hidden door that you feel the heat of the concealing flames scorching your skin. You step back, and you ask yourself, *Is this where I give up?* This is a crucial moment because at this point you can say "yes," turn around, walk back to the Grim Reaper and bow your head in shame as he takes your life with his scythe. Or you can say to yourself, *No, I have come too far, and I am willing to get burned.* Walk through the fire as you feel the flesh melt off of you, reach for the door with whatever strength you have left and walk through.

The beauty is found when you close the door behind you. The air is cool, your energy has returned. You look down to discover that you were never burned in the first place, you were restored.
I began my trip through Hell on Saturday, October 10, 2009. I did not open the door until Wednesday, October 21, 2009, and I did not close it until two days later.

To put into perspective just how sick I was, at some point during my trip through Hell, Irene came to visit. However, I was so ill during this period of time that I have absolutely zero memory of anything we discussed. I typically am very focused when I speak with Irene. I savor the moments because I enjoy our conversations immensely. But our entire (I would assume) hour-long conversation is lost in Hell because I had to focus all of my energy on not appearing sick. I did this because I did not want to worry Irene. Consequently, I am left with yet another silent video in my mind of Irene wearing a black and gray argyle top, with black leggings and boots, as she sat in a chair at the foot of my bed. I mention her visit because this is the one event that I cannot even guess what day it occurred. I was very drugged and I think I was just really happy to see someone who always managed to stay calm.

The following is the best I can do to piece together my trip through Hell. The dates and times may be severely off. The events may be completely out of order, but I can assure you that every other detail I am about to pour onto these pages is not only truthful, but also completely accurate. Like I have stated before, pain helps the mind remember everything.

Saturday, October 10 – Wednesday, October 14, 2009

I tossed and turned deep into the morning shortly after writing the October 9, 2009 entry. I couldn't sleep. I felt miserable. Hours later, I awoke around 10:00 AM to find myself covered in sweat. The only movement I could make were the shivers from the 101.8 temperature. I remember being alone in the room. My Swan was connected to the monitor, so I was able read all of my vitals. My vision was blurry, but when I was able to make out the "101.8" I was filled with disgust. I wanted to swear, but I didn't have it in me to even talk. The entire staff rounded that morning and immediately placed me on a large regiment of antibiotic medications. I rarely left my bed during this period of time. The infection showed no sign of improvement until an additional regiment of antifungal medications were added on top of the antibiotics. For the most part this entire period of time was a blur, mainly because each day was filled with the same nothingness. I would lay in bed where I would doze in-and-out of sleep as my mom would sit in a chair and crochet a blanket for my sister.

I only have two distinct memories from this dismal period of time. The first is of Dr. Krause and Dr. Gordon entering my room. They did their full analysis. Then Dr. Gordon turned to me with a look of deep sorrow on his face and began to tell me that I was going to be temporarily removed from the recipient list. He explained that the Swan will be removed and I will virtually be unplugged from the eyes of UNOS until the infection was cleared. I knew this would be the outcome—it was inevitable. I had been running extreme temperatures for three days, and the mere thought of having a transplant even seemed like a horrible idea to me at the time. Though I was expecting the news, I still couldn't help but feel crushed. I felt a lump in my throat begin to manifest. With tears building in my eyes, I turned to Dr. Gordon and said, "Can I ever get a fucking break?" Dr. Gordon didn't say much. He returned the same saddened look, rubbed my right knee and said, "We'll fix this." He then left.

I do not know when the other memory took place, but I remember it was one of my lowest points in this entire battle. I was lying in my bed. I had just awoken and I was alone. I stared at the ceiling as tears streamed down my face. "What do I have to do to prove that I want to live?" I began questioning the sky. I didn't receive a response, so I just continued to repeat the question over and over again. "I'm not going to die!" I said angered. Then I fell back to sleep.

Thursday, October 15 - Saturday, October 17, 2009

I had two major realizations during this three-day stretch. The first was that I am inches away from death. The second was that I was a Morphine addict.

I believe the Morphine realization came first. I was lying in bed. I had just received 4mg of Morphine to legitimately ease the pain. Ashley was my nurse. I remember that distinctly because Ashley has a very sweet, Southern bell, almost angelic voice. Her voice is the most calming, innocent sound I heard throughout my entire hospital stay. She is always happy and walks around the CCU with a big smile on her face. She is one of those people who can cheer you up just by saying, "Hi, my name is Ashley, and I'm gon'na be your nurse today!" I remember she was my nurse because I felt horrible for taking advantage of her sweetness. Like I said, I had just taken 4mg of the juice, the pain was gone. I was numb all over, simply riding the high. I knew every hour I was allowed to take the same dosage. I also knew that Ashley and I had become very close and she would do anything to make sure I wasn't sad or in pain. That was when I began to press the nurse call light every hour to get the same 4mg dosage of Morphine.

Like I said, I felt horrible for taking advantage of Ashley's kindness. In fact, to this day I feel like a prick. At the time, though, the high overcame my guilt. I liked it because it helped me escape. It took away the sadness and helped my mind preoccupy itself momentarily with thoughts other than, *How much more time do I have left on this Earth?* It wasn't until I had lied to Ashley and then pulled the same trick on my night nurse that I had the realization that I was indeed addicted to Morphine and general narcotics. I remember thinking to myself, *I really do not give a shit, either way I am probably going to die, then what does it matter? Or, if I miraculously am saved, worst-case scenario, I go into some Morphine Addict Anonymous program for a year.* The short-term benefits vastly outweighed the long-term potential consequences as I rolled the addiction dice.

The other realization I had in regards to how close to death I was came on a day that Natalie visited. I had been off of the list for a while and I had a brilliant idea to somehow persuade my doctors into letting me go outside. My argument was that I no longer had a Swan catheter in my neck, which makes my risk of infection much lower, and therefore I should be allowed to see the sun after nearly fifty days of hospitalization. My doctors agreed very quickly and I thought it was kind of strange (months later I would find out that my doctors had told my parents that I had maybe a week to live at this point). They were probably letting me go outside as a form of a "last wish" type of deal. Later this day, I found myself predicting that I had about three more weeks left in me. Either I was overestimating my body, or the doctors were underestimating my determination. Thank God we will never find out.

Regardless of my life expectancy, I went outside blissfully with the aid of Melissa, Natalie and my mom. Melissa was great. She dressed me up in all of her womens winter clothing and we departed for the streets of downtown Chicago. The walk lasted five minutes until I began to experience feelings of dizziness, fatigue and both my vision and hearing began to go. I was reliving everything from my days leading up to my hospitalization at Chicago General. My mom panicked and ran into the hospital. Melissa, Natalie and I sat on a ledge of a window as Melissa helped slide my hands into yet another article of feminine clothing, her spare gloves. My mom appeared with a wheelchair and I slowly sat down. I was then wheeled around the hospital roughly five times.

The weather was not ideal. It was drizzling, but after being locked inside of a CCU room for so long I wouldn't have cared if there was a monsoon. I was going to milk my time outdoors to its fullest. I believe Natalie pushed my wheelchair and Melissa pushed my IV pole for me, as we walked outside for a half hour. I came back and I remember a few of the nurses cheering for me. I laughed and then went back into my CCU room. This is where my memory of this event ends. I only remember the moment that I spoke of earlier.

I was lying in bed. It was probably 11:00 PM. The lights were off and I know for a fact I was alone. I stared at the blank television screen in deep thought. I then calculated that I had three weeks to live. The part that scares me most when I look back on this moment is that I was completely calm when I had that realization. I think it's because I was either cocky enough to think that I was inevitably going to be saved, or I had just hit the point where "death" had just become a word to me. Mentally, I disassociated it with any meaning.

So this is the set-up going into the next week. I think I have three weeks to live. My team of doctors think I have five to seven days remaining. My future donor is living a healthy life and has no idea who I am.

Sunday, October 18 – Tuesday, October 20, 2009

On October 18, 2009, the Chicago Bears played the Atlanta Falcons on Sunday Night Football. It is because of this game that I am fully certain that my account of this three-day period is in perfect chronological order. The reason being, because I was able to hear the audio from the game almost four hours after it ended.

Shelby was a Resident who was working on the floor this entire month. She had to work horrendous hours, typically from noon to 1:00 PM the following day. Throughout the course of the month Shelby and I became good friends. Many times, she would smuggle me food in from surrounding restaurants or pick me up a candy bar on her way to work. This particular night Shelby smuggled me in a sandwich and we watched the football game together in my room along with another Resident. The game ended and I headed off to bed thinking that the day had come and gone like many other days—uneventful, with no offers of a heart and kidney… I was sadly mistaken.

I awoke around 11:45 PM to my nurse, Polly, at the right side of my bed. I would describe Polly as being very spunky. She is probably no taller than five feet, from the Philippines and always on top of her game. Polly was my nurse only about six times between my initial stay in early August and this second elongated stretch, but I loved it when I had her. She was interesting to talk to and she was always very sweet. On this Sunday, I gave Polly a run for her money. I put her skills to the test and I would say she passed with flying colors.

"Go back to sleep, I'm just changing the bags on your IV," Polly said in her accent. "Nah, I really have to go to the bathroom and wash my face. Then can I have my Morphine and I will go back to bed?" I questioned. Taking Morphine really was not necessary, I just knew that the feeling was fun to fall asleep to and made it so that I wouldn't have to hear my dysfunctional heart beat through the pillow. Polly asked me what my pain level was. I, of course, lied as I slowly rose from the bed. That was when I felt an urge to vomit take over my body. I sprang forward and grabbed the nearest trash can. The trash can was gray and very large. I would estimate that it stood three and half feet tall because it came up to my navel. I began to dry heave into the can, nothing would come up, so I continued to push. That was when I heard a sound that I can only describe as an electric shock go off in my head. *Zap!* My vision went black for less than a second. I came to and my arms were slamming the trash can to the floor. The room sounded as though a dump truck had just rolled in. *Zap!* My vision once again went out. I came to and saw Polly's face in horror. "Bill, it is time to lay down!" Polly said with a shaky voice. "No, no I'm fine, I just need to throw up, wash my face, brush my teeth and then I will." I tried to play it off as though nothing out of the normal was happening to me. *Zap!* The lights went out for a third time, but when I came to I was catching myself from hitting the floor. "Armand! Armand! Get in here, I need your help!" Polly was screaming outside of my glass door. Armand rushed in. He is one of the few male nurses on the ward. He is taller and fairly built. I heard Polly explain to Armand that I was having awkward motions where my arms were flailing in the air. *Bullshit!* I thought to myself. I was very delirious and startled, but I continued to convince myself that nothing was wrong. That's when I had the fourth blackout. I came to and found Armand and Polly grabbing onto me as they guided me to my bed. I sat down, "It's not my heart, it's my brain… I'm having seizures." I finally gave into the notion that something was terribly wrong.

Armand left to get the Residents. Polly asked me if I wanted my parents to be called. It was when she asked this question that I began to rethink my three-week prediction. I changed my life expectancy to about two hours. If I surpassed that deadline I gave myself two weeks. Polly asked me for my cell phone, but then struggled to operate it. She asked me if I could dial my house, but as I was holding onto the phone I had another seizure. The phone fell to my lap. When I regained focus Polly was asking me if I wanted her to dial the number. "No!" I said abruptly. I was beginning to feel a mix of fear and frustration. I was determined to dial my home from the cell phone. I made it as far as opening the contact list and scrolling down to "Home" when another *Zap!* occurred. This one was different. This twitch was far worse than the others. My vision came back, but my arms and legs were still flopping in the air. My arms came down hard on the side rails of the bed. "Fuck!" I exclaimed from both pain and anger. "Just press send," I said to Polly in a defeated voice as I gestured with my head towards the cell phone. The seizures continuously happened almost every fifteen seconds. I listened to Polly cautiously speak with my mom, but I only caught bits of the conversation because my hearing was going in-and-out.

Polly hung up and told me that my parents were on their way to the hospital. It was then I noticed that every nurse and Resident were in my room. They were all staring at me. Some of them began to give their support. "It's going to be okay, Bill. They will end soon…" I heard a voice say from somewhere in the room. That was when another seizure occurred and I smashed my arms against the side rails for the second time. "Let's get some blankets and pad the sides of his bed!" the charge nurse yelled.

The head Resident who had been watching football with Shelby and me began to bark orders. She ordered that I be given a heavy dose of Morphine (to slow me down), the Neurology Resident examine me, and for an EKG to be performed (to make sure I was not having arrhythmias or that my defibrillator wasn't accidentally shocking me).

That was when I saw Lauren's face, she looked as though she had seen a ghost. She almost seemed mesmerized by something other than my tweaks. Lauren and the other nurses left and immediately re-entered with the EKG machine. The EKG came out negative and I was given a large dose of Morphine. I felt the warmth come over my body. It took over faster than it ever had. It felt really good, but I wasn't able to enjoy it. I couldn't when I was waiting to die at any second. That's when I began to hear the entire second half of the Chicago Bears game in my head. I relived every call…

Cutler down field to Olsen. I don't know about that decision, Chris.

Yeah you're right, Al. That was a gutsy call, but Cutler has always been known to be a slinger.

What the fuck?! I thought to myself. I tried to get the audio out of my head, but the harder I tried the louder the broadcasting seemed to get. The Neurology Resident entered and performed the same bullshit tests that the other Neurology Residents performed on me when I had my initial twitches the week I was admitted. He was very sheepish and came off as though he had no idea what he was doing. He said I was "neurologically fine" and vanished from my room. The twitches continued for another hour until I fell asleep from the Morphine. I awoke to a dark room and Shelby sitting in a chair. She looked as though she was going to cry. Her curly light brown hair was lit blue from the light of the computer monitor. Shelby calmed me. She did not say a word, yet her mere presence relaxed me and made me feel like I was going to be okay. I drifted back to sleep. I awoke again to the familiar voice of my mom. I do not remember what she said, but Gus was in the room wearing his letterman jacket and my dad was standing by the glass door with a cheesy grin on his face. (My dad has a tendency of wearing this stupid smile on his face when things aren't going well. He had worn it multiple times already during this stay, so I knew he was just trying to hide his sadness.) I think I told Gus to be quiet because any sound reactivated the seizures.

I felt crazed. I had more Morphine in me than I knew what to do with. I couldn't stay awake, and if I did try to fight the sedation, I would throw myself into a series of three to five seizures. After a few tweaks I chose to give into the Morphine. I fell asleep saying to myself, *This is just a minor hiccup. You will wake up tomorrow and this will all be over.* I listened to some more football and then fell into a deep sleep. I awoke to Ashley's soft voice, "Good morning, Bill. I heard you had a rough night?" *Zap!* My fists landed hard on the mattress. Ashley and I both knew then that I was going to have a "rough" day, too.

Before I continue, I should mention that a significant meeting had taken place on this day. The meeting was not in my CCU room. In fact, I did not even learn of this meeting until nearly three weeks after it had taken place. I am told that on this morning the nurses were all called in for a mandatory discussion about me. My death was apparently eminent at this point. The nurses were called in to discuss, "Who had become too close to Bill Coon to deliver life saving treatment if necessary." I am told that Karrie, Ashley and Melissa all stepped forward and admitted they had developed a close friendship with me. However, Karrie was the only one to admit that she feared she wouldn't be able to deliver the treatment if I was to Code Blue on her shift. When I look back now I can't help but laugh at myself for how oblivious I was to my surroundings. Karrie had been on vacation and she returned on this Monday. Karrie always took me as her patient when she worked. It was known throughout the ward that if Karrie was working I was off limits to the other nurses. Karrie would pop her head into my room and I would complain to her for not being my nurse. She would respond with, "I'm sorry, but there is a really critical patient down the hall and I need to work solely with him." I believed what she had said as I rationalized with myself that she was one of the veteran nurses on the floor, therefore she must get the severely ill patients. What makes me laugh even more when I look back on everything, is that the patient she was referring to left the hospital weeks before I did. I probably would have complained and interrogated Karrie further, but I still got to have Ashley as my nurse. Ashley made every day go by quickly, regardless if they were as bad as this particular Monday.

I have to go to the bathroom, was the first thought that came to my mind once the seizure ended. I expressed my needs to Ashley, and she replied with the response I was expecting, "It's not safe for you to get out of bed." Visions of a Foley catheter going into my dick flashed before my eyes, but I still pressed on. "I <u>really</u> have to piss." I said as I felt my right hand uncontrollably slide across the bed. Ashley paused, "I can get you a condom catheter?" she asked hesitantly. I giggled like a schoolgirl at the word "condom." "A condom catheter? What the fuck are you talking about?" I was very confused. Ashley started laughing at my immaturity and explained that it was like a Foley catheter, except it goes on like a condom and I would urinate into it. *As long as it doesn't go up my dick I'm totally cool with it*, I thought.

Ashley left and returned moments later with the condom catheter. She closed my curtain and gave me privacy as I struggled to hold on to the contraption. My hands were shaking ferociously. I kept dropping the condom. Each time, I would unleash a repulsive swear word at the top of my lungs.

This is one of those moments in my life that I wish I could have been a bug on the wall. I'm sure I was quite the sight. I was twitching as though I had Parkinson's Disease, swearing like I had Turrets Syndrome, and then just before the condom went on, I accidentally pissed on my left hand. (Don't ask me how, I twitched and a little shot out.)

Finally, I managed to use the device correctly. I must have really had to go because my next memory is of Ashley entering the room and staring at the bag. She started to laugh and said, "You weren't kidding when you said you had to pee." I smirked and asked Ashley for a pack of hand wipes so I could clean my recently soiled hand. Ashley

handed me the pack of wipes. *Zap!* I came to and heard a loud crash.
It sounded like a gun had just gone off behind my bed. I was startled.
I frantically began to search for the hand wipes, but they were gone. It
was then I realized that during my last twitch I had lost control of my
hand and involuntarily whipped the plastic container against the wall.
I can only imagine what I looked like because that's when I noticed
Ashley fighting back a smile. I could tell she wanted to laugh, but she
didn't want to offend me. Ashley later left the room and my mom
entered shortly after.

It was when my mom entered that I began to lose total control. The
twitches wouldn't stop. I tried as hard as I could to fight them, to gain
back my body's independence, but it was a freedom I had already lost.
The room was beginning to fade to white. Everything around me was
succumbing to the bright light. Eventually the room looked as it did on
the day I was visited by the many strangers at Chicago General. I knew
at this moment that I was about to die. Though I was twitching, my
body seemed to slowly go numb—I stopped feeling any form of pain.
It was as though my life was draining out of me, like a glass of water
with a small hole on the bottom. The numbing sensation was down to
my collar bone when I began to stare at the bright light on the ceiling. I
remember staring into the light. I was waiting to see angels.

The numbing sensation was just below my rib cage when I turned to
my mom and said, "Just let me die, leave me alone." I can't describe my
mom's reaction because she was blanketed by the bright light. I only
remember hearing her speak. "Bill, don't give up! Keep fighting! Fight
for the life you love!" She kept uttering that sentiment. The further I
drifted away mentally, the louder and more forcefully she would say it.
I don't remember how many times she had said it to me, but the numbing sensation had drained down to my knees when I finally understood
what she was saying. I felt my brain make its last push to feel reality for
the two seconds that it took for her to utter her sentiment.

 "Don't give up! Keep fighting! Fight for the life you love!"

It sounds so cliché, but I genuinely saw my life flash before my eyes.
Memories that I had remembered only through pictures suddenly
became first-person movies. I relived my life. Though my body was in
a bed at Mercy, my mind was at bat nervously awaiting a pitch in the

midst of a Little League baseball game. I blinked and my surroundings changed to my fourteen-year-old birthday as the smoke from the candles drifted into my eyes. The smoke cleared and I was with my friends dancing in a circle at prom. I blinked one more time and I was back at Mercy. The light was still around me, but I felt a form of mental power resurge in my mind as though the lights in my brain had snapped back on. I stared intently at the light. I summoned all of my Will and fought the light off. In the corners of my eyes, I could see the white slowly regress back into the ceiling. I felt the numbing sensation regress in my body, slowly working its way up to my scalp. The light finally left the room—it knew I wasn't going anywhere. The battle to stay on Earth depleted my energy. I fell asleep, but I was awoken later in the day when a woman from the defibrillator clinic came in to turn off my mechanical chest box.

My doctors sent her in as a precaution. The worry was that the twitches were actually miniscule, accidental shocks from my defibrillator. The "defibrillator theory" was proven to be a bust as the twitches continued. I knew this wasn't the case. My mom and I had already figured out that the twitching was a result of my failing kidneys and a Creatinine level that was near 3.8 (a good level should never be higher than 1.1). The problem was that my body was once again being overloaded with the toxins that my kidneys were too weak to excrete. But when you are in the hospital, every team must come in and every inch of your body must be examined. I knew the solution was another series of dialysis treatments. The operation to have a catheter inserted into the left side of my neck was already scheduled for later in the day. I waited in bed until a female Attending from Neurology entered with two Residents. She asked me a series of questions, which I struggled to answer. I struggled not because the questions were difficult, but because with each answer I began to jerk uncontrollably. The Attending determined what my mom and I had already known. She gave my mom a compassionate nod, turned and left the room.

It was finally time for my catheter operation. Ashley went with me down to the operating room much like Karrie and Irene did when I had my first dialysis catheter implanted. Ashley was allowed in the operating room. We talked (actually Ashley asked me questions, and much like my conversation with the Neurology Attending, I struggled to respond). The doctors and nurses took a while to prepare the room for the operation. I was then lifted from my bed and placed on the narrow surgical table. The nurse began to prep my neck with an alcohol swab. That's when she coughed. She wasn't wearing a mask, she didn't cover her mouth and she was standing directly over my head. I shot Ashley a look of disgust and anger. Ashley immediately understood, and if my memory serves me correctly, I believe Ashley asked the nurse to put a mask on. I asked the unsanitary R.N. for my usual cocktail of drugs. She obliged and the room went black.

I awoke in the middle of the procedure. I was only awake for less than a minute and I was so out of it that my entire body felt numb. I remember seeing a glass window. There were a lot of computers and a doctor was at each one. I remember seeing Ashley standing in the back of the room as she observed through the glass. She looked nervous. The room went black again.

I awoke in my CCU room feeling famished. My mom was sitting at the foot of my bed drinking a large coffee and Ashley was charting on the computer. I asked for food and both my mom and Ashley jumped with excitement. I had been so sick that I hadn't requested a meal since October 9th. I was given a green pepper that my Yia Yia had cooked for me the prior night. I don't recall eating the green pepper, so I do not remember if I required assistance in eating the meal, but I do remember throwing it up.

"I'm going to throw up!" I yelled out. My mom handed me a small bedpan. "Are you fucking serious?!" I screamed at her. When you throw up, you can usually gauge how much it is going to be just before it happens. I knew then that I was going to need a trash can, and that the shoe-sized container my mom had produced was simply not going to cut it. I had to make do with what I was given. My mom then handed me a larger plastic bin. I masterfully switched containers. I felt all of my abdominal muscles tighten and my eyes fill with tears. I vomited uncontrollably. *I am never eating green peppers again!* I promised myself. The feelings of nausea subsided and I fell asleep, exhausted from the turn of events.

I awoke hours later to the sound of the dialysis machine being wheeled into my room. The sight of the machine made my stomach cringe. If there had been anything left in my stomach it probably would have come up at that very moment. The technician went through the all too familiar steps as she prepped the machine to suck blood from my neck. Finally, she clipped the tubing to my new neck catheter and I felt the coldness consume every cell in my body.

The technician was a new face. I had not seen her before. She was older. I would assume she close to retirement. I remember thinking she looked like a younger Mrs. Claus. She had short, light brown hair, rosy cheeks, an aged complexion and a pair of ruby red glasses. I soon learned that though she looked like Mrs. Claus, she certainly was not as jolly as Old Saint Nick's wife. I remember I made a joke. I know it was funny because both Ashley and my mom laughed. Mrs. Claus didn't think so. Her face remained stone cold and she almost looked angry with me for speaking. My mom and I exchanged looks with one another that said, *What's her problem?* I then fell asleep for a short period of time.

I awoke to the tubing being disconnected from my neck and the smell of the alcohol swab sanitizing my catheter. I watched Mrs. Claus pack up and leave on her metal dialysis sleigh. It was then I realized the twitches had stopped. I stood up with a feeling of rejuvenation. I hadn't felt well enough to walk in days, so I did a victory lap around the CCU. The feeling must not have lasted long because my memory skips a few hours ahead at this point to 10:00 PM. I am lying in my bed, my entire body is aching and I am staring at the clock.

My dad enters the room with a large bag of food from the cafeteria. He hands me two cups of soup and tells me to choose the one I wanted. (Soup has high sodium content, so I was not allowed to eat both cups in one sitting.) I chose the cream of chicken in hopes that I could stomach the food. I took the leap of faith and consumed the entire cup within minutes. Time passed and my stomach remained settled.

I remember feeling weak, so weak that my vision was beginning to go. There seemed to be a white cloud over everything. A halo was over ever light and I started hearing static coming from the vents above. I have thought about this moment many times since it occurred. I believe that if my parents were not in the room this was the moment when I may have died. I had an eerie feeling for a good two hours. I felt like there was someone else in the room with me. I could not see them, but I felt that they were watching me, waiting for me to give up. I didn't give in. Instead I got cocky. I was so convinced that Death was watching. I wanted to show it that I still had life in me and that I wasn't going anywhere. I stood up from my chair. I felt my knees burn and my back crack. "What are you doing?" my mom questioned. "I'm going to go for a walk!" I said proudly. I remember announcing it, saying it with all my strength so that everyone in the room could hear me. "Walk with him," my mom whispered to my dad. My balance was off and she was worried I was going to fall and rip the Swan catheter from my neck. I remember speaking with Lauren as I passed the nurse's station. She was covered by the white clouds, but I remember hearing her say, "It's nice to see you're walking." Each step felt as though a nail was going through my joints, but I marched on, clutching my IV pole, talking to my dad about something I don't remember. I returned from my walk exhausted and craving Morphine for the pain. That's when I noticed that the eerie feeling had left the room. I felt a sense of accomplishment come over me. I felt that I had scared away Death. My parents noticed the late hour and kissed me good-bye. I fell asleep feeling alone that night. I was happy to be alone.

The morning of October 20th was a blur to me. My memory does not come back until the middle of the day when I had one of the coolest experiences of my life. The cornerback for the Chicago Bears, Charles Tillman, and his wife, Jackie, came to visit me in the hospital. Being the die-hard Chicago Bears fan that I am, I honestly would have crapped my pants from the star-struck feeling that I experienced had it not been for the narcotics, which caused chronic constipation.

The twitches were beginning to come back, my hands were starting to go, and I felt my legs tremor under the covers. My dad had brought my Xbox and a small LCD television set to my room in early September. I had the miniature home theater resting on a blue cart in front of my bed. Charles grabbed the remote, turned to me and said, "Wan'na play?" Without thinking, I replied something along the lines of, "Hell yeah!" We chose to play Madden NFL 2010, and he graciously let me use the Bears. Meanwhile, my mom and Jackie were discussing how to raise a child with a heart transplant.

Charles and Jackie run a wonderful charity, "The Cornerstone Foundation." The foundation focuses on aiding the families of critically and chronically ill children. They chose to make this their foundation's focus after their daughter was diagnosed with Cardiomyopathy and required a life saving heart transplant in July of 2008.

A good portion of the visit was spent discussing medications and my own personal experiences growing up. Charles and Jackie left, but not until Charles and I exchanged cell phone numbers, while Jackie and my mom did the same.

About an hour had passed when my cell phone went off. I looked at the screen and I was astounded to see the words, "Charles Tillman Cell," light up the miniature square. "Hello?" I answered in a confused voice. I was certain he had dialed the wrong number. "Hey, it's Charles, I was just calling to make sure you didn't give me a fake number," he said jokingly. I laughed pretty hard and thanked him for coming to see me. "No problem," he replied. "Hey, I actually went out and got you a gift to make the time pass a bit quicker in there," he continued. *Wow... this man is one of the nicest people I have ever met.* I thought to myself. We discussed his return, but then discovered it would be too late for him to make it back to the hospital in time. It was around 7:45 PM when he had called. Charles was on the other side of the city and the visiting hours were coming close to ending. He said he would bring it by in a few days or he would give it to Jackie and have her drop it off at my house for him while he was at practice. I believe I thanked him again before hanging up in sheer amazement. Once again, my memory fizzles away and my last recollection of this dark period of my life takes place around 11:00 PM.

Ashley was back. She was my night nurse on this day. I don't remember the reasoning behind it, but I believe she contractually had to work one night shift every few months. I would later find myself ecstatic that her one night fell on this evening. The seizures came back full force this night and Ashley's calming demeanor kept me sane. I was glad she was there. I was glad she was able to share a special moment with me. That night I fell asleep to warmth of the Morphine. While I dreamt of a brighter future, my dreams came true. Around 2:00 AM, the CCU received a phone call that the transplant team had found a perfect donor match for me.

I awoke the next morning to the start of my new life.

A Stranger's Heart

Wednesday,
October 21, 2009
-
Sunday,
November 1, 2009

CHEERS FOR A NEW HEART AND KIDNEY

When I was younger, someone told me that on the day you die, in your final hours, you would only be able to remember ten specific moments. They are the ten moments that changed the course of your life, made you the happiest, or made you cry the hardest. The morning of October 21, 2009, will be a moment in my life that I will certainly never forget. I was so happy, my life was changed, and when everyone left the room, I cried.

Wednesday, October 21, 2009

At exactly 6:59 AM, my life was saved. I awoke to the sound of my sliding glass door opening. I looked up and saw Dr. Gordon. He looked ecstatic, smiling from ear to ear. His glasses were hanging lower than usual on his nose. "Bill, I have some news for you. Last night, Dr. Getty accepted a heart and kidney for you." My body went numb. The feeling was a sensation I will never forget, yet I struggle to describe it. It was as though my entire body stopped. There was no sound. I couldn't swallow. I couldn't blink. I remember trying to breathe, but even my lungs stopped. My body finally recovered from its paralysis, and my brain began to work just enough to get out a one-word response, "Bullshit!"

Dr. Gordon's smile got even bigger. "No, no bullshit." This is when I knew he was for real. Dr. Gordon swore. Dr. Gordon never swears. He was so happy that he had broken out of his typical professional demeanor. He continued, "Seriously Bill, Dr. Getty accepted the offer, and you will be in surgery later this afternoon." That was when I noticed Ashley standing behind Dr. Gordon. Her smile was huge. It was always large, but on this morning it was enormous. They each congratulated me and then Dr. Gordon explained that it wasn't a 100% sure thing. He warned that there was still a chance the procurement team could arrive on the scene to find ailments that were not reported in the paperwork. Though he gave me the warning, I could tell even he knew that the offer was perfect. We both knew that I had come too far for an error in the paperwork to get in the way. Dr. Gordon and Ashley left the room to begin working on the consent forms.

I didn't think twice before dialing my house. I knew my dad wasn't home, but I wanted my mom to be the first to know. "Is everything okay?!" said my mom in a panicked voice. The numbing sensation hadn't fully left my body yet, and my voice came out surprisingly calm. "Yeah, everything is fine. Dr. Gordon just came in my room and told me that Dr. Getty found a match... I'm going to have surgery today." There was a pause on the other end. She then started to cry as she spoke through her tears. She told me she loved me and that she was going to throw her clothes on and rush to the hospital. We then began to pick whom we wanted to call. I chose my dad, Natalie and Aunt Patti. I left the rest for my mom.

No sooner did I hang up with my mom, I was speaking with my dad. "Hey Buddy!" he said. My voice was still relaxed. I can still hear myself speaking and I almost sounded stoned. "Hi... yeah so, I just found out they have a match for me and I am going to have surgery in a few hours." My dad didn't pause like my mom. He immediately went into a series of loud noises that were occasionally interjected with actual statements. "Wahooo! That's great! Heeewoooo! Oh, oh yes! Humi-nah!" I remember laughing at the noises. It was so awkward, yet I was able to feel his happiness through his ramble. I could almost hear his brain click back into reality as he regained his composure. "So when is the surgery?" he asked. "I don't know yet. Dr. Gordon only mentioned that it would be later this afternoon. I'd assume in the next four hours because that's how long the heart is good for out of the donor's body." My dad began to speak quickly. He explained that he was heading towards Wisconsin and would turn around at the next exit. We hung up and I continued making my calls.

I learned this morning that my mom was either a very quick dialer or my family was highly skilled at the telephone game. My news was already old news to everyone I spoke to from here on out. Yet each person talked to me for an extended period of time. Everyone was telling me that I deserved this and that God had answered their prayers.

There was one phone call I received that stands out in my mind the most. It was from my cousin Nick's wife, Alisa. She was sobbing. I remember hearing her voice shake and it sounded so real that I could visualize her chin quivering. She was at a loss for words as she told me how happy she was and that she loved me. It was really nice hearing from Alisa. She wasn't able to visit me when I was in the hospital because she had a son who was a year old (and consequently was a walking germ magnet). She was also pregnant with her second child, so it wasn't safe for her to come to a hospital. Our conversation lasted for about ten minutes, but it was cut short when Dr. Gordon entered with the paperwork.

Dr. Gordon was still smiling. He pulled up a chair and sat to the right of my bed. I did not read a single word on the consent form. I figured that it told me the risks of dying, but I knew either way I had nothing to lose. I focused really hard as I signed the papers and triple checked everything to make sure it was filled out appropriately. Dr. Gordon then went into detail about the necessary steps leading up to surgery. He explained that the Anesthesiologist would speak with me, I would undergo a thorough bath with a special soap, and that Dr. Getty would speak with me as well.

It was when Dr. Gordon left the room that I grabbed my laptop. I hit the power button. Before my desktop appeared, I began to cry. It was a short cry, but it was also a very deep and emotional one. Tears didn't pour from my eyes, they leaked. I was filled with such happiness and a degree of accomplishment that I had never felt before. I logged onto my Facebook account and posted a status that I had been fantasizing about posting for months. "ITS ONLY 99% OFFICIAL... BUT... I GOT THE CALL!!!! HEART AND KIDNEY TRANSPLANT!!!!!!!!!!!!!!!!!!!!!! THE 58 DAY WAIT IS OVER!!!!!!!!!!!!!!!!!!!!!"

After posting the status, I thought about e-mailing Peter. However, I was filled with so much confidence that I chose not to and shut my laptop down. I was alone in the room for nearly fifteen minutes. I sat in silence as I reflected on everything that I had been through. I looked at my IV pole and then began to rub the wires that dangled from my neck. *I'm not going to need this soon*, I thought to myself. I didn't smile though because as I felt the wires, it dawned upon me that someone had died the prior night. "Shit!" I said aloud. I felt a sinking feeling tear through my gut. "God bless the donor and their family," I muttered to the ceiling. I did my cross and rested my head on the bed.

I struggled to smile during the hours leading up to the surgery. I had to become so cold and focused the past 58 days in order to survive,

that I convinced myself I couldn't be happy until the surgery was over.
I had told myself so many times, *If you lose your mental strength, you
lose the battle*. The saying became my mantra. I had this belief that if I
lightened up before the surgery, my body would give out on the table.
I just stared at the wall in front of me, looking at the artwork for one
last time. It was the same artwork I had fallen asleep staring at for the
past 58 days. My wall featured work from a multitude of artists. I had
neon colored poster boards from Claire, Jack and Grace. They are the
children of Karen, my NICU nurse from when I was an infant. She
has been in my life practically since the day I was born and her entire
family has become an extension of my family over the years. The neon
boards read, "Get Well Soon Bill! We Love You!" They were written
in marker, and even though I had read each sign 20-30 times a day,
the signs still made me feel warm inside every time I'd read them. The
other artwork was on my dry erase board, it was drawn by (the much
older) Nicole. She had drawn several random designs. One of the
designs was a sketch of the White House. Above the Presidential palace
she wrote, "Cheers For a New Heart and Kidney!" I used to stare at the
words before I went to bed and angrily mutter to myself, "Psh! Yeah…
not today, Nicole." However, on this day, I was finally able to embrace
her message to me.

My quiet time ended when my nurses began to flock into my room.
They came in groups, all of them. I remember seeing Stacy and Lauren.
It was refreshing seeing Lauren that morning. The last memory I had
of her was from the night that I had my seizures. The image of her
petrified face was burned into my mind. Lauren's expression was the
exact opposite on this morning. It was as though she was compet-
ing with Ashley in a giant-smile contest. Ashley, of course, was win-
ning, but Lauren was giving her a run for her money. Even Stacy, who
always had a witty comeback, was at a loss for words. She was silenced
by happiness. Her facial expression was very distinct. Her mouth was
puckered, yet her cheeks were being forced upward by a smile. It was
as though she was searching for the perfect words to say. Eventually,
she spoke when the group of nurses began to leave. I do not recall
what she said exactly, but I remember it was flattering, yet filled with
sarcasm. I found it appropriate because Stacy and I had joked with one
another throughout my stay. We had developed a "guy friend" type of
bond with one another. Though I enjoyed her comment, I got this feeling that she was dissatisfied with what she had chosen to say. Lauren

wished me luck as well, and then she left. Ashley stayed in my room. She looked exhausted, as though she had just gotten out of a P.O.W. camp. Light gray bags were starting to form under her eyes and I could tell she was fighting her eyelids from fully closing. "I'm so happy for you," she said in a delirious but sincere manner. "I want to stay around here so bad, but I need to get some sleep. I am so tired." she paused, and then continued. "I'm gon'na check on you around the clock. I'm gon'na have someone call me with updates all day." I told her she was sweet and thanked her for everything that she had done for me. She replied with the same enormous smile and then left the room. That was when my family walked in.

I don't remember the order of arrival, but I do remember who came to my bedside that morning. My mom, Dad, Carissa, Gus, Aunt Patti, and Aunt Lisa filled my room. They made their final visit to the CCU an hour and a half before my transplant. They were congratulating me, kissing me and asking me every question that they could think of. They wanted to know if I was nervous. I told them I wasn't and explained how I have never once had a fear of this surgery. I knew the possible complications, I knew I could die on the table if the heart was not right, but I knew deep down that if I was given the opportunity to have this surgery, it would all go swimmingly. I had complete trust in all of my doctors, and given Dr. Getty's sensational track-record I figured there was no way my luck could be so bad that I would be the one heart he screwed up on. No sooner did I finish my explanation to my family, the man with the magical hands himself entered through my sliding glass door.

Dr. Getty is best described around Mercy Care as being "The Man." He is very tall in stature, you honestly couldn't miss him even if you tried. He has black hair and a matching goatee. He has a distinct accent. I know he is from Eastern Illinois, but to this day, I still think he sounds like a Southerner. Accompanying his monstrous stature is a monstrous reputation. Everyone knows he is a genius—an artist with medicine. Indeed, much like every genius, he intimidates everyone. There is not a single nurse I know in the entire hospital who is not petrified of Dr. Getty. He has a tendency of yelling when things are not done correctly, but then again, I can't blame him. He does extremely complicated procedures, so I'd assume that a minor error in preparation could result in major complications or death of the patient. Though Dr.

Getty scares everyone, he has never once frightened me. The few times that I had spoken with him, he was always very calming and genuine. Though he walks around with a drill sergeant persona, I can totally see him as a loving family man who enjoys a good walk around the park with his pet dog, as he sips on his Caramel Frappuccino. Dr. Getty was also very happy this morning. He explained to me the basic steps of the procedure, detailing when the heart will be out of my body and for how long. He explained that he is expecting a lot of bleeding due to the Plavix, and that there is a chance I will need a separate surgery when the kidney is implanted. None of this news fazed me. Even Dr. Getty seemed creeped out by the coldness in my expression. I wanted to show emotion, but I couldn't. I was still holding onto my mantra.

The Anesthesiologist entered in the middle of Dr. Getty's explanation. I don't remember his name, but he was younger, probably in his mid-to-late thirties. He detailed the drugs that I would receive. Then, of course, listed all of the possible complications of life support, such as deafness and the possibility that I may go blind. Once again, I remained cold. "Oh, okay," I responded. I then signed the last of the consent forms.

To my surprise, Mrs. Claus entered on her dialysis sleigh again. I questioned her if she had heard that I am getting transplanted. I asked if the dialysis was necessary. She responded with a very serious, "Yes, I did hear. And your doctor's still want you to have a quick treatment." I was shocked that someone could be that robotic. She never once congratulated me or even seemed remotely pleased in knowing that I wasn't going to die. I didn't let her buzz-kill the moment, neither did my family. My mom pulled out her camera and took a picture of me. The flash caused my hands to fly upwards, I had a mini seizure. "Don't fucking do that again!" I said panicked. I wasn't angry with my mom. In fact, I think I overreacted. I was just scared. I didn't like how unexpected it was. The flash threw me off and almost made me lose my serious composure.

Mrs. Claus hadn't lied when she said that it would be a short treatment. Only thirty minutes had passed when she began to shut down the machine and detached the tubing from my neck.

Bessie was my nurse this morning and she had the pleasure of being the one to wash my body with the special soap. Bessie had been my nurse only on rare occasions. I didn't know her as well as the rest of the staff, but she always treated me with respect. She also, was always very confident with every task she performed. Surprisingly, the bath was relatively quick. I had this image in my mind of me using a fine cloth to wash the inside of my ears, and another image of me scrubbing the inside of my butt cheeks with a buffer. Neither of these images ever became reality. The bath was comparable to my typical wipe-down in the morning, except the soap had rough beads in it, and it smelled like the fluoride treatment that you'd receive at a dentist office.

Everything seemed to happen quickly at this point. Before I knew it, three surgical nurses were in my room. They were dressed in powder blue scrubs. Each of them wore matching hair nets and a medical mask, one that I had yet to see anybody wear. It looked hard, almost concrete. It had three parallel lines flowing through the middle, the lines were wavy, ripple-like. I specifically remember one of the nurses. It was a male nurse and he was tan. The tan nurse asked me if I was ready to go, as he detached my bed from the wall and began carting me out my sliding glass door. I took one final look at the place that I had called "home" for so long. I smiled because I knew I would never be back in Room 810 again. The surgical nurses had a hard time pushing my bed into the hallway because the area outside my door was cluttered with so many of the people whom I had grown to adore over the past two months. I stared straight ahead and listened to the many familiar voices saying, "Good luck!" behind me. I was led down the same hallways I had taken on a multitude of trips, the same hallways that took me to my Swan catheters, the same hallways that were blurred on countless occasions when I could not see. On this day, the hallways were clear, so was my mind. I was incredibly focused. Since June 8th, I had been mentally preparing myself for this moment. It was the moment when the pain would stop and I could feel young again.

After a short elevator ride, I was wheeled into a new hallway, one I had never seen. This was the oddest part. The hallway was not how I had imagined it. The walls were made of white brick. They reminded me of the classroom walls in my elementary school. I was expecting something a little more regal. I was anticipating a golden light or for the Pearly Gates to open in front of me. Instead, I was wheeled through a cold hallway with multiple winding turns.

Finally, I had reached my destination.

The room was massive in size. The walls were white. In actuality, the walls were light gray but they were painted white by the overbearing bright lights that shined from above. Calling this room sterile would be an understatement. Two large monitors were staring directly at me from across the room. They had yet to be turned on. I assumed they were used to display all of my vitals during the procedure. There was a wall to my right that was dedicated to latex gloves and masks. The wall adjacent had plastic bins, which were marked with many words that I struggled to pronounce. Foreign machines stood to the left of my bed. It took me a few moments to realize they were the machines that would keep me alive. My analysis of the room was cut short when the Anesthesiologist stepped into my line of vision holding a large syringe. I was accustomed to seeing 5 mL syringes when my nurses would inject me with my diuretics and narcotics. This syringe was triple in size and filled to the brink. "Are you nervous?" asked the Anesthesiologist. "No," I replied, "but I'll take what's in there," I said jokingly. He laughed and quickly pushed the mystery fluid into my veins. I felt a rush of heat consume my chest as though the drug had ripped through my heart. In a matter of three beats, the warmth shot through my arms and legs. Every limb and every inch of my body was soothed with pulsating heat. I smiled. The room blurred and began to spin. The room wasn't bright anymore, it faded to gray. The tan nurse looked at me with squinted eyes. The room went black.

I awoke the next day with a stranger's heart beating inside of me.

REBIRTH

I had waited so long for the transplants. I had been struggling to stay light-hearted, yet remain cold and focused mentally. It was time for me to let go of the coldness. I finally stopped uttering my mantra.

I let go too early. This is why I was so angry during a time that I should have been elated.

Thursday, October 22, 2009

Oh that's hot, but it feels so good! I thought to myself as I began to regain consciousness. The fresh incision that stretched from my collarbone to my upper abdomen was burning from within. It was a different burn, a whole new kind of heat. It felt prickly, as though millions of miniature bubbles were going off simultaneously underneath my ravished skin. Then, my vision came back.

The room was blurry, At first I could only see blobs of color. I felt as though I was looking at a painting whose colors were running into one another, like a canvas that was left out in the rain. Slowly the images began to reveal themselves. I first began to see shapes, only of those that were in close range. Those shapes then became the buttons on the side of my bed. I understood what the buttons would do as I began to conform to my surroundings. My depth perception then came back. I saw my dad. He was talking to a girl. I knew that I knew her name. I knew I had talked to her several times in the past month, but in this moment her name escaped me. I looked around the room and saw my sister standing in the back corner. She was near a green leather chair. We locked eyes. I turned away. That was when I saw both my mom and Melissa talking at the foot of my bed. Melissa was on the left. My mom was on the right. She was gesturing with her hands. Melissa giggled. Her laugh, which I had grown to love, was the first sound I heard when my hearing came back. I smiled, before my head hit the pillow.

Every memory that I am going to describe on this day lasted in intervals of three to seven seconds. I had been under a great deal of anesthesia, and as the chemicals left my body I struggled to maintain consciousness.

I woke up again. The room was now covered in a blur. This blur
would consume everything in my line of sight for the rest of the day.
"I can't see!" I said to my mom. She and Melissa stared at me confused. "Honey, we can't understand you. You have a breathing tube in
your mouth," my mom said compassionately. "Fuck!" I exclaimed, but
nobody understood me. My mom handed me a pad of paper with a
pen so that I could communicate through writing. I stared at the paper
for a moment, admiring the sandy brown color of the stationary. My
head instantly grew heavy. I fell asleep again.

Whenever I would wake up, my brain would immediately return to
its previous thought. Regardless of how much time I was asleep for,
I acted as though no time had passed and expected everyone to be
thinking my same thoughts.

When I awoke this time, everyone was still in the same positions of
the room where I had left them. Because of this, I can assume I only
fell asleep for a few minutes. I began to write my prior thought down
on paper. I still have these papers today. My mom saved them because
she knew I was writing this book and she thought they would come
in handy when I began to write this section. My handwriting is very
sloppy, you can tell I am in duress, and you can clearly see when
I would fall asleep. The blue ink drags off of the letter. Letters that
shouldn't have tails have elongated scribbles connected to them. The
first note is one of the three that I remember writing. I remember the
reaction of both my mom and Melissa when I handed them the note.
"I can't see," my mom said aloud. Realizing what she had just read,
she began to panic. Melissa panicked, too. Her eyes dilated behind the
lenses of her glasses and her mouth dropped open. "What do you mean
you can't see?!" my mom yelled at me in fear. Melissa then regained her
composure, "Okay, Bill… do you mean that you can't see me right now,
or is everything a little blurry?" Melissa questioned slowly, sounding
every word very articulately. I nodded my head. Melissa continued,
"Yes, as in you can see and everything is blurry?" I returned the same
gesture. "Oh thank God!" my mom whispered loudly as she clenched
her chest. I then felt the cold pillow against the back of my scalp. I was
falling asleep again.

I awoke yet again. This time I was startled upon regaining consciousness. I awoke to Dr. Gordon smiling at me from the foot of my bed. He

startled me because my brain once again was attempting to return to its prior memory and Dr. Gordon's presence conflicted with what my mind was trying to recall. I immediately grabbed the pad of paper and began writing. I realized time was precious, at any moment I was going to be asleep again. I wrote, "Thank you for everything." I reached outward with the pad of paper, my mom grabbed hold of the opposite end. I felt my grip release as I dozed back to sleep. I remember writing this note, but it is one of the few notes that are no longer in my possession. My mom has since told me that she gave it to Dr. Gordon and told him that he should keep it because he had earned it. This was the first time I would agree with my mom in months.

I remember coming to and noticing that Dr. Getty was now standing where Dr. Gordon had been. I was awake for a bit longer this time. I remember hearing Dr. Getty's boisterous accent boom through the room. I once again grabbed my pad of paper and wrote, "You're a good doctor." It wasn't my most educated statement, but I was able to convey my message. I remember watching Dr. Getty read the note, tuck his upper lip under his lower, turn to me and as though he was fighting back a smile and say, "Thank you." I then fell asleep.

I have one last memory of my own. The rest is what I have been told by my mom and Melissa.

I awoke and had a sudden realization, *It doesn't burn where the kidney should be.* I slid the mint green gown upwards, towards my stomach and stared at my left hip. The spot where the kidney scar should have been was untouched—it was just how I had left it. I felt a form of rage consume me. My mom must have noticed that I was awake and staring at my hip because I remember hearing her voice in the background say, "Honey, they couldn't do the kidney yet, there was too much bleeding." I was so pissed off. I thought I was now destined to die on the table. I had gone hours without saying my mantra, I had let go of the coldness, and I knew I couldn't get it back. I had changed my way of thinking in such a short time. I had reprogrammed my brain to prepare itself for pain. I wasn't ready for another surgery. I was ready to heal. I fell asleep shortly after and I have no other recollection of this day.

I am told that I awoke several more times on October 22nd. Each time, I was furious. I would attempt to swear, as I would try to pull the breathing tube from my mouth. I was delirious. Supposedly, I would cry at times. I would pound on my bed in frustration, flick off nurses, and would give Dr. Getty dirty looks when he would tell me to stop touching the breathing tube. Eventually, a surgeon who I would never see, nor would I ever meet, came into the room. Supposedly, her name was Dr. Hanner (my mom was even unclear as to what her name was). I am told that I was very calm with her. I was not mentally sound enough to sign the forms, so my parents did the honors. I was wheeled away to surgery where I was once again knocked out. I did not awake until the following day.

Friday, October 23, 2009

Even though I do not recall anything that transpired on this day, I do remember a very significant moment that occurred on this night.

In my memory, I was alone in my room. This may be true, but I highly doubt this to be correct because I know Natalie and my mom never left my bedside. I remember falling asleep, but it was the first time that I dozed off slowly; I didn't just suddenly black out from the anesthesia. I had my right ear against the pillow when I heard a sound that I hadn't heard in almost a year's time:

"Thud...Thud...Thud...Thud...Thud..."

I had a consistent heartbeat, a healthy heartbeat. A tear trickled from my right eye. I smiled, and fell fast asleep.

Saturday, October 24, 2009

I like to refer to this day as "egg day." This was the first day that I recall eating a meal. The breathing tube had finally been removed and I was able to ingest meals of substance. I remember my dad being in the room. He was really excited to buy me food. Throughout my entire hospitalization, my dad seemed to feel a sense of accomplishment when he'd purchase a meal for me. At times, he was guilty of smuggling me meals that were completely against my diet. I had a safe in my room that was jammed packed with Doritos, Pringles and every imaginable candy bar. My nurses never once thought to check the safe. I am told by my ladies (Ashley, Karrie, Lauren and Melissa) that they all shared a big laugh when they cleaned out my room and discovered my secret stash.

"Well buddy, what do you want to eat?" my dad questioned with excitement in his voice. "Anything, I don't care," I responded. "Well, do you want soup, a sandwich, breakfast?" he continued. "Breakfast" sounded fantastic. Every morning in the hospital I was only allowed to eat Cheerios with milk. Occasionally, I would receive a hearty orange to go along with my meal. On those days I felt like I had won the lottery. I quickly thought of the most unhealthy breakfast food that one could order. I requested bacon, eggs, an English muffin (buttered of course), and milk. I can't recall if it was my mom or the nurse who interjected, but one of the two said that I couldn't eat the bacon. I must say, I was in agreement with them. I really didn't have any intentions of eating the bacon. I only ordered it because I could. I also knew my dad would have purchased it without thinking twice.

Before I continue, there are two details that must be mentioned. The first is that I was able to stay awake on this day for roughly two to three hours at a time. The anesthesia was wearing off steadily. I was only sleeping because my body was so tired and traumatized from the operations, that after holding conversations with my visitors, I would be overcome with extreme fatigue. The second detail is that my voice was extremely light. I tried to talk, but my vocal chords had been so stressed from the breathing tube, that my voice came out sounding light and breathy. I spoke as though I was doing a poor Michael Jackson impersonation.

My dad hastily threw on his jacket. My mom did the same as they merrily strolled out of my room in search of a small diner where they could relive their youthful dating days with one another. As they left my room, a husky male nurse entered. He was tall and had dirty blonde hair. He wore silver glasses, had a very bold European accent, and an even bolder European name. "Hello! I am Biorski!" he exclaimed. He rolled the "r" when he said, "Biorski!"

Oh shit, this guy is going to be rough, I thought to myself. However, I was wrong. Biorski's job was to remove one of the chest tubes that were dangling from my torso. Biorski proved to have the gentlest pair of man-hands that I have ever encountered.

Resting below my green gown was a multitude of foreign plastic and copper objects. I had five long white tubes with three sets of copper wires woven into three of them. The wires had metal pellets dangling from them; this device was to serve as a temporary pacemaker. My body was decorated in unnatural objects. I felt like a Christmas tree covered in cheap ornaments, all I was missing were the lights. The tubes were stitched into the skin and each stretched about a foot and a half long. At the other end of the tube hung hollow plastic balls. They were the same color as the tube, but they were ribbed, their texture was rough to the touch. On this day I looked down to find two of the plastic balls were filled with blood. Biorski grabbed the two blood-filled balls and dangled them over a yellow bucket. He unscrewed the balls from the tube and then began squeezing the excess blood into the bucket. After reconnecting the balls with their original tubing he looked at me, and in broken English said, "I'm going to remove one-of chest tubes." My heart began to race. I was petrified. I realized that this is was the moment I needed to man-up. I had pre-planned for this moment. I realized that in giving up my mantra I had allowed my brain to accept pain.

"I want you to take deep breath… then, I pull the tube, and you blow out as I pull. Do you understand?" Biorski questioned. "Yeah, lets do this," I responded. I began taking deep breaths as Biorski masterfully cut the stitches with a small blade. He didn't even prick the skin. "Okay, now… breathe!" Biorski screamed at me. I sucked in air, I could feel my eyes enlarge. "Now blow out!" I felt like I was in the midst of a scene from a horrible World War II movie, in which my Russian submarine was about to be struck by a missile. Biorski was my Four-Star General. I was his Lieutenant. His spit splashed against my face as he scream his final command, "Blow Har-dar!" I did as he said, his dirty blonde hair whisked against his face as though he was taking a jog into the wind. Finally, the tube came out. The feeling surprised me, it felt good. The sliding of the tube had scratched the area of the incision, relieving a tickling sensation that had been slowly festering. Biorski threw out the tube, looked around the room with a proud grin on his face, turned to me and abruptly said, "Good-bye." Biorski left. I sat upright in my bed, admiring the newest addition to my scar collection.

There was now a new hole on my body. It was in the shape of an eye. The center of the hole was bright pink, it looked glossy. The outer circumference of the hole was bright white. It looked like I had just been sitting in a pool with an open cut. The skin was raw, very fresh.

My parents entered and I proudly showed them my battle wound. Smiling, my dad handed me a bag. I was too weak to unload the contents on my own, so my mom assisted me in the preparation of my food tray.

My first bite was of the eggs. It had been so long since I had tasted cholesterol, let alone grease. It slid down my throat slowly. Part of me didn't enjoy it. I felt like I had made a mistake. My throat felt slightly thick from the unnatural coat of butter. However, the other part of me loved it. *This has been long overdue,* I thought to myself. I felt the eggs hit my empty stomach, splashing in the abyss of digestive acids. My stomach felt as though it had erupted. The acid tore up through my esophagus, reaching my lower neck, until it trickled back down its original path. I later learned the breathing tube had irritated my throat. This sensation would not leave until the day of my discharge.

I have always had a weird hang-up with food. If I am given multiple types of food in one meal, I must eat each food separately. Sometimes, I go as far as not letting different food groups touch one another on my plate… I think I have a problem.

I wanted so badly to eat the English muffin, but I held back the temptation as the abnormal part of my brain forced the fork to continuously grab eggs. Eventually, the scrambled yolk was a distant memory. I grabbed hold of the muffin and that's when I saw my dad. He was standing in the right corner of the room, smiling from ear-to-ear. He was like a proud father watching his child take its first steps.

My memory of this day ends with the meal. I may have been awake the rest of the day, or I may have taken a lengthy nap. Either way, nothing too eventful happened. I know Karrie came to visit because I woke up the next day to find a plastic bin that you place in a toilet to collect stool resting near the window in my room. Karrie and I had an inside joke and she had written me a note on the collector. I believe it reads, "Get well soon. And don't you ever leave this in my mailbox again!" This plastic collector is still in a box that is stored in my basement today.

Sunday, October 25, 2009

My first memory is of the Chicago Bears playing the Cincinnati Bengals. Sadly, this memory doesn't begin on a happy note. I was very angry as I watched the game. The Bears were simply obliterated. They lost 10-45 on this day. Fortunately, I did not have the ability to watch the full game, for I was stricken by a heightened sense of fatigue. I dosed in-and-out as I watched the game. I couldn't stay awake. I felt powerless.

I must have given in to the exhaustion on this day because my next memory occurs around 8:00 PM.

Stacy entered my room. I was alone. (My family typically never went home before 10:00 PM during these initial days, so I can only assume they went to the cafeteria for dinner). Stacy stared at me. She looked serious, almost as though she was thinking really hard. "How are yah feeling, buddy?" she asked warm-heartedly. "I'm feeling good," I responded. Stacy continued to stare at me as though she was examining every inch of my body, looking for a movement that was out of the norm. "I just wanted to tell you that I am really happy for yah…" she said seriously, "…you look great, I'm proud of yah." I realized then that this was one of the first times that Stacy wasn't carrying on our typical joking relationship. "Thanks so much," I replied. "Yeah, no problem," Stacy said as she started to smile; she looked like she was pleased with what she said. It was as though she had finally told me what she wanted to say before I was wheeled away into surgery. She only stayed for a few more minutes. I showed her my scars and then she left.

Monday, October 26, 2009

Monday, October 26, 2009 was simply a blur. I have only one memory from this day in which two nurses were assisting me out of bed.

"No… no… uuuugh… fuck! No!" I pathetically whimpered to the two nurses. One of the nurses was Biorski, the other nurse was a young, brunette female with faded freckles on her cheeks. They were grabbing at my legs. I had been lying in bed this entire time. Biorski had just informed me that Dr. Getty wanted me to get out of bed. "I don't give a shit… just let me sleep," I muttered under my breath.

"Okay, now Bill… grab hold of my shoulders…" Biorski said as he propped my body upright on the side of the bed. The freckled nurse stood behind me. I could feel her hands on my shoulder blades holding me up from behind.

"Where? Wh- where the fuck are we going?!" I was starting to get mad. I had been awakened several times the night before. My IV pole had gone off on a multitude of occasions. Each time the blinking light read, "AIR IN LINE." I would then have to hit the nurse call light, wait for a voice to respond, and then lay awake for five minutes until she corrected the situation.

"Bill! You are going to stand up. We are going to put you in that chair." Biorski said, as he pointed to a green leather chair that he had positioned to the right of my bed. I understood what I had to do. I recalled following the same routine with my dad during my first week of hospitalization. I also knew that the second I stood up, my knees were going to buckle, much like they did when I grabbed a hold of my dad. "Grab my shoulders!" Biorski asserted again. I put my arms around him, as though we were slow dancing at a middle school dance. I pushed myself up, but I could only raise myself an inch or two off of the bed. That was when Biorski put his hands under my armpits, lifting my frail body to my feet. "Stand! Stand!" Biorski grunted. I tried to, but as anticipated, my knees gave out. I watched my hands slip from Biorski's shoulders. I managed to cling onto two fistfuls of his shirt, saving myself from landing ass-down on the ground. The freckled nurse ran over. She grabbed my left arm as Biorski slid my body to the chair. "All right… now you sit here two hours." Biorski said as he gasped for breath. "Two fucking hours?! Are you serious?!" I replied sounding distraught. Biorski didn't respond. He knew I was too weak to leave the chair. I was stuck.

The room was quiet, but it was obnoxiously loud at the same time. Before the freckled nurse left, she turned on my television and raised the volume to the highest level. I'm sure she was just trying to be nice, she probably assumed I would like some entertainment. Unfortunately, she seemed to subconsciously change the station to a program that she enjoyed. For two hours, I was kept awake by the obnoxious voices of three middle-aged women bickering about their favorite Halloween costumes, recipes, and "tips on how to still make your house spooky

during a recession!" I sat in my green chair furious, pathetically shooting the nurses dirty looks as they passed by my sliding glass door. My
mom then entered.

I remember she was carrying two handfuls of bags. She smiled as she
walked in. She seemed excited to show me the bag's contents. At that
moment I didn't care what she had brought. I had an extreme desire to
share my thoughts with her. "I don't like them." I said, as though my
comment was brilliant. My mom looked at me with a smirk. "They're
assholes." I said after a pause. My mom continued to smirk, "Well
honey, they're not going to be as nice to you as the girls on the CCU.
They're not supposed to be. The CCU's job was to get you to transplant.
This floor's job is to make you get better. They're supposed to push
you." I replied with another delirious comment before drifting off to
sleep.

Tuesday, October 27, 2009

This was a day that I felt a miracle occur within me. I felt my body
regenerate. I believe it was on this day that my body adapted to my two
new organs. Not only did my voice steadily grow stronger as the hours
would pass, but the muscles in my body seemed to strengthen.

My first memory of this day is one in which I am lying on my back,
staring at the ceiling. That was when my Nouna entered the room. She
entered smiling, excited to see me and to give me the meal that she had
cooked. To be honest, I am a bit hazy on what the meal was. I have an
image of pasta, an image of chicken, and an image of broccoli. I may be
remembering three separate meals, but there is also a strong likelihood
that it was all one meal (the three combined would be quite delicious).

It was when I woke up that the miracle began. I noticed my voice
was beginning to sound stronger. Nouna and I spoke for a while. We
discussed how I was feeling and the date that I was anticipating my
discharge to be. I told her that I was shooting for Halloween night. She
looked at me as though my prediction was a bit overzealous. That was
when my nurse entered the room, his name was Bradden. Bradden was
very thin. He had a beard and shaggy brown hair. At first I thought he
was a bit effeminate, but as the hours passed I learned that he was just a
really soft-spoken guy.

I remember the blinds on my window being closed. The room was dark, and both my mom and Nouna wanted sunlight. I enjoyed the darkness though. The dark atmosphere allowed me to sleep whenever I chose to. Bradden said he was going to remove another chest tube. Both my mom and Nouna left the room squeamishly. They announced that they were going to get coffee from the cafeteria, as they quickly threw their purses over their shoulders and fled from the scene. "You've done this before, so you know what to expect," Bradden said. "Yeah, I know. It really isn't that bad," I replied. Sadly, I was mistaken. My frame of reference of a chest tube removal, was a removal of a tube that was stitched into the skin. I didn't realize that one of the tubes was lodged between my ribs.

"Are you ready?" Bradden questioned. "Yeah, lets do this shit," I joked back. Bradden didn't find it too funny. "Deep breath… now blow out!" Bradden said as he tugged at the tube. The chest tube didn't move. Instead, I felt a sharp sting tear through my chest cavity. "Ah, what the fuck! What the fuck, man!" I scream at him. Timidly, Bradden let go of the tube and looked at me puzzled, "I don't know… it's not coming out." "What?!" I said in disbelief. "Take a breather, I am going to go speak with the Resident… we may need to get a surgeon in here to take this one out," Bradden uttered under his breathe. He looked scared.

I put my hands over my eyes, waiting for the pulsation of pain to fade away. That was when the social worker, Carla, entered. Carla wanted to see how I was feeling. I informed her of my current predicament and her face instantly changed to an expression of disbelief. We spoke for a while, as Carla desperately tried to change the subject to one that was more uplifting. I could tell she was trying to get my mind off of the pain. Bradden re-entered with the Resident. She was blonde and didn't wear makeup. He began to explain that the au-naturale Resident has had a great deal of experience removing these types of chest tubes. "It's the same procedure. You are just going to need to hang in there for a bit longer. It will definitely be a little less comfortable than your first, but if you want me to, I can prescribe some Morphine for the pain," she said. "Morphine" was all I had to hear before giving my consent. I was still quite addicted at this point.

The Resident began to pull. The same pain re-surged, but this time Carla grabbed my hand. She was standing to the left side of my bed as

I screamed every cuss word into the sky. "Okay, that's it," the Resident said as she showed me the tube. Blood was running down the white plastic. "Bradden will bandage the area and I am going to go put in the order for the Morphine."

I can't explain what happened next. It was as though my body reset. Any form of fatigue or pain magically left my body. At that moment I felt renewed. Both Nouna and my mom were back in my room. We began to converse and as we spoke, they each would continuously tell me how much better I was. They were both in awe by my sudden change in behavior. My mom went as far as making phone calls to my dad and some of my aunts to report my good spirits. That was when I had a thought that even surprised me, *I want to walk*. I expressed my latest idea to my mom and she helped me out of bed.

I had an elongated cord attached to my body. The wire was roughly five feet long and it connected the leads on my chest to the monitor above my bed. The leads displayed my heart rhythms on a continual basis. I mention this now for two reasons. The first being that this cord limited my range of movement; it forced me to stay in my hospital room during this initial walk. I paced the room for five minutes, walking from my window to my sliding glass door. The second reason I mention this cord, is because this wire would get me into trouble with Dr. Getty twice in the next twenty-four hours.

The rest of the day was spent experiencing my new body. My brain seemed to process thoughts faster, my motor skills strengthened, and my lungs even felt as though they were inhaling more oxygen. My visitors left early this day. By 6:00 PM, I was alone.

I was feeling so healthy at this point that I managed to go on my laptop for the first time since surgery. I used my food tray as my desk, and began responding to the countless e-mails I had received offering me prayers and well wishes. While I was responding to the e-mails, I began chewing gum. I stood up to throw out the wrapper. As I did, the five-foot cord wrapped around my leg, bringing me tumbling to the ground.

As I mentioned, my thought process seemed quicker. I remember instantaneously thinking to myself, *Whatever you do, land on your back! Do not catch yourself with your hands. Your chest is way too fragile right now!* I spun my body mid-fall, landing on the plastic footrest of my bed. I landed perfectly on the footrest. The force plowed my butt crack. Slowly, I slid down the plastic as though the footrest was a credit card and my cheeks were the register.

I was on my knees at this point, desperately trying not to move. I heard a creaking noise coming from my left. I looked up to find the IV pole slowly tipping over. It was coming down on me. I reached up with my left arm and held the pole in the air. Seconds later, three nurses ran in. Two grabbed me and pulled me onto the bed, while the other untangled my legs and moved the IV pole. "What are you doing?!" said one of the nurses. I could clearly see that she was the oldest of the three. I could also see that she was pissed. She had curly red hair, bags under her eyes and a wrinkly forehead. I couldn't help but laugh at the sudden change of events. "I was just trying to throw out my gum wrapper," I said smiling. My nonchalant attitude only infuriated the fiery nurse further. "Do you realize how stupid that was?!" I continued to laugh, I couldn't stop, even though I was telling myself to keep a straight face. "I was just trying to keep a tidy room," I replied like an ass. She rolled her eyes and the three nurses left. Each of the nurses exchanged looks of disgust and began whispering to one another. I knew they were talking about me, and the fact that I knew they clearly did not like me only made me laugh harder for the rest of the night, especially when they would pass my room, glaring at me through the glass door.

Dr. Getty was on his way out of the hospital at this point. He received word of my tumble and made a pit stop in my room.

"What are you doing?!" he asked. I remember thinking, *Does everyone on this floor begin conversations with that phrase?* Dr. Getty didn't even try to hide his anger as he continued to reprimand me with his accent. "Don't you understand that the surgery to correct the damage that you could have caused is not only ten times more complicated, but it is ten times more painful?!" I knew that I was feeling great at this point when my gut reaction was debate. "I know, I'm sorry Dr. Getty. Yah see, I was trying to throw out my gum wrapper..." Dr. Getty cut me off, "I don't care what you were trying to do..." I then cut Dr. Getty off, "No, but really, it was the cord's fault. I'm not used to having a five-foot cord near my feet." Dr. Getty realized this conversation was going nowhere, sighed and said, "Alright... well just be careful, okay?" I nodded and watched as he walked down the hall shaking his head in disgust. The night was still young. I had one more act of rebellion left in me.

I went to bed around 11:00 PM. I believe it was because my kidneys were finally working correctly that I had an urge to piss something fierce by 12:30 AM. I got out of bed, but realized when I sat down on my toilet that the five-foot cord was getting in the way of me removing my pants. I disconnected the cord from my leads and was pleasantly surprised to find that the monitor didn't begin sounding alarms. I went back to bed and awoke the next morning to Dr. Gordon entering my room.

Wednesday, October 28, 2009

Dr. Gordon was in extremely good spirits this morning. I would say that it was the happiest I had seen him since the day that I met him in late July. "You are doing extremely well. Everyone on the team is very pleased with your progress," he said. As he spoke he paced from my sliding glass door to the window on the right side of my room. Dr. Gordon began detailing my day. He explained that I would undergo my first post-transplant biopsy to verify that rejection hadn't begun. If all went well, I will be transferred to 11 West. 11 West was to be the final stop. Once I made it to that floor, it would only be days until I could return home. No sooner did Dr. Gordon finish his explanation, Dr. Getty was back at my door, looking angrier than before.

Dr. Getty looked as though he had prepared a speech, yet he seemed to be at a loss for words. "Do- do you- what are you doing?!" he said. *Oh shit, I'm in trouble.* I thought to myself. "Last night, you took your leads off?! Don't you understand that we lost that entire period of time to have data on your heart?! There could be a complication right now and we wouldn't even know about it!" I looked over to Dr. Gordon. He was staring at the wall and avoiding eye contact with both Dr. Getty and myself. I knew then that Dr. Gordon was siding with Dr. Getty. I was on my own. "I'm so sorry. I truly did not mean to do that. I meant to take them off, but I forgot to put them back on. I had to go to the bathroom and it wasn't working too well with the cord. I couldn't get my pants off..." Dr. Getty had heard enough. He began talking louder over me. This in turn caused me to speak over him. "I really respect what you have to say! I truly am sorry. It won't happen again. You have no idea how much I appreciate everything that you have done for me. It was a misunderstanding." Dr. Getty once again gave up on the argument. He shot Dr. Gordon a look as if to say, *What are we going to do with this kid?* Dr. Getty then left. Dr. Gordon looked at me baffled as though he had no idea that I had removed the cord. "Uh... well... just try to not do that again," he said.

Bradden was my nurse again on this day. He later entered to remove the remaining chest tubes, leaving only the temporary pacemaker in place. He told me that I would be taken down to the lab for my biopsy momentarily. Sure enough, like magic, a bed was soon waiting for me outside of my room. My mom entered only minutes before my departure. She waited for me in my room while I was wheeled down the all too familiar halls of Mercy Care. The procedure went flawlessly. I was wheeled back to my room where I spent the next two hours coming out of the sedation.

I awoke to find another bed waiting to escort me. It was 4:00 PM when I was wheeled away to 11 West. I was finally stable enough to not require Intensive Care. Though I want to write about how "glorious" my room was, I can't because I had been on this floor for roughly five days in the early weeks of September. I knew what it was going to look like. There was no surprise. I was on this floor when Irene sent me the letter telling me that I was inspirational to her, the night she kept me afloat. I will say, however, I was ecstatic to have a door on my bathroom. It had been a long time since I was able to enjoy that type of amenity.

The remainder of this day was spent visiting with family. I believe my cousin Estelle came to visit, along with Aunt Patti. I remember gorging on everything that was brought into my room. I had an uncontrollable feeling of hunger. I went to bed counting the days. I was so close to home. I could taste it.

Thursday, October 29, 2009 – Friday, October 30, 2009

I chose to bunch this forty-eight hour period of time together because nothing happened. Honestly, if I even tried to write about these days in full detail, I would bore myself to sleep. Therefore, I can only imagine how painful it would be from a reader's perspective. Truthfully, I felt incredible. I felt like my old self. (If my old self had absolutely no muscle mass and wasn't allowed to lift anything more than three pounds.) I did have a great deal of back pain though. I was apparently positioned awkwardly during surgery. My arms were tied behind my head for nearly twenty hours. Consequently, I had horrific knots in my back. My multitude of visitors happily massaged the knots out of me during this period of time.

These days were spent talking to doctors, watching television and spending time with Karrie, Ashley and Melissa. I also ate everything in sight. Because Halloween was approaching, I received many gift baskets of candy. I ate so much candy, that at one point, my glucose level had reached 540 (an incredibly high level, technically diabetic).

I did have a minor complication, which caused a bit of concern during these days. My groin leaked profusely. The right side of my groin was used not only for the dialysis treatment just before my heart transplant, but it was used a second time for the biopsy. There was a hole in my skin, which would not stop seeping fluid. The hole would not close because the force of the water never allotted the leg an opportunity to heal. Dr. Getty assured me the hole would close in two weeks time. Unfortunately, I had to spend these days going into my bathroom, almost hourly, to tape different types of bandages to my groin.

Any event that merits any attention on these pages occurred on Halloween and the day after.

Saturday, October 31, 2009 - Halloween

Why was Halloween interesting? Well, I certainly wasn't frolicking door-to-door dressed as a pirate yelling, "Trick-or-Treat!" Halloween was interesting because I woke up weaker than I had been throughout my entire battle with this illness, including my days at Chicago General. When I say "weaker," I don't mean physically. I felt healthy, like a stallion. I was emotionally weak. I was mentally tapped. There was nothing left in the tank. I was running on fumes.

I awoke on my own. Dr. Gordon wasn't there, my nurses were not there, nobody, just me, myself and I.

I went to the bathroom where I began to poorly bathe myself with a washcloth. I threw cold water in my face and when I looked up I saw every scar. Five holes, they looked like bullet wounds. A six-inch scab where my chest was sliced, and my entire abdomen was stained blue. (The 11 West floor routinely gives its patients Heparin shots in an attempt to thin their blood. The worry is that the patients will develop blood clots from being so immobile.) My shoulders were blue as well; I saw the small circles where needles had gone in. My hands were trembling. I had been on my new anti-rejection drug, Prograf, since October 22, 2009. Hand tremors are a very common side effect of Prograf. This particular morning, I had no control. The last time I looked in a mirror and saw the same sight was the day I realized I was going to die; the day that I chose to fight. I realized this morning that I had come so far. It had been so long since I had been at home, even longer since I had felt healthy at home. That's when I broke down crying. I truly lost it. I cried so hard that my entire body shook. I wanted to go home, I didn't want visitors, and I especially didn't want small talk. I only wanted a warm shower and my own bed.

On this day, my mom's friend, Derrick, and his wife were planning to visit. I rarely ever see them, so I don't know them very well, nor do they know me. I probably only speak to them two, maybe three times a year. Like I said, the last thing I wanted on this day was small talk.

I was under the impression they were coming in this weekend not to see me, but to spend time with Derrick's parents. I was told my hospital room was nothing more than a stop in their trip. I picked up the phone and immediately called my mom. Keep in mind, I was sobbing as we spoke.

"What's wrong?" my mom said concerned. "I can't take this shit anymore, I need to get the fuck out of here!" I yelled into the phone. I was beginning to hyperventilate. "Calm down, relax, oh Bill… I know, I know, you have been there for so long, you are almost out. You are so close," she said in the most motherly voice imaginable. "I don't want visitors, I really do not want visitors. Can you please call Derrick and tell him that I don't want people here and to just go straight to his parent's house?"

She quickly responded with, "Yes honey, I'll do that." I heard my dad in the background, "What's going on? What's wrong?" My parents began talking, I couldn't make out what they were saying. Finally, my mom remembered I was on the phone, "Your father is getting dressed now, is it okay if we come? Aunt Patti was planning on coming today, too. Should I tell her to not come?" Aunt Patti was probably one of the few people who I could have handled speaking with on this day, so I told my mom to only grant Aunt Patti visitation.

My Halloween nurse was Kristen. Oddly enough, Kristen was a good friend of Karrie. Karrie used to work on Mercy's fourteenth floor with Kristen before they each transferred departments. Kristen walked in to find me crying at my chair. She was really cool about it. She comforted me and then went on a mission to find the on-call doctor to see if she could push for a discharge. Unfortunately, Kristen's attempts failed. I was informed the only doctors who could discharge me were either Dr. Krause or Dr. Getty. Both doctors did not work again until Monday. I was screwed.

My parents arrived about two hours later. My dad entered like always, bearing food. My mom walked in with two bags of chips and left over candy. She first comforted me and then began to complain about the weak traffic flow of children. She said she felt old because she realized our neighborhood had grown up, and the once large amounts of trick-or-treaters had grown into college-aged students.

My parents did their best to occupy my mind. They did so for nearly four to five hours until Aunt Patti arrived. It was like a changing of the guard. My parents gave up. Aunt Patti was their reinforcement.

I enjoyed my time with Aunt Patti. This part of the day seemed to go by much faster. We spoke for a while until Melissa showed up. Somewhere in our conversation, I mentioned to Melissa that I was experiencing horrific muscle pain. Melissa got excited and offered to show me a massage trick she learned at her yoga class. She had me lay down on the bed, and in some weird, mystical way, she jarred my muscle and I heard my entire spine pop. The pain was gone. I was literally speech-less. I had to remind myself to swallow my saliva. Melissa got a kick out of my reaction. She laughed with her infectious giggle. The three of us continued our talk in which Melissa invited me to her upcoming wedding the following summer. Melissa's fiancé then texted her; he was outside waiting to pick her up. Melissa left and Aunt Patti and I continued our conversation.

We spoke about my future. Aunt Patti began telling me how she only sees a brilliant 2010 ahead of me and asked me for my predictions on what the next year of my life has in store. I told her that I wasn't expecting to be fully recovered until after Christmas. I assumed that by my birthday in April, I would not only be 100% recovered, but I expected to be in talks with a publisher or at the very least finalizing this book. Finally, I pledged that next Halloween was going to be much better than this one. Aunt Patti smiled. She was in total agreement.

Sunday, November 1, 2009

I awoke at exactly 11:55 AM. I know this because I panicked when I realized the kickoff to the Chicago Bears/Cleveland Browns game was on in minutes. I didn't bother to bathe until the game was over at 3:00 PM. During this period of three hours, both my dad and Peter came to visit. I would also receive a very interesting message on my Facebook wall.

Much like I have always done on game day, I turned on my laptop about fifteen minutes into the game. I logged onto my Fantasy Football account and watched real-time stats fly across the screen. Once I was fully situated with Fantasy Football, I checked Facebook.

Before going to bed on Halloween night, I changed my status. I wrote, "CANNOT TAKE THIS SHIT ANYMORE… I NEED TO GO HOME!" This was the first time in 68 days that I complained via Facebook. I never once searched for pity from the outside world. I thought it was weak to even do such a thing. But as I said, Halloween was my weakest day.

For those who read this and do not understand social networking websites, a "status" is simply your current thoughts and activities. You tell the public what you are doing, thinking, or sometimes, what you wish you were doing. Anybody who sees that status has the ability to comment or share his or her opinion on your thought. It is basically an open forum on your mind. As the Internet has evolved, so has the practice of social networking. Etiquette has developed, but much like any form of etiquette, you basically just need common sense and a conscience to not break social networking etiquette. I learned on this morning that Derrick's wife has absolutely zero etiquette.

Derrick's wife is a nurse. She works on a floor similar to the one that I was in post transplant. She is the "Biorski" of Michigan. Because of her profession, she apparently believed that she was qualified to make her comment.

For the purposes of this book, I wish I had saved the comment. I would have italicized it and shared it with my readers so that the ugliness of her comment could be fully understood. But on this Sunday morning, I was so hurt, shocked and appalled by what she had written, I had to delete my entire status along with the comment just so I could log onto Facebook again that day and not experience the same "knife in my stomach" feeling.

She wrote something to the affect of: I have ABSOLUTELY NO RIGHT to complain. She then went into a two to three paragraph reprimand in which she told me that I should think about the donor family and imagine the sorrow that they are feeling. She then reminded me that I should be grateful to be leaving, and that I could be in the situation where I was going to die and never leave the hospital.

I was taken aback, mostly because she had me so wrong. She had no idea that since the day I found out about my need for a new heart and kidney, I had done nothing *but* think about the donor family. She didn't know about the nights where I would go to bed praying for life and then feel horrible at the same time for wishing death upon a complete stranger. Had she even taken the slightest interest in my life over the past four months, talked to me, or at the very least, sent me an e-mail, she would have known that I *was* grateful to be leaving. She would have known that I had been in the situation where I realized I was going to die. In fact, for quite sometime, I was convinced that I was never going to leave the CCU. I believed the faces of Karrie, Ashley and/or Melissa were going to be my last sight on this Earth as they attempted to resuscitate me.

The rest of this day is a blur, not because I was sick or unconscious. It was a blur because she reminded me that someone had died for me to be living. She launched me into an emotional haze. Her reminder made me feel horrible about being alive. I didn't need the reminder; I had already vowed to live the rest of my life honoring this stranger's life. I knew my recovery was going to be painful. I promised myself to do my best to only complain of my pain in these pages. If I had to, I would only cry to my mom.

From here on out, I returned to my journals.

The following is my documentation of how I returned to the life that I had been longing for.

The Journals:

Recovery

Monday, November 2, 2009 –

Monday, February 22, 2010

SURVIVAL

How did I survive? This is a question that I have been left asking myself repeatedly since the moment I came out of the general anesthesia. I knew the answer; I just didn't want to admit it because I was so ashamed of it being the truth. Though as much as I try to hide from the truth and sweep it under the carpet in my mind, the truth is too ugly to conceal. I had to become a different person. I was not myself the entire hospital stay. I became a two-faced rendition of myself. I was myself only to my doctors and nurses. To my biological family, I was a prick. I took everything out on them, mostly my mom. My mom was the easiest target. I knew deep down she was never going to go anywhere. I could shovel as much shit as I wanted at her, and I had the comfort of knowing she'd always be by my bedside.

I referred to my mom as being a part of my "biological" family. I say this because in order to survive, I made my nurses and my doctors my family. I treated them like gold. I considered my conversations with them to be more valuable than my conversations with my parents. Their advice seemed more logical and they seemed to understand me more than anyone in my other family could.

What most disgusts me about my survival technique is the way I manipulated so many people. I took complete advantage of members from both of my families. The hospital family's manipulation was a tad more innocent than what my biological family endured. I only took advantage of their kindness and eventually their admiration for me. Besides lying to them about my pain levels so that I could get a Morphine fix, I would vent to them. The slightest issue that would arise with my mom or any biological family member would be expressed to my nurses. Eventually, I noticed a couple of my nurses began treating my mom a little colder than they had in the past. The nurses began joining my side, a force against establishment and the individuals who I thought were insensitive.

My biological family was emotionally brutalized by my actions. I took everything out on them. No matter what they said, in my mind, they were completely wrong. I would continuously say, "You have no idea what I am going through!" Because they knew I was right, they could say nothing. This is why I progressively grew angrier with my mom as the weeks went by. My mom would be the only one who would say, "You don't know what I am going through as a mother!" This, in turn, would anger me, thus beginning the vicious cycle of the venting to my nurses. My nurses would then get angry with my mom, which would then make me feel better about myself. Meanwhile, the underlying problem was that I was looking for something to control.

My need for control was the culprit. I had control over nothing. I couldn't control my kidneys, I couldn't control my heart beat, I couldn't control my fate. I lived everyday with the fear that I was going to die. I would take naps in the middle of the day, and before I fell asleep, I'd have the realization that I may never wake up.

I did what I had to do to survive. I am not proud of it. I know I will probably spend the rest of my life angered by my actions. However, if I were to go back, I would do it all over again. It's because on December 28th, I am moving into my studio apartment. On April 24th, I will be turning twenty-one. Next May, I will graduate college. Someday I will get married. I am not proud of what I did, but I am going to live because my insensitive actions are what saved my life.

I'm doing everything I can to revert back to the person that I once was. I don't ever want to be the ugly person I became. Never again will I manipulate. Never again will I be the Puppet Master.

Monday, November 2, 2009

I cried a lot today. However, for the first time since June, the tears were those of joy. I was finally discharged after 70 days (ten weeks) in the hospital.

The discharge process is very monotonous. Every doctor, from every team, has to come in, say their final peace, and arrange a follow-up appointment for sometime in the coming month.

Appropriately, the first team of doctors to visit was Dr. Krause, Dr. Gordon, and Chloe. Dr. Krause was a bit skeptical about discharging me because I have had an elevated white blood cell count for the past three days. His concern was that I might be developing an infection. Due to the fact that I have not had a fever and I am on large amounts of Prednisone, (which has raised my white blood cells multiple times throughout my stay) it was agreed that I could be discharged with an assortment of antibiotics.

I waited a few hours, anxiously staring at the clock. I found out that I was being discharged at roughly 10:00 AM. I did not leave the hospital until 4:00 PM. The six hours felt like an eternity. Fortunately, my cousin, Estelle, visited at 2:00 PM. Estelle, along with my mom, helped break up the time as I fantasized about breathing fresh air.

Around 3:00 PM, a hospital pharmacist delivered my pills. I was lectured on my new regiment and told when each individual pill was to be taken. I am currently on sixteen different medications. Each drug has a different function ranging from anti-rejection to (believe it or not) Viagra. It was during this time that both Karrie and Ashley entered to say good-bye. Ashley walked into the room, but then immediately turned around when she began to cry. She was so genuinely happy for me that she was unable to contain herself. It is moments such as those that make me excited for the future, as I look forward to continuing my friendships with my nurses.

The pharmacist exited while my nurse entered. She removed the IV from my arm. I felt like a prisoner being freed from Death Row. The ball and chain that was my IV pole had finally been detached.

I bent over. My back was to the door. I began to pick up a bag, which was filled with boxers and toiletries. That was when I heard footsteps enter the room. I turned around to find Dr. Gordon and Dr. Krause. They had come to say their final good-bye. This is when my day began to get emotional. Dr. Gordon stood there. At the same time we each reached out and hugged one another. "Thank you so much for everything," I said in his ear. I felt a lump in my throat begin to build. I turned my head as though I had heard something come from the other side of the room in an attempt to buy a few seconds to collect myself. I looked back, and Dr. Krause was standing there, his arm stretched out waiting to shake my hand. I shook it and thanked him for all his hard work as well. We briefly discussed how a Home Healthcare nurse would be coming to my house tomorrow to draw blood. We said good-bye once again before they left. My mom and I picked up what was left of my possessions, said farewell to Estelle, and exited the hospital room for the final time.

My mom and I were alone on the elevator. It was then that reality sank in. I flashed back to July 30th, the day that I met Dr. Gordon and Dr. Janpour. I was so ill that I had almost blacked out walking from the car to the elevator. I was now a changed man. I was cured. I began to cry. This time I couldn't stop the tears. This time I didn't try to. The walk back to the car was roughly four minutes long, the tears poured down my face the entire time. Bystanders looked at me sadly. I figured they must have assumed I had just lost a family member. I continued to cry and did not stop until I was in the car and on the road heading home.

I returned home to a great surprise. My entire neighborhood was decorated with heart-shaped balloons and signs leading to my house. I pulled into the driveway to find nearly sixty people, all friends and family. They gathered with cameras as they cheered and whistled. I was handed a bouquet of flowers and asked to pose with the group. I was speechless the entire time. I mouthed, "Thank you," repeatedly. I celebrated with everyone for fifteen minutes until I began to grow cold and slightly weak. My mom noticed my fatigue and pulled me into the house. Only my close family members were granted access to my home. (I was too immune compromised to have many visitors. Even my family had to wear masks when they were in the house.)

I spent the next two hours with my family as we ate food and discussed my plans for the future. It was then I decided to take a shower. I hadn't taken a shower since August 23rd; I had been fantasizing about the sound of the shower head for weeks.

The walk upstairs was difficult for an assortment of reasons. The first problem being, I do not have a fully functioning leg at the moment. My left groin currently has twenty staples in it from my kidney transplant. The staples begin at my belly button and make a horseshoe pattern down to my groin. Due to the placement of the staples, I have a great deal of discomfort when I take steps with my left leg because the waistband from my boxers rubs against the staples. Another issue I am dealing with is my leaking leg. Because the area requires so many bandages and a great deal of surgical tape, the mobility of my right leg has been compromised. The walk upstairs took a total of three minutes. When I reached the top of the stairs I felt as though I had achieved greatness. I was exhausted, but I felt like a champion.

Never in my life had I removed my clothes as quickly as I did. I ignored the fact that surgical tape is extremely adhesive when I ripped all the bandages off of my groin. I turned on the shower head. I anxiously waited for the perfect temperature as I periodically grazed the water with my hand. When the water was just how I had imagined it, I entered the shower, taking my time as I pulled each damaged leg over the tub carefully. That was when I felt the water hit the back of my neck and slide down my frail body. I lifted my head backwards and stared at the ceiling. The water crashed against my scalp, and I instantaneously broke down sobbing. "I fucking did it!" I said gasping for air. "I survived… I fucking made it!" I felt a rush of heat consume my body, like a wave of blood had filled every one of my veins at the same time. I looked down, and through my tears I could see the water was gray, gray with white spots. My skin had been so dirty and poorly managed for so long, it was shedding as the dirt ran off of my body. Even in my emotional state, I could not help but find the beauty in the filth that was the water. I had completed the darkest chapter of my life. I had been through Hell. I had watched all of my dreams slowly fade away. I witnessed countless deaths, countless tears, and developed more emotional scars in the past seventy days than I had in a lifetime. But there I was. At the end of it all I was still standing. The final piece of skin fell off of my body and the water became clear. It's time to begin the next chapter in my life.

It's time I find happiness.

Tuesday, November 3, 2009

As I sit around in my house and look toward the future, I find myself constantly looking backwards in time. I begin to relive the painful moments. The moments when I was depressed, anxious, or even close to death. I started thinking about all the people who pulled me out of those moments, the people who saved my spirit and were able to pull my mind away from the dull existence in which I was living. I began to compile a list. The list featured everyone who I could think had helped me at some point in the past five months. The list is already sixty strong and I know there are many names I have yet to think of.

To write a personalized letter to every individual on the list will not only take a great deal of time, but it will require a lot of energy that I do not have. I worry about the time factor because I want to say thank you to all of the people as soon as possible. I am filled with such gratitude that I almost feel my mental recovery cannot begin until I give thanks. I chose to write a standard letter, which I can send to everyone on my list. Then, if I had received a gift at some point, I would handwrite a thank you on the footer of the letter.

The following is the letter that I am sending to everyone who saved me:

What does it mean to "Swim?" I have spent a great deal of time over the course of the past five months reflecting on the very word. To me, "Swim" means to fight, it means to persevere, to never give in and push until the day that your life has been restored and you can find inner peace through normalcy.

However, one cannot swim alone; it is merely impossible. There are days where you find yourself sinking, drowning into the abyss of the unknown. It is on these days that you need to reach out and find something to hold onto in an attempt to keep yourself afloat.

If you have received this letter, you helped me swim. At one point in the past five months you gave me hope, you made me smile, and you helped keep me alive. You gave me the momentum that I needed to fight for another day and reminded me of all the amazing people in my life. For this, I am forever grateful.

Thanks for the push,
Bill Coon

It felt like an emotional release writing this letter. It's important to give thanks.

Wednesday, November 4, 2009

Today was unexpectedly spent at Mercy. Early yesterday morning, I had a Home Healthcare nurse come to my house and draw my blood. It took a long time for the results to come back. Today, I received a call from one of the outpatient coordinators who informed me that my white blood cell count was at 26. I know from my days at the hospital, a white blood cell count is not supposed to be any higher than 13. Dr. Krause was uncomfortable with the number and asked me to drive into the city so he could run a few tests.

The first test was a simple blood draw to collect vials for lab work and blood cultures. I then had to fill yet another cup for a urine analysis. I went to the 19th floor where I met a really nice woman named Vonna. She really took her time to assure that the blood draw was as painless as possible. She seemed really affected after I told her that I had been in the hospital for seventy days. She saw how bruised and battered my arms were from the countless needles, IV's and picc lines. The entire stop lasted maybe five minutes. My mom and I then headed down to the 18th floor to meet with Dr. Krause.

Dr. Krause looked very concerned. I could see in his face that he was thinking of every possible cause for an elevated white blood cell count. Finally, it was determined I would need to get a CT scan before I could leave the hospital. The belief is that I might have a pocket of infection somewhere in my body that my immune system is naturally trying to fight off, thus increasing my white blood cell count.

An hour and a half later, I found myself getting into the CT scanner. The technician was a young Asian woman. I asked her, "I just had a kidney transplant, so I have twenty staples that stretch from my stomach to my inner groin. This isn't going to be a problem with this scan, will it?" She assured me that I'd be fine and pressed a button that slowly raised the bed of the scanner off of the ground. The machine started to spin and began prompting me when to breathe. "Breathe deep," the CT scanner said in a robotic voice. I took in a large breath of air, but then found myself gasping when I felt each of my twenty staples vibrate and shock me from within. *That lying bitch!* I thought. The scanner continued to go back-and-forth through the machine three more times. I noticed there was a clear bar at the center of the machine, which caused the vibrations and shocks to occur whenever my staples passed through. With each pass, the pain worsened. I did my best to focus on the voice prompting me, but by the time I made the final pass, my brow was shimmering with sweat and I had a single tear running down my face. I left the hospital limping. With every step, my staples would tingle.

The ride home proved to be a horrible continuation of the CT scan. Every pothole and abrupt turn felt like another pass through the bar. I have given in to the fact that I am physically spent. My once superb pain threshold is now a distant memory. I cannot take any more pain. I need at least a month off from any procedures.

Thursday, November 5, 2009

My entire day was spent at the hospital again. I awoke around 8:00 AM today and had an hour to shower, wash my face, brush my teeth, bandage my groin and get dressed. That was when I received a call from Mercy informing me that yesterday's CT scan showed a large pocket of water around my new kidney. I was informed that the entire Cardiology staff is concerned, and they want me to come in and have a procedure called a "tap" performed. I spoke with my mom before obliging the Cardiology team's request.

It took roughly an hour and fifteen minutes to get into the city, and another twenty minutes to get upstairs. Something I forgot to mention, was that I awoke this morning with another episode of Gout in my right ankle. Because of this, my mom had to run into the hospital to find a wheelchair, as I hobbled along after her.
Before I went in the operating room for the tap, I had to first get my blood drawn on the 19th floor. I then headed to the 18th floor for a visit with Dr. Shao. We discussed my right ankle. She said I would

either be given Colchicine to treat the Gout or some Dilaudid to ease the pain. She mentioned that she would discuss the options with Dr. Getty and then she'd bring a script to me in the waiting room.

My mom then wheeled me to the fourth floor where I strapped on a gown, had an IV placed into my left forearm, and then had an "Allergy Alert" band placed on my wrist. I had just gotten done wearing the red allergy band for seventy days. The band itself nauseated me to the point that I could not stand the sight of my own wrist.

The surgeon then entered from behind the curtain. He was of Latin decent. He spoke very slow and calmly. He explained the procedure in great detail. He described how a needle was to be inserted into the side of my torso, where he would then attempt to suction the fluid. He explained the process could take up to an hour and then he left to prepare for the procedure. His nurse entered and wheeled me into the operating room.

I asked for a great deal of Fentanyl when we entered the room. I explained to the nurse how I no longer have a tolerance for pain. She must have sympathized with me because moments later, I tasted the bitter tang of saline and I began laughing. "I think you drugged me!" I said hysterically. She smiled at me as though I was making an ass of myself. She reached into her pocket, pulled out another syringe, and injected a clear solution into my IV. That's when I fell asleep.

I do not know how long I was asleep for, but I woke up when the surgeon entered. He was scanning my stomach with a portable ultrasound as he rambled off numbers and words that I had never heard before. "Okay, I'm going to give you some Lidocaine," he said. I felt the familiar Lidocaine needle pierce the skin. "I can't take any more pain! Can I have some more sedation, please?" The surgeon nodded his head to the nurse. I fell asleep again.

I woke up one more time and saw a syringe in the left side of my body filling with a clear liquid. I didn't feel a thing, but the sight of the procedure startled me. "Holy shit!" I exclaimed. My language must have offended them because I immediately tasted saline and once again fell asleep.

I awoke in the recovery room. My mom was sitting by my bed. I lay there for an hour until I was finally placed into the wheelchair and sent home.

The ride home today was painless. I can thank the leftover sedation for that.

Monday, November 9, 2009

I have been dealing with a great deal of discomfort at the spot of my two incisions. The staples in my groin continue to ache with every step. Fortunately, tomorrow I have a clinic appointment with Cardiology and they have agreed to remove my staples, as opposed to me scheduling a separate appointment with Nephrology.

The other discomfort that I am experiencing isn't necessarily pain. It's more obnoxious than anything. My chest is very mangled. Not only do I have three old scars from my infant transplant, but I now have an additional five holes on my chest from the chest tubes that I had the initial week after surgery. The holes are scabbing nicely. Actually, one scab has already dried up and fallen off, leaving a very small scar that is only noticeable if you closely examine my body. The other scar is about six inches long and stretches from my collarbone to the center of my chest. This scar is healing extremely well. I'd estimate that of the six inches, there is only four inches of scabbing remaining. I am healing quickly, but within the healing lies the discomfort.

I am experiencing these sensations. I can only describe them as pulsations. It's as though both my kidney and sternum will randomly heal, causing a wave of pain to shoot through the scar. The pulsations occur at random times and there seems to be no way of predicting the pain. There have been times that I have been mid-sentence, when I am suddenly stricken with a pulsation. I just sit there clenching my fists. Sometimes I moan from the pain until it leaves. The scars also itch. However, I cannot scratch the scars because the areas are too delicate. Unfortunately, I am not allowed to put any ointments on the scars either. My day was spent trying to preoccupy myself and forget about the tickling sensation.

I feel like an asshole as I sit here and complain about such trivial problems. A month ago today, I was experiencing my final good day before my downward spiral of infection and kidney failure began. I could be so much worse off right now... I could be dead.

God bless my donor.

Tuesday, November 10, 2009

I had my first biopsy today since being out of the hospital. I do not remember the procedure because I opted to receive sedation. I only recall meeting with Dr. Krause. He lowered my Prograf dosage and scheduled my second post-transplant biopsy for next Thursday.

The true highlight of the day was my return to the leasing agency of my studio apartment. My mom surprised me this morning when we got into the car by offering me the opportunity to go sign a lease after the biopsy. I excitedly accepted, and around 3:00 PM I returned to my studio apartment.

I met with Wendy, the same woman who gave my mom, Aunt Patti and me a tour back in July. She remembered me and recalled my entire situation. She showed me a unit on the seventh floor. It was the exact model I was forced to give up on the ninth floor. I was ecstatic! I had dreamt of stepping foot into my studio apartment for so long, and today it all became a reality. I felt this feeling of satisfaction come over me. I had beaten the disease, and now I will soon enjoy the splendors of success.

My mom and I went to Wendy's office where we discussed the lease and the fine print of the paperwork. I signed a 15-month contract and chose to move in on December 28th. I figured this would give me enough time to move everything in and get situated before the New Year began.

My life is all coming together. On Thursday, I sign up for classes at Columbia, today the staples came out, and tomorrow Irene is coming to visit me at my house. I am really excited to see her. It has been so long. I miss spending time with her.

Wednesday, November 11, 2009

Irene visited today. It was so nice to see her, especially in street clothes. Irene arrived at my house around 12:30. Fittingly, we immediately went for a walk together outside. I hadn't walked around the CCU with Irene since late September, so it was such a rewarding feeling being free from the IV pole and feeling fresh air as we walked around the block reminiscing about our CCU laps. When Irene and I used to walk around the CCU, we would always talk about hanging out when I was discharged. However, when Irene and I would discuss plans, it would always seem more like a fantasy, as though the possibility of us grabbing lunch one day was so far into the future that it almost seemed unlikely.

"Hey you need to slow down, you're walking too fast," Irene said with a smile on her face. It was then I noticed I was walking at least two steps ahead of her. "I'm sorry," I replied. "I guess I'm just not used to walking with you without having to push a ten pound IV pole," I said happily. Irene smiled at the realization as we continued our walk, eventually making it back to my house.

We began to talk as we sat on my couch petting my dogs. Soon, close to three hours had passed. Upon realizing the time, it occurred to both of us that we each had a great deal of homework to do. We then said good-bye.

Today was the best day since returning home. It certainly went the fastest. I notice that Irene is really good at making time pass. I look forward to seeing her again.

Saturday, November 21, 2009

Today is my one-month anniversary of receiving my lifesaving heart transplant. I was thinking about what I wanted to say in this entry, how I could possibly express my gratitude to my donor. That was when I realized I couldn't. The best I could do is simply describe how wonderful I feel.

I have come a long way since surgery. In fact, I have come a long way since last week. I feel revived. I run up-and-down stairs without effort. I can eat anything I want without thinking twice about sodium. The only pain I experience is muscular pain in my shoulders, and even that

is decreasing as the weeks go by. My life is back on track. My future has
been restored. I am finally happy again.

As much as I want to bask in the glory of my survival, I can't. There is
a thought, which has dawned on me several times throughout the day.
Even though my entire family has been writing me e-mails congratulating me on my "one-month," I know somewhere in the country there
is an entire family in pain. They are faced with the gloomy realization
that a month ago today they lost their loved one. Obviously, I don't
know what the family looks like, but I continuously get this image of
four women sitting at a table as their tears fall on the picture of their
lost family member. I can't shake the image. It's just stuck in my mind.

Sunday, November 22, 2009

I must say, throughout my battle, I witnessed a lot of sadness and pain.
Not only with my situation, but also with the battles of others during
my seventy-day stay in the CCU. There was a lot of death and darkness.
However, through it all, I have witnessed many miracles. I witnessed
God's plan and my strong faith was made even stronger through the
process.

It sounds crazy, but even though I had to literally come a week from
death, knowing what I know now, and after meeting the amazing
individuals who I met, I can see how my life has changed for the better.
God literally repositioned every aspect of my life. To be honest, I
would do it all over again to have the same results. There were times
when I was in the hospital that I felt as though I was singled out by
God and cursed. Now that I have been home for twenty days, I realize
that God did indeed single me out, but I was not cursed. I was chosen
to do something bigger and help people with what I have learned. For
this I am grateful.

Thursday, November 26, 2009 – Thanksgiving Day

What am I thankful for on this Thanksgiving? I should definitely start
with the obvious, I am thankful for my donor. I am thankful for the
unselfish generosity of his/her family. I am thankful they were able to
look outside of themselves during their darkest hour and make a deci-

sion, which saved not only my life, but I can only assume, the lives of many others.

I can imagine they spent this day struggling to find something to be thankful for. Everything positive in their lives must have no comparison to the sadness they felt on October 21st and the sorrow they are still, without a doubt, experiencing. I wish I could do something to help ease their pain, but I know I can do nothing. This thought tore at me as I tried to indulge in the ham and turkey throughout the day. It's 4:02 AM and I still haven't been able to shake the thought from my mind.

The only miniscule comfort I can find for the donor family, who saved my life, is the fact that they have forever joined a community. They have joined the community of those touched by organ donation. The same loving and supportive community who reached out to me during my time of darkness, offering their support, stories and words of encouragement. The very community to whom on this Thanksgiving, I give thanks to.

On this Thanksgiving, I am thankful to no longer feel pain when I move my legs. I am thankful that I no longer have a catheter protruding from my neck, and that I no longer have to take Morphine to get through the day. I am thankful for my unbelievable support system of family and friends. I am thankful for the staff at Mercy Care, who took a man in shambles, and with the power of modern day medicine, pieced him back together stronger than he has ever been.

On this Thanksgiving, I am thankful to be alive.

Friday, November 27, 2009

A great deal of my day was spent cleaning my room and unpacking my winter clothing from storage, as I repacked all of my summer attire.

I realized today that I am going to face a problem this winter. None of my clothes are going to fit me the way they used to. For whatever reason, eighty percent of my winter clothes are tighter muscle shirts. I no longer have muscles, specifically any muscle in the pectoral region. I do not expect to gain this muscle back until the spring, when my winter clothing will have been packed away for months. This realization had me thinking about the concept of time.

It dawned on me that I have been a victim of time since June. I had to wait for a summer to pass until I could meet with Mercy Care. I was depressed by my poor performance during my first cardiac rehabilitation workout when I was only able to walk for a short amount of time. I had to wait fifty-eight days for a lifesaving double organ transplant, which I needed because my twenty-year expectancy was up. I had to spend twelve days recovering until I could go home. Now that I am home, I have to wait out the flu season until it is safe to go in public. I feel like I never have complete control. I'm never in the drivers seat. I'm always riding shotgun to time.

Monday, November 30, 2009

I have been given a lot of shit about my use of narcotics in the hospital. Mostly from my parents, but my five aunts thought they should chime in as well. I will admit they were right when they said I was taking too much, and they were completely right when they said I was addicted in October. But I hate when people judge when they haven't walked in the other person's shoes.

What brings me to this topic today was my conversation with my friend, Marie, over the web cam. I mentioned to her that tomorrow I will be going in for another biopsy and then I have a Urology appointment to remove a stent from my kidney. I told Marie I was going to be receiving sedation for both procedures and she responded jokingly, "You're such a drug addict!" I'm not mad at Marie by any means. I know her sense of humor and I let it slide. However, her comment left me thinking for a long time about how my family viciously judged me when I was in more pain than they could possibly fathom.

I keep finding wonderful changes in myself that were sparked by this disease. In the past, I used to judge people, too. I used to be the first to point fingers, the first to make a joke. But now, fuck that! Unless I have been there, I have no room to say anything. Too bad my aunts never had this realization. It would have saved me a lot of stress.

Saturday, December 5, 2009

I'm very torn inside. I have two conflicting thoughts that have been fighting for dominance over one another throughout the course of the day.

The first is that I feel amazing. From the moment I wake up until the second my eyes shut at night, I feel completely healthy. I have minimal stress. I am twenty-three days away from moving back into my studio. In a little over a week, my friends return from college for winter break. My life couldn't be any better.

However, even though I feel this way, I still have a second thought that makes me feel selfish. I feel like this amazing feeling hasn't peaked. I feel like the quality of my life is being tarnished by the side effects from my medications, specifically Prednisone. Prednisone is one of those drugs that will save your life, but it will take a lot out of your life in return. The drug makes me angry. I hate how I am not myself inside. At times, I am so irritable I feel as though I am going to erupt on the next person who speaks, even if they are not speaking to me.

Prednisone makes you hungry. Today alone I have consumed two bowls of cereal, two grilled cheese sandwiches, a tube of Pringles, an orange, a bowl of pasta, a large serving of green beans, 64 ounces of grape juice, a sundae and a fairly decent sized serving of my mom's beef stew. The majority of my meals were gorged between the hours of 1:00 PM and 7:00 PM. I realize at this pace I am destined to become obese. I am going to need to work on eating a bit healthier when the urge strikes.

When I am not stuffing my face with calories, I am looking at myself in the mirror. I have the pleasure of staring at my puffy "moon face" (as the doctors call it) or at my chest and shoulder cavity, which is completely broken out with acne.

It is when I look in the mirror that I begin to complain about the side effects and I feel selfish. Not only do I feel bad because I know that the alternative is being six feet below ground, but I know someone had to die for me to have the first happy thought. I want to complain to my doctors and have them lower the dosage, but they won't budge until

I am three months post-op. Even then they are saying they will only reduce the dosage 2.5mg a month. I am currently on 20mg. My goal is to debate with my doctors and have the initial tapering be 5mg. I think this is a reasonable request.

Until then, I am stuck at 20mg and I am on eight other pills, which all give me side effects of their own.

I hope I don't come off as ungrateful, I truly feel blessed. I just want to be my easygoing self again and live this life to the fullest. It is just frustrating when you are being held back from achieving your highest potential.

Wednesday, December 9, 2009

I returned to St. Adrian Hospital today. It felt rewarding to not leave in an ambulance. I went to St. Adrian for my first cardiac rehab session.

The room was filled with nurses and two physical therapists. My therapist's name was Anna. She is younger. I'd guess that she is in her late twenties. She is very down to earth and laid back. I began the rehab session by walking on the treadmill. I instantly had a flashback to early summer when my "doctors" at Chicago General had me begin rehab after my defibrillator surgery. As I began the workout at 2 MPH, I recalled how I struggled to complete the test in the early summer months. Now, 2 MPH is a joke. Then, I struggled to breathe. Now, I am able to last the entire thirty minutes, reach 3.5 MPH with no problem, and walk on a 3-inch incline. Then, I lasted just over seven minutes and when it was over, I wanted to cry from my feelings of defeat.

I have come a long way. I was starting to forget about how horrible I felt this past summer. Today was a good reminder. It made me appreciate the minimal physical strength I currently have.

Monday, December 14, 2009

It's funny how people react when I tell them I had a heart and kidney transplant. Everyone goes through the same series of emotions in the exact same period of time, about 50 seconds.

I don't offer the information up to everyone. It's not that I am embarrassed about my transplants, I just don't find the need to flaunt it and fish for some form of sympathy/pity/admiration, or whatever the typical human response may be.

Like I said, everybody's reaction is the same. The person goes through a series of emotions before my very eyes. It's almost as though I can see their mind literally crap out in front of me.

Stage 1: Shock
Total Time: 3 Seconds

This part is very quick, but for some reason I get a sick feeling of pleasure when I see it. Their mouth drops open. It doesn't fully extend, but it gets low enough where I can see their tongue. As their mouth drops, their eyebrows simultaneously begin to slowly creep upward. For whatever reason, the left eyebrow always seems to lift a tad bit higher than the right.

Stage 2: Disbelief
Total Time: 5 Seconds

The eyebrows begin to lower, but the mouth remains open. The eyes start to tighten. Then the individual begins to stare me down as they look deep into my eyes, almost as though with a single blink I am going to tell them the truth. Their head then immediately snaps backwards and the skin on their neck folds. This is where they finally speak. They say the same two words, "No… really?" The "no," is said in a deeper, raspier voice. The "really" follows about a second and a half later, but it is said in a squeaky, high-pitched tone. They almost sound embarrassed.

Stage 3: Dumbfounded
Total Time: 10 Seconds

Stage 3 is my favorite part, but it does not begin until I answer their initial question of "No… really?" "Yeah, on October 21st and 22nd," I respond. I try not to act cocky when I say this, but I feel like it always comes out sounding very nonchalant. The individual then cocks their head to the side (typically to the left, but this seems to change with each person). A noise that I can only describe as "gargling" comes from their mouth, which is then followed by a series of irrational words and statements. "Uh…. are you o-…. can you d-…. so you nev-…. wait… a heart <u>and</u> a kidney?!" I can't help but smile at this point, sometimes I laugh as I respond, "Yeah, the heart was put in on the 21st and the kidney went in the day after." Their eyebrows then scrunch upward again as they say their one-word response, "Woah!"

Stage 4: Curiosity/Concern
Total Time: 25 Seconds

Their brain begins working for them again at this stage. A million questions are then thrown at me all at once. "Are you okay now? Why did you need those transplants? Does it hurt? So can you still go to school? Are you on a lot of medicine? Can you still have sex?" I answer the questions and typically, because this conversation happens in passing, the conversation will end with my answers and a quick good-bye. Eighty percent of the time, the person I ran into will go into the final, fifth stage as I walk away.

Stage 5: Tell Somebody!
Total Time: Unknown, but I typically hear the first 5-6 Seconds

It's interesting how everyone loves to gossip. It's human nature to want to be the one with the big news. I always hear the person grab somebody they are with and start talking about me. "Can you believe that? Do you think he's serious?" I was at an electronic store today, where I went through the stages with an acquaintance who worked there. As I walked away, I began to hear whispers. I turned my head and saw five employees at customer service staring at me. When I locked eyes with them, they all turned their heads and began to pretend to do work.

I love human nature. It's so simple and so sweet.

Wednesday, December 16, 2009

Never has the Christmas tree looked as beautiful as it does this year. The white lights seem to have a life of their own as they illuminate the ornaments that gently rest upon the branches. Each ornament brings back a memory from a Christmas past. The tree itself seems taller,

almost mammoth-like. It stands tall and proud even with the absence
of presents. The uncovered space below the Christmas tree caused me
to ponder on what I want this year for Christmas. Anything that can be
store bought seemed so meaningless and cold. It was then I realized my
Christmas had come early this year, and that I have already received
the greatest gift of all, the gift of life.

This Christmas, I wouldn't be able to stare at this magnificent tree if
it were not for my donor. This Christmas, I get to watch old holiday
films. This Christmas, I get to feel the same excitement I did as a child
on Christmas morning when I'd dash frantically down the stairs to see
what Santa had brought me. I would have never been able to do any of
this if it were not for the family of my donor, who in their darkest hour
mustered the ability to step outside of their pain so that they could take
away mine.

I have thought about it, and I realize what I want more than anything
this year for Christmas. I want the donor family to be happy. Though
it will be extremely difficult, I want them to be thankful they have each
other. I want their holiday to be filled with the same traditions, and for
the New Year to bring them only happiness because they gave me happiness. I am thankful for them, and I am thankful to be alive.

Thursday, December 17, 2009

I have not-so-great news for today.

During my last appointment, the Nurse Practitioner failed to mention
that I would not only be having a heart biopsy today, but I would also
be put through an angiogram and a heart graph exam. This changed
both mine and my mom's day drastically. The procedure lasted two
hours as opposed to the typical forty-five minutes. I then had to be on
four hours of bed rest afterwards instead of the usual one.

I arrived at the hospital and was given my own personal room. I knew
something was weird at this point because I typically am given a bed
in an open space with a curtain. My mom and I were very confused
until my nurse entered and explained that I was going to have multiple
procedures performed. "We were never told any of this!" my mom
said angrily. The nurse paged the on-call doctor to speak with us.

Fortunately, that doctor was Dr. Gordon. He entered along with Dr. Shao. My mom was very upset and began to complain about the lack of communication that we are receiving from the outpatient program. I chimed in with my mom because I too have been very dissatisfied; though my complaints are due to the high Prednisone dosage and the Nurse Practitioner's stupidity. Both Dr. Gordon and Dr. Shao apologized for the Nurse Practitioner's error and answered our main question, "Why the Hell am I having these tests done?" It was explained to us that if a baseline angiogram is collected at eight weeks post-transplant, the data could be compared to the one-year anniversary angiogram. The comparison can help predict any future problems, mainly Transplant Vasculopathy, and pills can be given to prolong the inevitable.

"I'm sorry you guys, I really don't mean to be difficult and take it out on you two," I said. My mom agreed as Dr. Gordon replied jokingly, "You've always been a challenge, Bill."

I was then taken to a different room by a technician where I underwent a simple echocardiogram. Meanwhile, Dr. Shao stayed behind to field more of my mom's questions regarding the procedures. I returned, where after a wait, Dr. Smithison (an Attending from Cardiology) came by to explain the procedure. We discussed how an angiogram had to go through either my groin or my wrist. Unfortunately, each side of my groin is not accessible. My right side has been deemed "off limits" by myself and Dr. Getty due to the excessive leaking that I experienced in my first three weeks after surgery. My left side is not an option because my kidney is in my lower left abdomen. We determined the left wrist was the best bet and I was wheeled into the catheter lab.

I saw the usual staff of cath lab nurses. I know their faces, but I am just now beginning to pick up on their names. There was a new face today. She was young and seemed very excited to see me. I offered to walk into the lab because I have had a multitude of prior experiences where the nurses struggled to get the bed through the doors. When the new girl saw me walk into the room under my own power, she was ecstatic. "Bill! It's so nice to see you!" she shouted. I was confused. I knew I had never seen her in my life, but just to be polite I responded, "It's nice to see you, too!" I tried to match her excitement, but I failed miserably. I was then given a warm blanket and strapped down by two large strips of Velcro. The new girl leaned over the bed. Her brown eyes were squinting from her smile. "I was with Dr. Getty when he put in your heart!" she said proudly. I felt relieved that I wasn't supposed to know her. But I felt like an idiot upon realizing that I was caught in a lie when I said it was nice to see her. The nurse then administered the drugs and I was out.

I awoke when I felt a feeling of warmth come over my left hand. It felt like a ball of fire had just flushed through my skin. I looked over and saw Dr. Smithison sticking a catheter into my wrist. I was so drugged that I thought, *Hmm, that's kind of cool.* I then proclaimed to everyone that I would like some more Fentanyl. Dr. Smithison seemed startled by my announcement. I remember hearing him speak as I drifted back to sleep.

I awoke in my room with my mom on the left side of my bed. She was speaking with my nurse. My arm was pulsating with pain up through my shoulder. I had an air cast on my wrist that was pressing against the incision spot. "It's filled with air. Every couple of hours, I will release some air and the pain should get better," the nurse said when she heard me moan. She left and I bitched about the pain for the next four hours to my mom.

As promised, the nurse released some pressure periodically, but the pain didn't subside. She gave me Dilaudid to numb my arm, but she only gave me .5mg. She was unaware of the fact that I am very immune to all painkillers and .5mg of Dilaudid is like taking an Aspirin to me.

I was eventually discharged and told to keep a close eye on my wrist. If it were to begin bleeding, I was to apply ten pounds of pressure and call "9-1-1" immediately. *Fun*, I thought. *I get to tempt death again.* It had been two months since my last face-off, so I left the hospital excited about the challenge.

It is now 10:45 PM. I still have Fentanyl in my system, along with Versed, Dilaudid and a Norco that I happen to have left over from my Chicago General days. Each of these drugs are supposed to make me tired, but I cannot sleep because the pain is still throbbing in my arm.

I don't have to go back to Mercy until January 7th. I am looking forward to the vacation.

Friday. December 18, 2009

I am trying my hardest to move on. I want to let go of the hospital.
With each passing day the memories seem to fade. They are not as
colorful in my mind. I am actually beginning to forget the names of the
nurses (except Karrie, Ashley, Irene, Stacy, Lauren and Melissa. Those
are names I will never forget).

My friends and family are helping me rediscover myself. They each
are helping me in a different way. My friends bring out my sense of
humor. They inspire my funny side to claw itself out from underneath
the rubble of the ugly me. I feel myself again when I am with them.
My friends don't talk about the hospital, I like that. Instead, they let
me mentally regress back to a time in my life when I was on top of the
world, a time when I didn't have to think about biopsies or my glucose level. We joke as we share stories from high school and college.
Together we plan for a brighter future.

My family helps me, but in a much different way. My family gives me
inspiration and drive. Though all of my cousins do this, Natalie serves
as the prime example. She tells me on a consistent basis that I am "her
hero" and reminds me that the days of Prednisone will someday end.
She tells me to look forward and to never lose sight of the fact that
everything is temporary.

Monday, December 21, 2009

I had a realization today—I wasn't exhausted. It may sound weird, but
today was the first day that I truly understood just how great I actually feel. It was as though I experienced a flashback and I was mentally transported back into my old body. I remembered how I would
feel earlier in the summer after a day of overexertion. I recalled how
I couldn't stay awake, how my breathing would worsen and my feet
would swell to skin-splitting sizes.

Yesterday was my first day since being home that I had plans, which
didn't involve a blood draw or a biopsy. I went to breakfast with Sara
and my former coworkers from Harper College. I later returned home

to work out on the treadmill, where I ran four miles in an hour's time. After showering, Jo picked me up and we spent the night at Jen's house with a large group of friends. I didn't return home until 1:00 AM.

I find it funny that I feel like gloating about not coming home until 1:00 AM. I'm twenty years old and that is a major accomplishment for me. Though the bigger accomplishment to me is that I never once lay down to take a nap today. This time five months ago, breakfast with Sara alone would have done me in for the day.

2010 is going to be great.

Tuesday, December 22, 2009

Today I found out that a childhood friend of mine had died. His death wasn't quick and painless and it didn't happen today. It happened eight years ago.

His name was Brent. We had known each other since we were kids, technically babies. He was the third infant heart transplant in the Midwest and I was the fourth. I surprisingly have many memories of Brent. I remember his thick glasses and his brown hair that was always shaggy, never styled. I remember running up-and-down his basement stairs, playing with his toys and making fun of our younger brothers.

I remember losing touch with Brent. We just stopped hanging out. Years went by and I would quietly wonder to myself why our families had stopped talking. I never questioned my mom. I just assumed they had moved away or our parents had gotten into an unresolved dispute.

Brent's family's Christmas card arrived in the mail today, but Brent wasn't in the family portrait. That's when I learned of Brent's passing. He was thirteen when he went into heart failure. His disease was slightly different than mine. He developed Coronary Artery Disease.

During the past few years I have been trying to reconnect with Brent. I have searched for him countless times on a multitude of social networking sites. Each time the search results returned empty. My parents chose to hold this information from me because they didn't want me to live my life in fear. They didn't want me to think I was going to have

the same fate as Brent. I respect their decision. At the age of thirteen, I would not have been able to handle this information. It is only now that I feel I am able to cope with his death and take the news in a calm manner because I have already survived Brent's tragic fate.
I couldn't fathom going through Hell with the mind of a thirteen year old. The battle would have been lost before it began.

R.I.P. Brent. 1989-2002

Friday, December 25, 2009 – Christmas Day

I will never forget Christmas 2007 because that was the year I cracked my head open when I stupidly jumped off a table and hit the top of my skull on the recessed ceiling of my basement. As a gift from St. Adrian that year, I received seven staples, two hours in the Emergency Room, and a five hundred dollar medical bill.

I don't anticipate me forgetting this year's Christmas either because this Christmas, I learned that I lost the ability to cry.

My Nounó (Greek for Godfather) gave a speech this year. It was very moving and I was genuinely touched by what he said before Christmas dinner was served. He told me how proud he and the rest of the family are of me. He began crying as he said, "I don't think I, or any of us, would have been able to do what you did at the age of twenty." I have never seen him cry before, so I was taken back. I glanced at the crowd of family members and noticed there wasn't a dry eye in the room, except for mine.

I wanted to cry. I knew that I should. I even tried to force it at one point in the speech, but I couldn't shed a single tear. I determined then that I have officially released all of my sorrow. The pity I once felt for myself is now gone. I now feel a sense of strength and accomplishment when I think about the last six months of my life.

This was a very merry Christmas.

Monday, December 28, 2009

I AM FINALLY WRITING A JOURNAL ENTRY FROM MY STUDIO

APARTMENT!

I feel elated. The silence of this room is so peaceful. I haven't experienced solitude since the beginning of May when my nightmare began.

The move-in process began yesterday when my Aunt Deme, Aunt Lisa, Aunt Patti, Carissa, Gus and my parents helped me move into my studio. I wasn't able to stay here last night because I had to come home for a blood draw.

Today, my mom and Carissa helped by bringing the last of my possessions to my studio. I wasn't able to help any of my family members move a single object because I am still limited to a low weight restriction.

As I stood in my apartment watching my family haul in box after box, I couldn't help but think about how far I had come. Two months ago I was experiencing intense pain at both the site of my kidney incision and throughout my back. Three months ago, I was lying in a hospital bed roughly twelve blocks Southeast of my current location with a Swan catheter protruding from my neck. Then, my heart rate was kept at a steady 140 BPM by two Inotropic drugs. Now, my heart rate is 110 BPM... A tad fast, but that's due to my current excitement level.

I remember staring out my CCU window everyday, trying to look as far Northwest as possible. I used to pretend I could see my apartment, that the tall buildings standing in the way were just a figment of my imagination. I used to envision what this room would look like. I'd picture where I wanted my television and desk to stand. I thought about the minor details, too. I pictured where I would store my cups and silverware. I basically pictured my heaven on Earth. A place that I knew I would someday be if I could put every ounce of my energy into staying mentally strong and alive.

This studio is just how I imagined it.

I completed my long-term goal.

Friday, January 1, 2010 – New Year's Day

The past week has been filled with hosting my friends and showing off my new studio apartment. Doug and Marie spent the night. This morning Doug and I walked ten blocks to a parking garage on North Broadway to retrieve his car.

We had been walking for nearly ten minutes when it occurred to me that the last time Doug and I had walked together in the city, I was unable to walk more than twenty steps without needing to stop. I would be hunched over from the pain.

Today, I had to walk slower so that Doug could keep up.

2010 is going to be a much better year. I think I am going to accomplish many goals. I already accomplished one by writing "2010" at the end of today's date. Four months ago I promised myself I would see 2010. Goal accomplished.

Tuesday, January 5, 2010

When I was sick, there was a song that helped me make it through many bad times. I made mention of this song only on rare occasions throughout this book. Which to me is odd because I titled this book after the song. The song is "Swim" by Jack's Mannequin. Andrew McMahon, a survivor of Leukemia wrote it. The lyrics are the most inspirational words I have ever heard or read. They pushed me to stay strong on days when I felt weak and helped me hold onto the hope of a brighter future. When I was in the hospital, I wanted so badly to write Andrew to thank him for writing the song. I was never able to find a link to him, not even through the band's website.

The world is very small. You never know who you will meet and who that individual knows. There is a really great guy named Vince who works for Donate Life Illinois. He reached out to me through Facebook and asked me to begin blogging about my experiences from the hospital bed. He kept in touch with me, and I, in turn, sent him excerpts from this book. When I was in surgery, Natalie posted the music video of Jack's Mannequin's "Resolution," (a song about moving on with life) on her Facebook account and wrote, "So proud of my cousin Bill… this was one of his theme songs for when he made it through the surgery… thank God we've made it to today! Can't wait to have our 'old' Bill back!" Vince saw Natalie's video post and informed Natalie that he was a friend of a representative of Jack's Mannequin's management team. On Halloween night, I turned my laptop on to find a message from Andrew McMahon. I was dumbfounded, but ecstatic. He wrote that he was glad his songs could inspire me and that he and the rest of the band are sending their continued thoughts and support. I wanted to write him back at that moment, but I truly did not know what to say. I figured that I would wait until I left the hospital and would compose a message then. I had a sticky note on my desk at home for months that read "McMahon," reminding me to respond to his letter. Every time I looked at it, I would try to think of how I could express my gratitude through written words. Every time I attempted to write the letter, I'd go blank. It wasn't until tonight, after hours of pondering around my studio, that I found the words. The following is my long-awaited response to Andrew:

Dear Andrew,

Let me begin by thanking you for the letter that you wrote me when I was in the hospital, and let me apologize for taking so long to respond. I received your letter on Halloween night. Since then, I have had this burning desire to write you back, but I haven't because I have been lost for words as to what I wanted to say to you. I can't possibly put into words the connection I felt with your song, "Swim." However, I can whole-heartedly tell you that "Swim" was one of the driving forces that kept me alive. If it were not for your lyrics, I truly believe I would not be here today.

I was initially introduced to "Swim" at the end of June when I saw you play at The First Midwest Bank Amphitheater with The Fray. A little over a month later, I was hospitalized and told that I needed both a new heart and kidney. I later spent seventy days in the hospital; fifty-eight of those days were in Intensive Care. I mention all of this because on each one of those days, when I was awake, I listened to your song. Your lyrics gave me strength and kept me going. There were times when I would be laying in bed and I would want to give up, but I would whisper to myself the first lyric that would pop into my head. Each time, the random verse would get me through the bad moment. I actually hummed your song as

I was being wheeled into surgery.

It meant so much to me that you took the time out of your busy day to write me that message. I wanted to contact you throughout my entire stay in the hospital, but I never seemed to be able to find a direct link to you through a website. You can only imagine just how ecstatic I was when I discovered that you contacted me.

Thank you again, Andrew, for your letter and for the gift of "Swim." You probably never thought that you would save a life when you wrote that song, but you truly did.

I am going to try my hardest to make it to your February 22nd or February 23rd show in Chicago. I am currently on three drugs that basically eliminate my immune system. Consequently, large crowds are not the safest place for me to be. However, I am hoping I will be lowered on many of the drugs and I can make it to your show just in time.

I hope all is well with you and the rest of the band. Good luck with the tour!

Sincerely,
Bill Coon

I sent the letter to Vince's friend asking him to forward it on to Andrew. I really hope Andrew gets it. I just want him to hear from me personally. He doesn't need to respond.

Wednesday, January 6, 2010

I'M GOING TO THE JACK'S MANNEQUIN CONCERT! Andrew's Manager responded to my e-mail offering me opera box seat tickets to the show! The seats are far away from the crowds, so the risk of being near germs and anyone who may potentially be sick is reduced greatly. I am so excited for this! He said I can bring two other people with me. Carissa has already claimed one of the tickets and I think I am going to give the other to Peter. Last year, he took me to a lot of Chicago Blackhawk's games and I know he will have a great time at this show. I can't wait to hear "Swim!"

Thursday, January 14, 2010

I received my official grades from last semester today. I had enrolled in four online classes, each worth three credit hours. I had written before my elongated hospitalization that I was going to make, "Earning a 3.75 GPA" my new short-term <u>Will</u>.

Once again, I failed my short-term <u>Will</u>. I earned two B's, one C, and an F.

However, this is the first short-term goal that I am not distraught over failing. I am actually quite impressed that I was able to transfer three classes to Columbia this semester. Looking back, I was very naïve to even think that I could pull off anything higher than a "B." I didn't understand the pain that I would feel or the emotional anguish I would face during the preceding three months of my life.

For the record, the F was from a literature class that I never bought the books for. I couldn't see when I was in the hospital, so I never bothered to turn in a single assignment for that class.

Now I know I failed three short-term goals, but I accomplished two of my crucial long-term goals.

1. **Make it to my studio.** COMPLETE
2. **Survive.** COMPLETE

Thursday, January 21, 2010

I had a kidney biopsy today. It was the first biopsy for this organ that I have had to undergo since the transplant. I was not sedated, so I was extremely nervous for the procedure.

A kidney biopsy is much different than a heart biopsy. There is very minimal privacy involved. I was one of the three patients in the room having the procedure performed within ten minutes of each other. I didn't get their names, but the other two patients were from completely different walks of life. The first was a Latino woman. She was in her late thirties and was accompanied by a boyfriend who was dressed in baggy jeans, an oversized Yankees jersey, and a flat-billed hat that was crooked to the side. The other patient was an older gentleman. I'd estimate that he was in his mid-sixties. His wife joined him for the procedure. She was plump, her hair was graying, and until our dividing curtain was pulled shut, she continuously smiled at me and said, "Hi."

The two operating doctors entered. I recognized both of them. They had visited me countless times when I was waiting for my transplants in the CCU. I don't recall their names, but they are both very nice, sincere people.

I was given a large dose of Lidocaine. The gel soothed the skin, making everything in my hip numb. It was then that a hefty green tube was removed from its air-sealed packaging. The tube had a large needle at the end of it that I would assume stretched three inches long. "Okay, you are going to hear a click noise, try not to jump," one of the physicians said to me in a calm voice. I then watched as they inserted the needle into my kidney. I'd estimate that an inch and a half of the needle went into the skin. "Click!" The needle jerked inside of me. I saw a piece of tissue shoot into the tube. "We need one more," the same physician told me. The tube screamed out one last time, "Click!"

They wiped the blood away from the spot, and a nurse applied fifteen minutes of pressure to the wound. I was then given six cups of water and a bottle of apple juice. I was told that I could not leave the hospital until I could piss without blood coming out. I figured that this would not be a problem and I drank as much as my stomach would allow me to in a forty-minute period. To my surprise, it was very difficult to stop peeing blood.

My first attempt was a complete failure. Red blood poured into the toilet. *Holy shit!* I thought to myself. I returned to my bed and continued to chug. This process repeated itself two more times over the course of another hour.

Finally, my piss was an acceptable shade of "peach," and I was sent home and told that I would be contacted in twenty-four hours with the results. I will be shocked if anything is wrong. I am on a hot streak of successful biopsies.

Friday, January 22, 2010

My journal entries in this book have been growing less frequent since I have begun living in my studio apartment. My life has been steadily returning back to normalcy since the beginning of 2010. It's crazy how fast time can pass when you are not busy occupying your mind with the thought of each day being your last. I have not taken a single day of my new life for granted, but I have noticed that as I continue to grow stronger, I begin to easily forget how fragile my body is. In a way, I almost needed a wake-up call. Today, I received that call at 3:29 PM on the corner of State and 8th St.

My phone rang. A number that I had never seen before was displayed on the miniature screen. I answered and heard the familiar voice of the Nephrology Fellow. It was the same doctor who had performed my biopsy yesterday. She began to inform me that the results of the biopsy came back poorly. They believe my body is beginning to slowly reject the new kidney. Fortunately, the level of rejection is very minor and can be reversed. The Fellow continued by telling me I would need to be admitted to Mercy Care for the weekend, and that I would need to undergo rounds of IV medications to correct the situation.

I was truly stunned. I stood in shock. I couldn't imagine something going wrong with any part of my body. I have felt so incredibly good for months now that something rejecting seemed almost out of the question, no longer a possibility. Her parting words to me were that she was going to work on getting me a room and that I needed to speak with my parents to make arrangements for the weekend.

I called my mom, and much like myself, she was shocked. We discussed driving arrangements and I told her to wait until a room was ready for me before she rushed down to the city. She agreed and we both anxiously awaited instructions from the Fellow.

Two hours passed until I finally received a phone call from Nephrology's Nurse Practitioner. The range of emotions I experienced within that two-hour span was eerily chilling. I remembered feeling each of the emotions while I was sick, and I had flashbacks to my journey. It was as though I was living each stage of emotion from my battle in intervals of 30-45 minutes.

First, I experienced the anger. I flashed back to the days at Chicago General. I remember walking around my house, feeling dazed from the Isosorbide, knowing something was wrong, and deep down feeling that I was progressively growing sicker.

I then felt confused. I wondered why this was happening to me. I tried to find an explanation as to why I would be forced back into a hospital during the final three days of my winter break. I searched for a reason, but I never found it. It was this stage that brought me back to Mercy Care. I remembered staring at Dr. Gordon and Dr. Krause when they did their rounds one weekend. I looked them in the eye and told them I felt my body was crashing and I was soon going to be in the CCU again. Dr. Gordon looked as though he believed me. Dr. Krause seemed slightly less convinced. I then remembered the warmth of the tears flowing down my face as I looked at Dr. Shao, Dr. Gordon, and Chloe through watery eyes a few days later, when they told me I was indeed sicker, and I needed to be removed from the list.

Finally, I experienced acceptance. I had returned to my studio at this point. I was staring out the window when I began to pray. "God," I said. "I don't know why you chose for this to happen to me, maybe it's for the book. Maybe you want the readers to see that there are bumps in the road when you are recovering, I understand this. But please, don't let this become my life. I am grateful for the second life that I have received, but please, don't make me spend this life in constant fear of being hospitalized." That was when the phone rang. It was 5:47 PM. The Nurse Practitioner told me that the heads of the Transplant Nephrology team had reviewed the results again, and the condition was very minute. She told me a Home Healthcare nurse was being sent to my house in Lake Zurich, and I would need to receive only twenty to thirty minutes of IV medication for the next three days.

It's funny how the symbolism of a ringing telephone has changed throughout this journey of mine. At first, I prayed to hear the sound; it represented life. Now, I dread to see an unknown number come across my miniature screen.

Monday, January 25, 2010

I must admit, when I envisioned my triumphant return back to college,

I never in a million years would have guessed that it would follow a weekend of IV medications and a kidney rejection episode. Nonetheless, I didn't allow the grim weekend to rain on my parade.

My last dose of IV medication finished at 9:45 AM. After removing the IV from my arm, I immediately jumped in the shower and began washing my body as though I was preparing for a hot date. While I was showering, my mom was busying herself as she anxiously awaited a return call from Dr. Shao. I had awoken with a dangerously high blood pressure (164/100) and my glucose was not stellar by any stretch of the imagination (234). My mom was worried. I was filled with comfort in knowing that Dr. Gordon had assured me over the phone last night that both conditions are side effects from the IV Solu-Medrol (IV Prednisone). He was certain my body would regulate itself by Wednesday evening.

I began to hastily put on my pants when Dr. Shao called my cell phone. I explained my current predicament. Just as Dr. Gordon had done the night prior, she assured me, in a calming voice, that my body would return to homeostasis by Wednesday. The only factor that truly concerned Dr. Shao was my high blood pressure. Since last speaking with Dr. Gordon, both my systolic and diastolic numbers had risen twenty points each. Dr. Shao prescribed a blood pressure management pill and requested that I call in with an update the following day.

It was 10:30 AM now, my mom and I seemed to have traded emotions. She was calm and I was panicking that I would miss my first day of school. We still had to make a trip to the pharmacy to retrieve the newly prescribed pills before we could begin our hour-long commute into the city. Miraculously, the roads were wide open. The trip lasted only forty-five minutes and my mom was able to drop me off a block away from the classroom.

Before I left the car, my mom told me she loved me and that I should take in the moment to its fullest because I had fought so hard for this day. She was right. This was yet another dream coming true for me. I stood at the corner of State and Congress awaiting the light's permission to walk. I turned and quickly glanced back at my mom. I could see her white smile beam through the tinted windows and I believe she may have been crying. The light then changed and I began my walk towards the building.

The building looked completely different from what I remembered. There was a new paint job on the West side of the building. It had been washed light purple. In olive green lettering, the building proudly read, "Columbia." A class had just let out and students began pouring out of the revolving door. This was a surreal moment for me. In the past, I had been able to recognize the majority of the students who came out of this particular building. They were all usually from my major, the students within my major are very tight knit. Today, I didn't recognize a single face. They were all new. It made me feel old, as though I had lost a step.

No sooner did I recover from the shock of the unidentifiable faces, I was getting off the elevator on the 7th floor when I bumped into a former classmate of mine. He was extremely excited to see me. "Bill!" he exclaimed. "Wow, buddy. I was just thinking about you this morning on the way to class. I had been following your story in the school paper and when I got home I was going to run a search on your name to see if I could find out what happened to you," he paused. "But you… damn, dude. You look great! How do you feel?" he asked sincerely. I responded with my typical line. It's the most truthful statement that I can make without having to go into length as to how crappy I had once felt. "I feel amazing," I said. "Honestly, I have not felt this good since December of 2008." He responded just like everyone else does, with a look of amazement as though he had just seen a dead man rise from the grave. He then uttered the same verbal response, "Wow… that's truly amazing." We briefly compared schedules and then parted ways.

Ten minutes later, class had begun. I was sitting in my chair, unpacking my notebook and folder from my briefcase when the room suddenly froze. I had a flashback to a day in the hospital. I couldn't remember the exact date, and it was the first time I was having this vision.

Ashley had her back toward me. She was holding an empty syringe, so I can assume I had just been given either Morphine or a diuretic. I watched her walk out my door, closing the sliding glass behind her. I turned my head towards my window, staring out into the city. *You're not going to die Bill!* I thought to myself, *Come January, you will be in class and this will all just be a bad dream.*

The classroom then began to operate at its normal speed. I smiled and thought to myself, *You were right Bill... you did it!*

After class, I returned home to my studio and engulfed every piece of food that I could find with low sugar and carbohydrates. It is now 1:25 AM. I am heading off to bed. I recently checked my vitals. My sugar has dropped to 190 (still not great, but a major improvement). Also, Dr. Shao's pill did the trick. My blood pressure has substantially dropped to 127/74.

Three months ago, I completed my first long-term goal of surviving. Almost a month ago, I completed my second long-term goal of living alone in my studio apartment. Today, I completed my final long-term goal.

I became twenty again.

Friday, January 29, 2010

I have officially completed my first week of school. Every day my first class begins at 12:30 PM. I board bus #46 at 11:30 AM and arrive on campus at exactly 12:02 PM.

I am beginning to see familiar faces on the bus in the morning. There seems to be a group of us who are on the same schedule. These familiar faces are not always happy. Everyone seems pretty upset in the morning and nobody appears to enjoy public transportation.

I find myself dissimilar to everyone else on bus #46. Simply because, unlike the other passengers, I can't help but find the beautiful poetry within the route.

The bus departs from a stop that is kitty-corner from my studio. The bus then travels south on Lake Shore Drive and exits on Michigan Avenue. Eventually, the bus makes a stop at Michigan and Superior. At this point in the ride, I like to make sure that I am sitting on the right side of the bus. That is because if the windows are not covered in condensation, I am able to see the 8th floor of Mercy Care's in-patient building. If I am sitting at the correct spot, I can quickly count the rows and columns of the building to find my old window in the CCU. As the bus pulls away from the Superior stop I can clearly see the large

Mercy Care decal on the side of the building. I watch it fade away in the distance as we approach the final location, the corner of State and Harrison. Last school year I lived at the corner of State and Harrison. The route takes me on a personal journey through countless memories. The stop in front of Mercy Care humbles me before I begin my day. It reminds me of how lucky I am to have the privilege to take public transportation, to go to school, or to simply be outside.

I just may be the happiest patron of public transportation in the city of Chicago.

Friday, February 12, 2010

Today I awoke at 10:30 AM, stared at the clock, and questioned if I should reset my alarm and go back to bed. I vetoed the notion and took a shower.

After I lathered, rinsed and repeated, I walked around my studio, slowly dressing as I listened to the entire Jack's Mannequin album. I then grabbed my keys and headed for the bus stop on Belmont. There I boarded bus #46 and got off roughly twenty minutes later. I walked two blocks, entered Mercy Care, and went to the Cardiology floor. Dr. Gordon had written me a letter of recommendation for a scholarship I am applying for through Columbia. I had to pick it up from Heart Failure secretary.

I left Mercy Care, purchasing a large hot chocolate on my way out. I then had to travel to Columbia's Advising Office to pick up another letter of recommendation from my counselor. The distance between the two locations is roughly twenty blocks. I had the choice of walking the distance or taking a bus.

I chose to walk.

I later picked up the letter, boarded the Harrison Red Line, and got off at the Belmont stop. I then chose to once again negate the bus and I walked twenty minutes home. On the way home I stopped off at a convenience store to purchase a gallon of milk.

When I arrived home, I picked up my mail. There was a Valentine's

Day card from Aunt Patti and a letter from Gift of Hope. They had sent me organ donation Valentine's Day stickers because I participated in one of their promotions on Facebook two weeks prior.

I then poured myself a glass of juice, went online, and spoke with Jo via my webcam. I signed off with Jo and prepared dinner. I had mini frozen tacos.

After dinner, I finished writing one of the scholarship applications I am applying for and began watching the opening ceremonies to the Olympic Winter Games in Vancouver. While I was watching the ceremony, I lifted weights and then used the milk that I had purchased just hours before to make a protein shake.

I drank the shake, took a shower, and now I am writing this journal entry.

Why did I bother describing this rather uneventful, meaningless day? Well... because it was an uneventful, meaningless day. Overall, there were zero highlights. Not a single interesting event that is slightly original or out of the norm occurred. The point I am trying to make is that I am just like you. My life is now unbelievably plain. Why do I like this? Because at the moment, it is 12:37 AM, so technically it is now Saturday, February 13, 2010. Exactly five months ago today I was moved up to 1A status, something that is very far from the norm.

Monday, February 22, 2010

What does it mean to "come full-circle?"

To me, it means to end where you began, to take a journey you never once anticipated, a journey that takes you into the depths of your mind and forces you to stare at your soul and discover who you truly are.

However, this journey can only be considered as "coming full-circle," if at your return to the starting point of your journey, you return as a changed individual. You should be able to look at yourself in the mirror and see a different person, a better person, a stronger, rebuilt rendition of your old self.

Tonight, I came full-circle.

I began my writing on July 5, 2009. On that day, I struggled to put on a shirt. I sat in my chair crying, shaking and looking for a way out; an escape from my life. On that day, I listened to Jack's Mannequin's "Swim," as tears poured down my face. I was terrified, unsure of where my life was going to take me. At that moment, I was certain I was going to die. I was convinced my swim was going to end and that I was inevitably going to be crushed by the tides.

Tonight, I sat in the balcony of the House of Blues and watched my hero perform live. Tonight, I was able to hear the empowering lyrics of "Swim" one more time, in a different way than I had ever heard them before.

Andrew performed the song alone, on stage, under a spotlight. Every lyric echoed through the halls of the venue, into the ears of the audience, and into my heart. Tonight, I sang along with Andrew.

Just as I once mouthed the lyrics in my bedroom on the faithful day that I began this project, I did so tonight, in perfect unison with Andrew. There we stood, two survivors of two different diseases. Two people, who in their early twenties had their lives ripped from underneath them. But there we were, he was living his dream, and I was living one of mine. I was once again hearing the song, but this time I was in a different chair, a much better chair, and the one tear that slowly formed in my left eye was a tear of accomplishment, not sorrow.

I sat there and relived everything in a flash. I saw the IV's, I tasted the medications, I felt the heartache, the stomach pains, the chest pains, and I relived the seizures. But then I saw many faces. I saw Karrie, Ashley, Melissa, Irene, Lauren, Dr. Gordon and countless others. I realized in that moment I had met so many incredible people throughout my journey, people who have enriched my life or have taught me a lot about myself. These people, whom I would have never met had I not been stricken with this disease, have all impacted me and have made me a completely different person than I was on July 5, 2009. My life is better now than it ever was because of these people.

Before any of this transpired, I thought I was happy. I convinced myself that my life was perfect, that I had zero room for improvement. I was certain I enjoyed spending time with individuals who have no idea what life is really about, simply because I, too, had absolutely no understanding of the meaning of life.

Now that I have retuned to my beginning, I feel that I can easily share with you the secret to the meaning of life. I can answer the age-old question with one simple word and tell you what you should strive to achieve every day.

Happiness.

It sounds simple, but is it really?

Are you happy right now? If so, what makes you happy? Did you just purchase an item that you've had your eye on for weeks? Did you just get a promotion and now you will have a much larger salary, which in turn, will afford you the opportunity to live in a larger house?

Are you happy because you just passed an exam? Did you just trade a stock option last second, thus saving you a large sum of money before the price bottomed out? Or are you just happy because you think that shirt looks good on you right now?

Unfortunately, that is not happiness; that is merely temporary satisfaction. Now don't feel bad if you answered "yes" to any of the above questions. I too used to think the same way. I once believed that if I built a strong resumé, I could get a better job than my peers out of college, which in turn would set me higher than the rest of the people my age, thus allowing me to earn a larger salary, a larger house, and I would inevitably retire younger. I pictured that to be the perfect life, the golden standard. I was an idiot.

Now please indulge me as I pose to you a few more questions.

Did you ask that cute girl/guy that you bumped into and had a great conversation with at the book/convenience/drug store out to lunch? What was the last favor someone asked you to do for them? Did you do it?

Really quickly, think of the last time you were doing work when a friend called and asked you to go somewhere with them. Were you responsible and did you finish your assignment? Or did you put the pen down and go on an adventure? Who was the last person you hugged? Was it a genuine, warm, open armed embracing hug? Or was it an awkward, one armed, sideways pat on the back?

Now think about your immediate family. Are you on speaking terms with all of them? Have you spent the last few years or decade arguing with them over a series of minor disputes? If so, do you even remember what those fights were about? Have you told one of your family members that you love them in the past week? Finally, and most importantly, has anyone called you in the past two weeks just to talk or to tell you they were thinking of you and that they loved you?

Something I have learned is that you won't know for sure if you have truly achieved happiness in life until you are facing death. It is then that you can recap all of your mistakes. You can see where you went wrong and in that moment realize that you either achieved happiness, or you lived your life jumping from one temporary satisfaction to another.

As I have alluded to in prior entries, this disease was a blessing. I no longer spend my life hopping between temporary satisfactions. I don't even value money anymore. It's nothing more than green paper to me. I was able to see what I did wrong and now I can live my life achieving true happiness.

If you have read every single page to the left of this one, you have been a witness to my transformation. You have gone inside my head and you have seen what it takes to overcome extreme adversity. I hope you have learned from me, not only from my successes, but also from my major failures.

If you are in good health and without a single stress resting upon your shoulders, I hope you have enjoyed my story. I hope that you take it to heart and are moved to make a difference in the world regardless of size. I hope you help another person whom cannot help themselves. I hope you hold the door open for a person with a disability or give up your seat to someone who looks fatigued. I'd especially hope that after reading of my struggles, you become an organ donor.

If you are one of the people who I intended this book to be read by, you are most likely sick, not yourself. You just finished this book and are staring at these words wide-eyed, hopefully thinking, *I can do it, too!* But I do realize the strong likelihood that you are more than likely saying, "He did it, but I don't know if I can." I am here to tell you that you can beat this. You just need to trust me when I give you my final words of advice. Take <u>everything</u> that I say to heart, and <u>do not</u> question what I am about to say.

1. **It's okay to be taken care of.** As much as you want to do everything for yourself, there will come a time in your journey, if it hasn't already, that you will not be able to do simple, remedial tasks. For me, it was eating, walking and peeing. You are going to feel older than you really are and you will potentially become severely depressed by the feeling. Please, <u>do not give in to the feeling!</u> Just understand that when this is all over you are going to be able to do that remedial task better than you can currently remember <u>ever</u> doing it. When you do complete that task, you won't be able to stop smiling.

2. **Treat your nurses with the utmost respect.** If they treat you kindly, you give them back the <u>exact</u> same kindness, <u>REGARDLESS</u> of how horrible you feel. Your nurses will single-handedly save you from sadness. They will potentially save your life by giving you a reason to smile, thus making you live long enough for the medication to take effect.

3. **Do not forget who you are!** Write it down <u>right now</u> if you have to. This rule is one that my mom taught me. I later explored the rule and added to it. She taught me that you need to hold onto who you are so that when you win your battle, you can rebuild yourself by only picking up the pieces of yourself that you like. You can rid the new you of any bad traits or personality flaws. Though this is true, I later learned that you need to remember who you are so that you can have something to fight for. Consider it a mental reference point for what you call "Life."

4. **Be your own advocate.** This rule is huge. Please reference the section of this book entitled "Baby Steps" if you need examples. You need to remember that you know your body more than anyone else. Your doctors may say they understand, but you must always keep in the back of your mind that they likely have never taken the drugs that they

are prescribing. If a drug makes you feel miserable, ask for a change. Like I was once going to say to Dr. Wiezien, "What's the point in living if your quality of life isn't worth living for?" If your doctors cannot give you a good enough reason or if you ever feel that you are being mismanaged, by all means, get a second opinion, or a third if you see fit. However, I must warn you. A large portion of being your own advocate is not being stupid either. You must <u>always</u> do research. Go online, read medical journals, talk to people, make phone calls. Research <u>EVERY SINGLE PILL</u> that you are prescribed <u>before</u> you consume it. In the end, be <u>ALMOST</u>, if not <u>AS</u> smart, as your doctors.

5. **Take Your Medicine!** When you beat your illness, and <u>you will</u> beat your illness, daily pill consumption will likely be a requirement to sustain your current health and/or to avoid a relapse. After roughly two weeks of consistent pill consumption, your body will begin to adjust and receive the full benefits of the medication. You will begin to feel great, just like your old self. Inevitably, you will be like 99% of patients and feel that you are cured. You will begin to believe that you can get lazy with your medication. Sadly, you are not cured. You have only become dependent upon those pills. <u>TAKE THEM!</u>

6. **Road bumps happen.** Much like life in general, recovery is never going to be 100% smooth. There will be hurdles to jump. You need to face each of these hurdles with vigor and the same mental strength that got you through your original prognosis. Though you may be scared and you may feel that your life is never going to be the same again, you just need to fight those thoughts off, push them to the back of your mind and later bury them in the realization that you grow stronger with every hurdle that you leap.

Please trust me when I give you these warnings. They may be hard to stomach now, but I promise you, if you follow them, they will save you from hours, days, maybe even weeks of mental anguish.

Today, I have found the horizon at the end of my swim. My battle is over. I wish you the best of luck with yours.

This book played a major role in my battle. It allowed me to pour all of my deepest and sometimes darkest thoughts onto the blank white pages. As I wrote Peter in a letter from the hospital, I feel this book has given me a great deal of strength. This book helped me stay positive about my condition.

Because of this, I ask you to journal your story. I have shared mine with you in extreme detail. Now please, do me the honor, and share with me, yours...

_____

_____

_____

_____

_____

_____

_____

_____

_____

_____

_____

_____

_____

_____

_____

_____

_____

_____

_____

_____

_____

_____

_____

_____

_____

_____

_____

_____

_____

_____

_____

_____

_____

_____

_____

_____

One Last Word of Encouragement:

On Sunday, September 13, 2009, I was moved up to 1A status in the CCU.

On Monday, September 13, 2010, this book was released nationally.

Like I once wrote, "One year from now, this entire chapter in your life will all just be a faint memory… you can't forget that."

Are You Currently Swimming?

As I mentioned, I began writing <u>SWIM</u> with the intention of helping others. On my website (www.BillCoonBooks.com) you will find a direct link to e-mail me. I realize that I was very fortunate to have an incredible support system. I also realize that not everyone is as fortunate as I was. I firmly believe a support system is crucial to survival. Please feel free to contact me if you need someone to talk to.

In 2009, while waiting for the gift of life, I watched my family spend over $7,500 on non-medical expenses, such as bedside meals, parking at the hospital, gasoline to drive to-and-from the hospital and lodging.

This book was later read by thousands of people. Some of those people invited me to speak to their various support groups. In doing so, I learned that the average family spends between $5,000 and $10,000 on these non-medical expenses when their loved one grows critically ill.

These expenses added stress to an already stressful situation.

I wanted to do something about it. Finally, in 2018, Keep Swimming Foundation was born.

Keep Swimming Foundation's mission is to help families of critically ill individuals afford these non-medical expenses.

If you are interested in learning more, volunteering or making a personal or corporate donation, please visit our website:

KeepSwimmingFoundation.org

Special Thanks to...

Mama Coon
Aunt Patti
Natalie
Peter
JoWo
Estelle
Carissa
Dr. Gordon
Ashley a.k.a. "ADS" a.k.a. "The Show"
Karrie
Irenaay
Mrs. Clement
Yia Yia
Michael
Nicole
Candice Glicken
Brittany Kaback
Sara "Tink R Bell"
and Nouna

... for being my first readers, critics, and most importantly, for believing in this project since day one.

Also, to my dad, for his countless hours of printing and binding several volumes of this book until I finally got it right.

ABOUT THE AUTHOR: BILL COON

Bill Coon's mother took this picture on October 21, 2009, just before his heart transplant. This very picture is mentioned in "Cheers For A New Heart and Kidney".

After obtaining international success with his debut book, <u>SWIM: A Memoir of Survival</u>, Bill Coon became an acclaimed motivational speaker. To learn how you can obtain Coon for your event, please visit his speaking website at: BillCoonSpeaks.com.

OTHER BILL COON PUBLICATIONS:

"Imagination: A Short Story"

CONNECT:

Facebook: www.facebook.com/thebillcoon
Twitter: @thebillcoon
Instagram: @thebillcoon

PLEASE BECOME AN ORGAN DONOR:

If you are interested in becoming an organ donor, please log on to:
www.billcoonspeaks.com

Click on the "Become An Organ Donor" tab. There you will find information regarding organ donation, as well as links to donor registries.

GIVE THE GIFT OF LIFE.

51446818R00148

Made in the USA
Columbia, SC
19 February 2019